Capitalism on the Frontier

CAPITALISM

ON THE FRONTIER

Billings and the Yellowstone Valley
in the Nineteenth Century

¤

Carroll Van West

University of Nebraska Press

Lincoln and London

The paper in this book meets the mini-
mum requirements of
American National Standard for Information Sciences – Permanence
of Paper for Printed Library Materials,
ANSI Z39.48–1984.

Library of Congress Cataloging-
in-Publication Data
West, Carroll Van, 1955–
Capitalism on the frontier: Billings
and the Yellowstone Valley in the
nineteenth century / Carroll Van West.
p.   cm.
Includes bibliographical references
and index.
ISBN 0-8032-4755-9 (cl)
1. Billings (Montana) – Economic
conditions.
2. Yellowstone River Region – Economic conditions.
3. Capitalism – Montana – Billings –
History – 19th century.
4. Capitalism – Yellowstone River
Region – History – 19th century.
1. Title
HC108.B49W47   1993
330.9786'39 – dc20
92-15982 CIP

DEDICATED TO
WESTERN HERITAGE CENTER
BILLINGS, MONTANA

Contents

Ⓧ

Contents

ILLUSTRATIONS

Following Page 132

Map

Early settlements along the
Yellowstone River, c. 1880

Figures

TABLES

Acknowledgments

◻

During this eight-year project, I have incurred debts to many institutions and individuals. First and foremost, I thank the Western Heritage Center of Billings, Montana. Since 1982, I have worked with members of the center's staff in several different projects, and their interest in knowing more about the early history of the Yellowstone River Valley launched my own investigations. The former directors June Sampson and Bryan Berghager and the current director Lynda Moss have been most encouraging and helpful. I especially thank Lynda for her unwavering faith in this manuscript. The former curators David Carroll, Virginia Heidenreich, Carol Kemmis, and Marcia Wolter took time out of their busy schedules to share their insights about early Yellowstone history. I must also thank the center's former secretary, Joan Ware, and center volunteers, like Bobbie LaBard, for their help through the years.

Staff members at the Montana Historical Society further aided my research. Bill Lang, the former editor of *Montana: The Magazine of Western History*, encouraged my Yellowstone research and graciously published the first fruits of my work. Portions of chapters 2, 3, and 4 have been adapted from "Coulson and the Clark's Fork Bottom: The

Economic Structure of a Pre-Railroad Community, 1874–1881," *Montana: The Magazine of Western History*, 35 (Autumn 1985): 42–55. Tables 1–6 have been reprinted from the same article by permission. As the society's resident expert in all things about Montana, Dave Walter helped to correct my errors and sharpen my analysis. The archivists Sue Jackson, Bill Summers, Ellie Arguimbau, Christian Frazza, Lory Morrow, and Becca Kohl supplied me with a steady stream of valuable archival evidence. Sue Near, the museum curator, and Janet Sperry, registrar, guided me through the society's collections, providing a valuable artifactual perspective on the Yellowstone's past, and Jennifer Jeffries Thompson, education curator, gave encouragement and friendship throughout my research in Helena. I'm also grateful for the assistance of past and present staffers Marianne Keddington, Rick Newby, Dave Girshick, Diana Wilkison, Bob Clark, Laurie Mercier, and Patty Dean.

Three other institutions deserve special thanks. Dave Donath and Janet McIntyre Houghton at the Billings Museum and Archives in Woodstock, Vermont, provided me with copies of correspondence between Frederick Billings and Benjamin Shuart, letters that opened the doors to a totally unknown aspect of Billings history. The James J. Hill Reference Library in St. Paul gave me an opportunity to understand better the machinations behind the reorganization of the Northern Pacific Railroad in the 1890s. Tom White, curator of the library's Hill Papers collection, shared ideas and suggested research areas. The Center for Historic Preservation at Middle Tennessee State University has also been a source of support. Deepest appreciation goes to my colleagues there: James K. Huhta, Caneta S. Hankins, and Ed Johnson. Thanks go as well to the center's research assistants Susan Skarbowski and Erin Beth Dower, who helped me get the manuscript under way in the summer of 1989, and Jennifer Martin, who helped prepare the bibliography in 1991.

Public and private agencies also have been generous in support of this project. Funding has been forthcoming from a 1983–84 American Association of State and Local History Research Grant, a program funded by the National Endowment for the Humanities; a 1987 research grant from the James J. Hill Reference Library, St. Paul, Minn.;

and a 1987 Travel to Collections Grant from the National Endowment for the Humanities.

My acknowledgments would not be complete without recognizing several other research institutions: the Montana Collection of the Parmly Billings Library of Billings and especially the help of Librarian Jim Curry; the Western History Center/Archives at the University of Wyoming in Laramie; the Library of Congress; the National Archives; the Minnesota Historical Society; the Montana State University Archives in Bozeman; and the Montana State Library in Helena. Other individuals who have helped me in different facets of my research include Senia Hart, Harley O'Donnell, Larry Jensen, and Joyce Jensen of Billings; Robin Winks of Yale University, who graciously shared the manuscript copy of his biography of Frederick Billings; Marcella Sherfy of the Montana State Historic Preservation Office; Clyde Milner II of Utah State University; Ross R. Cotroneo of Western Oregon State College; Bob Frame of the James J. Hill Reference Library; and Adrian Heidenreich of Eastern Montana College.

Finally, and most important, I would like to acknowledge my greatest debt—that I owe Mary Sara Hoffschwelle, my wife. Reared in the East, but born in Billings, she persuaded me to go to Montana for four wonderful years. Without her help, support, and love, the manuscript would have never been completed.

Introduction

◻

Capitalism on the Frontier: Billings and the Yellowstone Valley in the Nineteenth Century is about the meaning and significance of economic change in the Yellowstone River valley during its first century of exploration, settlement, and development. Stretching from headwaters high in the Two-Ocean Plateau of Wyoming until meeting the Missouri River at the Montana and North Dakota border, the Yellowstone River valley possesses a striking, distinctive beauty. As it winds eastward, the valley is narrow and barren at some places but wide and fertile at others. My story focuses on one of those broad, productive places, a twenty-five-mile stretch of the valley, roughly between the present-day towns of Park City and Billings, that the pioneers called "the Clark's Fork Bottom." Here, during the nineteenth century, Crow Indians, fur hunters, pioneer homesteaders, audacious entrepreneurs, railroad executives, and eastern tycoons all played significant roles in laying the economic foundation for a future urban center of the northern plains, the city of Billings.

The Yellowstone's history of economic activity did not suddenly begin in the nineteenth century; rather it has amazing chronological depth, dating to the centuries of barter, subsistence transactions between the region's prehistoric inhabitants.[1] A rich anthropological literature exists about the economic traditions of the Mountain and River Crows, who occupied parts of the Yellowstone Valley for at least a century before white settlement.[2] Both bands of the Crow nation were great traders, traveling hundreds of miles to Native American trade centers where they would exchange the products of the hunt for Indian-produced vegetables and material goods acquired from the faraway American and Canadian worlds. These late prehistoric trading patterns significantly affected plains societies. My story refers to those days by exploring how ancient Native American trading traditions shaped the nature of the transactions between Crow Indians and trappers, both American and Canadian, during the fur trade era.[3]

Next I trace how the social and economic relationships of the fur trade era rapidly changed once permanent white settlements appeared in the valley, especially along the alkali flats of the Clark's Fork Bottom where the tiny hamlets of Coulson and Canyon Creek were established in the late 1870s. Consider what happened. In 1877, only months after the Battle of the Little Bighorn, the first squatters and buffalo hunters moved into the Bottom. The following year brought the initial farming families and the beginnings of a mercantile trade. Next came the arrival of merchants and entrepreneurs from Bozeman, then the hub for trade in southeastern Montana, and the Bottom's settlers entered the world of the market economy. The next three years witnessed meager, but steady, economic expansion and population growth. The local market economy was drawn into the economic orbits of Fort Benton, Bozeman, and Helena in Montana Territory and Bismarck in Dakota Territory.[4]

Then came the tracks of the Northern Pacific Railroad in 1882. A frenzy of speculation preceded the arrival of the Northern Pacific. Boomtown businesses multiplied; men even fought to the death over prime town lot locations. The Northern Pacific introduced the power of the American industrial revolution to the Yellowstone Valley, signaling its absorption into the mainstream of American capitalism. And, most important to this story, the railroad sold almost thirty thousand acres of its land grant to the Minnesota and Montana Land and Improvement Company, a corporation controlled by past and present railroad officials; the company established the town of Billings at the eastern end of the Clark's Fork Bottom.[5]

All of this happened in six years. In 1877, a barter economy—or what the historian John Faragher has called the "borrowing system"—best defined the economic relationships of the Yellowstone Valley. As settlement increased over the next four years, the farmers, hunters, and storekeepers created a local market economy, although the region's "inland towns" were tiny places of a few crudely built residences and a rough-and-tumble business or two. By the spring of 1882, those days seemed like ancient history in the Clark's Fork Bottom. In firm control of the region's economic destiny, the Northern Pacific Railroad and the Minnesota and Montana Land and Improvement Company replaced initial settlements with entirely new, and professionally planned, urban grids at both ends of the Bottom. The capitalist revolution, which had already transformed much of the agrarian landscape of the East, South, and Midwest, had finally reached the Clark's Fork Bottom of the Yellowstone.[6]

My story does not end there; rather it continues to search for the people, institutions, and economic forces that guided the settlement and development of Billings through the end of the century. When Billings initially strived to become the "second Denver" of the West, its major landlords, the Northern Pacific and the Minnesota and Montana Land and Improvement Company, failed to provide the capital and public improvements many residents expected. From 1882 to 1884, the two companies were often at odds, with the railroad considering Billings merely a minor stop along the Yellowstone lines. Its officials were more interested in boosting Livingston, the "gateway" to Yellowstone National Park.

Then in the spring of 1884, Frederick Billings, a major stockholder in both the Northern Pacific and the land company, with his son Parmly and his nephew Edward G. Bailey, stepped forward to take charge of the destiny of Billings and the Clark's Fork Bottom. Many local entrepreneurs welcomed the intervention of the Billings family; certainly these eastern capitalists could provide enough leadership and cash to keep the town's economy prosperous and expanding. Throughout the remainder of the decade, the Billings family gave the town not only leadership but also quite a bit of money. Frederick Billings owned more land in Yellowstone County than any other individual. A paternalistic landlord, the Billings family established a private bank while donating money for new schools, churches, and other public improvements. The family became part of a tradition of civic capitalism that shaped the region's development throughout the late nineteenth century.[7]

Yet the family's money and goodwill managed only to slow the town's slide into economic stagnation; the population of Billings, according to a reliable estimate, dropped by almost 50 percent from 1885 to 1890. In other western communities, such a severe population loss typically marked the beginning of the end: the town was fated to become just another minor railroad town at best or a western ghost town at worst. But Billings avoided both fates. Determined leadership from local civic capitalists, despite the unexpected deaths of Parmly Billings in 1888 and Frederick Billings in 1890, provided part of its salvation. Another contributor was the corporate reorganization of the American railroad system after the depression of 1893. Billings and the Clark's Fork Bottom found themselves selected as the meeting point for the three railroads—the Northern Pacific, the Great Northern, and the Burlington—that controlled the region's transportation network. The corporate alliance between the international banker J. P. Morgan and the railroad magnate James J. Hill laid the transportation foundation for the emergence of Billings as the Yellowstone's leading city in the twentieth century. Consequently, the history of Billings during the 1890s provides a case study of how the corporate reorganization of the American economy could affect a small town on the northern plains.[8]

The history of the initial development of Billings, from 1882 to 1900, also sheds light on early urban maturation in the American West. Over the past generation, an impressive group of community and regional studies of western urban history, including those of Duane Smith, Robert Dykstra, Don Doyle, Lawrence Larsen, John Reps, John Faragher, Kathleen Underwood, and Timothy Mahoney, has substantially increased our understanding of western town formation, decline, and consolidation.[9] Little attention, however, has been directed at the northern plains. The region in general, and the Yellowstone Valley in particular, lies well outside the national urban core that extends southward from Boston to Baltimore and westward to Milwaukee, Rock Island, and St. Louis. The few existing northern plains studies cover larger geographical areas and belong to more recent time periods. The geographer John Hudson has studied town development in North Dakota during the early twentieth century, and the historian Paula Nelson has used that same time frame to study homesteaders and town builders in western South Dakota.[10]

This study of the heart of the Yellowstone Valley, and the struggle of Billings, Montana, to become a small urban railroad center of three thousand residents by 1900, adds more than a different regional and chronological context to the question of urban evolution in the northern plains. The town's two-decade struggle to establish itself as an urban place also adds an interesting perspective. Unlike Kathleen Underwood's Grand Junction, Colorado, where the local land company worked with the railroad corporation, Billings suffered from bitter disputes between the land company and the Northern Pacific. Also unlike other well-documented western cities, Billings grew in spurts and failed to reach its full potential until the early twentieth century. Here was a western town that initially experienced a boom, then a severe bust, before a final boom put into place the physical, psychological, and economic infrastructure that helped Billings become the region's major urban center in the twentieth century.

Perhaps most important, this book provides a different perspective on the issue of regional economic development. The early urban evolution of Billings can best be understood as part of a larger process of economic change in the Yellowstone Valley during the nineteenth century. The region's nonmarket trading system was transformed into a corporate-dominated capitalistic system in less than eighty years, with the most rapid changes taking place in the last two decades of the nineteenth century, at the time Billings began its urban development. The rapidity of these economic changes magnified their collective impact, leaving little of the Clark's Fork Bottom of 1880 in the Billings of the new century. The influence of capitalism on the northern plains frontier of the Yellowstone Valley proved powerful indeed.

CHAPTER I

Patterns of Exchange

◻

[The Crows] seemed to desire that I go away. I had in my possession twenty-three beaver skins; in their opinion, that is a very large number and a great many more than we needed.—FRANÇOIS-ANTOINE LAROCQUE, JOURNAL ENTRY OF AUGUST 6, 1805

The Yellowstone and its streams, within that district beyond Clark's fork, abound in beaver and otter; a circumstance which strongly recommends the entrance of the latter river as a judicious position for the purposes of trade. . . . the mouth of the Yellowstone might be considered as one of the most important establishments for the western fur trade.—WILLIAM CLARK, JOURNAL ENTRY OF AUGUST 3, 1806[1]

Winding eastward out of Yellowstone National Park, the Yellowstone River possesses a unique beauty. Mountains loom over the riverbanks at the western end before the peaks recede into the background and the river valley flattens out, dotted here and there by cottonwood trees and native fauna as other famous western rivers, such as the Stillwater, Clark's Fork, Little Bighorn, and Tongue, empty their waters into it. Then, between the Yellowstone's confluences with the Powder and Missouri rivers, badlands dominate the landscape, giving the river an eerie, almost unworldly, appearance.

The earliest written accounts of the Yellowstone Valley were left by a Canadian, François-Antoine Larocque, who visited in 1805, and by the famous American explorer William Clark, who came a year later. The grandeur of the landscape may have momentarily caught their eye, but their gaze remained fixed on the country's vast economic potential. Their journal entries are blunt reminders that the fur trade was never far from their minds. Only months after their initial visits to the Yellowstone, the river became an important resource base and transportation corridor of the western fur trade.

The beginning of the fur trade era also initiated the capitalistic transformation of the Yellowstone Valley. In the first decade of the nineteenth century, fur traders introduced the Yellowstone's Native Americans to the ways of western capitalism by involving them in the worldwide market economy for animal furs. For the next sixty years, the Crow Indians, or Apsaalookes,[2] and fur traders wove together patterns of exchange that bonded the two cultures into a reciprocal relationship sometimes characterized by distrust and envy but often distinguished by trust, friendship, and mutual dependency as well.

This first chapter will rely on the many excellent secondary studies of the western fur trade to review the early history of economic exchange among the peoples of the Yellowstone, not only because the fur trade represents the intrusion of capitalism on the peoples of the Yellowstone but also because this early trade established patterns and assumptions that guided the economic activity of the Yellowstone Valley into the last quarter of the nineteenth century.

Historians once believed that Pierre de La Vérendrye, an agent for the Canadian North West Company, was the first white man to enter the Yellowstone region. Led by Assiniboine Indians, La Vérendrye in 1738 came south to the villages of the Mandans and Hidatsas along the Missouri River near present-day Bismarck, North Dakota. The French-Canadian trader hoped to discover a "western sea" and new potential areas for the fur trade, but instead he found himself enmeshed in an ancient Native American trade network based at the Mandan-Hidatsa villages. The disappointed La Vérendrye returned to Canada, leaving two expedition members at the villages to learn more about trading patterns and practices among the northern plains tribes.[3]

During their winter stay, La Vérendrye's two employees met many tribes, surely including members of the allied bands of the Mountain Crows and River Crows, as the Indians traded at the Mandan and Hidatsa villages. In a sense, the Native Americans of the upper Missouri region held trade rendezvous long before American fur traders and mountain men coined the phrase in the 1820s. Even before western goods entered the market, tribes such as the Crows traveled to the Missouri River villages to exchange products from the hunt for agricultural goods produced by the Mandans and Hidatsas. This barter trade between largely hunting groups such as the Crows and gardening peoples such as the Mandans and Hidatsas allowed both groups to supplement their way of life with valuable commodities, benefiting both groups almost equally.[4] The Native Americans at first viewed the fur trade with the Canadians and then the Americans in a similar fashion. The fur trade proved most successful when Canadian and American traders grafted themselves to the existing aboriginal trade network.

Recent scholarship has emphasized the extensive nature of these early Native American trading centers.[5] Economic exchange among the plains tribes had few of the attributes of a market economy. Craft specialization rarely existed; population densities were low; and the distances to travel were very great. Yet, a remarkable amount and diversity of goods moved back and forth across the country. A single archaeological site in South Dakota, for example, yielded beads from the Tennessee River valley, pendants from the Gulf Coast, Florida, and the Atlantic Coast, and dentalia from the Pacific Coast. A Haida carving from the Northwest Coast even appeared in a Crow medicine bundle. The Crows were active in two major Native American trade centers. They participated in the Shoshone rendezvous in southwestern Wyoming, trading with the Shoshones, Utes, Nez Percés, and Flatheads. Here they acquired their first horses. Probably the Crows' traditional friendship with the Nez Percés dates to these earlier trading relationships. The Crows also exchanged goods at the Mandan and Hidatsa villages on the Missouri, often trading items obtained at the Shoshone

9

rendezvous. Anthropologists have described this Yellowstone-to-Missouri circuit as an ancient trade route.[6]

The trade with the Mandans and Hidatsas also reinforced ancient ties between the tribes.[7] Anthropologists have concluded that the Crows were once either allies or one people with the Hidatsas. Archaeological evidence suggests that the Hidatsas and Crows moved into the Yellowstone country on several occasions before the final separation occurred sometime around 1600, A.D. leaving the Hidatsas growing crops along the banks of the Missouri and the Crows pursuing buffalo along the Yellowstone River.[8] The Crows retained one horticultural practice by growing tobacco for ceremonial purposes.[9]

In their trade with the Mandans, Hidatsas, and other northern plains tribes who participated at the Missouri trading center, the Crows obtained corn, beans, squash, and other vegetables in exchange for horses, dried meat, skins, buffalo robes, and other animal-derived items. An interesting facet of the exchange was its sexual division: women tended to trade only with women (food for, perhaps, moccasins) and men with men (which typically involved horses, weapons, and buffalo robes).[10] What the Canadian traders observed in the mid-1700s, in other words, was an active, healthy economic network.

In 1742–43, La Vérendrye's sons visited the upper Missouri region. Compared with the earlier expedition, their travels extended farther to the south and west—as far as the Big Horn Mountains of northeastern Wyoming. The La Vérendryes reached only the outskirts of the Yellowstone country, but their visit solidified the first contacts with the northern plains tribes, expanding the existing Native American trading network while opening the door for other Canadian fur traders and trappers to establish trade relations at the Missouri River villages.

Both the North West Company and the Hudson's Bay Company, two Canadian fur companies, periodically sent men to the Mandan and Hidatsa villages to tap into the native trade network. In 1777 or 1778, Pierre Menard came to live with the Mandans. A decade later René Jusseaume joined him. These two served as guides for Canadian trading parties and took part in the annual aboriginal rendezvous. Menard visited the Crows and Gros Ventres several times and also traveled along sections of the Yellowstone.

By the late eighteenth century, the Canadians began to consider pushing the fur trade westward into the Yellowstone Valley. Reliable traders such as David Thompson asserted that rich beaver country lay west of the Mandan and Hidatsa villages; others recommended that a permanent trading post be established at the junction of the Yellowstone and Missouri rivers. Nothing much happened, however, until the Canadians learned of the forthcoming Lewis and Clark expedition in 1804. This American venture, supported by the federal government and led by Meriwether Lewis and William Clark, was partly scientific and exploratory but was largely political and commercial in its mission. The Americans wanted a better idea of the wealth of resources in their newly acquired Louisiana Purchase as well as an opportunity to cement trading relationships with the region's native peoples. Reacting quickly to the economic challenge posed by the American expedition, the North West Company in June 1805 sent François-Antoine Larocque from Fort la Bosse, its trading post on the Assiniboine River, to the Mandan and Hidatsa villages. There he was to await the Crows, return with them to the Yellowstone Valley, and establish a new, direct source of furs. Larocque wanted to locate valuable beaver areas, teach the Crows how to prepare beaver skins for the commercial market, and retain their trade for his company, in much the same way that the Hudson's Bay Company controlled the Blackfeet trade for many years.[11]

The Mandans and Hidatsas correctly read Larocque's mission as a direct threat to their own monopoly control over the Crow trade, and the Indians did everything possible to persuade Larocque to stay out of Crow country. They warned him that, at best, the Crows would lie and steal everything he had or, at worst, murder him. Larocque knew that these warnings were largely self-serving. The Missouri tribes cared little for his well-being; what they wanted to stop was any direct contact between the Crows and Canadian traders. If Larocque was successful, he could bypass their middleman position in the aboriginal trade network—a place in the Native American economic system that brought prosperity and prominence to the Missouri river tribes.[12]

The Crows arrived at the Missouri villages in 1805 loaded with trade items. They obtained their first large number of guns, exchanging 250 horses, large packets of buffalo robes, clothing, and dried meat for 200 guns with 100 rounds of ammunition apiece, 100 bushels of corn, ket-tles, and other items. Impressed by the Crow bounty, Larocque ignored the Mandan and Hidatsa warnings and announced his desire to leave with the Crows. Interested in what this Canadian might mean to their trade, the Crows agreed to take Larocque to their home. They escorted Larocque through the southern portion of the Yellowstone country be-fore returning to the river near Pompey's Pillar. Larocque then floated down the Yellowstone to the Missouri villages.

During his stay with the Crows, Larocque taught their women how to prepare beaver skins in the preferred European manner. The women proved quick learners, for soon "Crow beaver" would rank among the best in the country. He further noted that the Crows were sharp traders. "They are not so stupid as Indians are thought to be," he remarked. "They reason justly enough on such subjects as they have occasion to see and be acquainted with. . . . They know very well to make advan-tageous bargains in their sales and purchases."[13]

Larocque shouldn't have been so surprised; the tribe's long experi-ence with trading accounted for this expertise. But the Canadian was only the first to document his ignorance of the tribe's trading prowess. Throughout the nineteenth century, traders, then settlers, would ex-press surprise, even shock, at the Crows' skill in trading. Today the no-tion still persists that the plains tribes in general were stupid traders, not prepared to participate in economic exchanges. Recent scholar-ship, however, has questioned this assumption. If the Indians believed they had been shortchanged or offered inferior goods, they might well choose to take their trade elsewhere or not trade at all.[14] The plains tribes understood different media of exchanges, with Made Beaver (a measure of value in fur equal to one prime beaver pelt) being especially well documented, and actually used such items such as dentalia as a type of money. However, they had difficulty understanding the ab-stract idea of interest accumulation on invested capital—a key compo-nent of the fur traders' capitalistic economy. In these types of ex-changes, the Indians were often shortchanged.[15]

Close on the heels of Larocque's 1805 visit to the Yellowstone came the 1806 visit by a party from the Lewis and Clark expedition. William Clark headed this foray into the Yellowstone country, hoping to obtain useful information on Indian commerce and the region's resources. Unfortunately, his trip was not very enlightening. Problems with building boats and with losing horses to the Indians (probably either the Blackfeet or Crows) turned his journey into a rather superficial exploration, although Clark did name "Pompy's Tower" (later known as Pompey's Pillar), placing his name there on July 25, 1806.[16]

The most significant contribution of the Lewis and Clark expedition to the future development of the Yellowstone region was its later reports, which emphasized the large number of fur-bearing animals in the area. To tap the Yellowstone's potential, and keep the Canadians out, the Americans recommended the construction of a trading post on the Yellowstone and another, larger post at the river's confluence with the Missouri. The Yellowstone, in Lewis's opinion, was a natural site for a fort "both in regards to the fur trade and the government of the natives."[17]

But Lewis and Clark also had an immediate and direct impact on the region. Before they even returned to St. Louis, they encouraged other Americans to hunt along the Yellowstone River. On the way back, at Fort Mandan in 1806, John Colter received permission to leave the expedition and join Forest Hancock and Joseph Dixson, two American trappers, for a Yellowstone hunting expedition. More than the number of beaver attracted the Americans. As Colter told his partners, the Yellowstone was largely free of the Blackfeet danger; moreover, the Crows would offer protection, hardy friendship, and, perhaps most important, the expertise of their women in preparing beaver pelts. Little evidence exists about the success of this first American venture, but after the winter, the three trappers dissolved the partnership, and in the spring of 1807, Colter floated down the Yellowstone and the Missouri. While heading for St. Louis, he met another group of trappers, led by Manuel Lisa, a St. Louis businessman, and assisted by George Drouillard, who had served with Lewis and Clark. Colter readily agreed to return to the Yellowstone as a member of the Lisa expedition.[18]

Manuel Lisa listened attentively when the members of the Lewis and Clark expedition talked of the rich fur lands of the upper Missouri region. The land of the Crows was uncommonly valuable, he heard; some expedition members claimed that beaver there "could be taken from the streams with clubs." As his biographer Richard E. Oglesby has observed, Lisa quickly envisioned "the Northwest as a giant fur empire, a great source of wealth for himself and his adopted land." And beginning in 1807, Lisa "dedicated his life to exploiting it."[19]

In the spring of 1807, Lisa organized the first major American commercial expedition to the Yellowstone, and for the next decade he attempted to establish a profitable fur trade in the region. His success as a trader—"an art which required creativity, good luck, and meticulous attention to detail"—was due to his abilities as a salesman, his thorough knowledge of the tribes, and his relative sensitivity to Native American culture. Lisa's reputation for fairness, courage, and reliability also served his expeditions well. His desire and ability to maintain friendly relations with all tribes, except for the Blackfeet, strengthened his alliances with the Crows, Mandans, and Hidatsas.[20]

Heeding Colter's report that the Crows were active and fair traders, Lisa directed the expedition to the heart of the Yellowstone Valley. In late November 1807, at the confluence of the Yellowstone and Bighorn rivers, the trappers built Fort Remon, the first permanent structure constructed by whites in Montana. The new fort's location stood in the midst of plentiful game, near a traditional Crow wintering ground. Cottonwood trees and surface coal were also available near the riverbanks, making the winter camp much more bearable for Indians and traders alike.[21]

Arriving so late in the season, the trappers met with little success of their own, and Lisa decided to encourage the Indians to come to Fort Remon for direct exchanges. He sent John Colter in the dead of winter to find the Indians and bring them back to trade. Historians still argue over Colter's exact route, but there is little doubt that his grueling trip over mountains, rivers, and the natural wonders of the upper Yellowstone expanded Colter's knowledge of the region's terrain and resources far beyond any other American trapper. He became one of the great explorers in the fur trade.[22]

Yet his heroics meant little at the time because Colter brought few Indians to the fort. The Native Americans were not interested in trading out of season or outside their traditional trading patterns and alliances. Lacking the type of consumer mentality already well developed among whites, the Crows and other tribes had no intention of answering Lisa's summons. Before returning to St. Louis in the spring of 1808, Manuel Lisa again sent Colter into the Yellowstone country. This time, Colter traveled beyond the Three Forks of the Missouri to the Beaverhead River country, where he met a group of Flatheads who agreed to trade with the Americans. Before they reached the trading post, however, Blackfeet warriors attacked, and only some timely reinforcements on the part of the Crows saved the trading party from disaster.

Blackfeet antagonism to the American presence on the Yellowstone dated to the ill-fated 1806 meeting between Meriwether Lewis and eight Blackfeet warriors along northern Montana's Two Medicine River, where shots were exchanged and two Blackfeet were killed.[23] From then on, a generation of American and Blackfeet traders hated and feared each other. And the violence would escalate, because the antagonism involved more than revenge for the Two Medicine River fight. The Blackfeet did not want American goods flowing to the Crows and Flatheads, and they considered the American incursions into the Three Forks area as trespassing on prime tribal hunting grounds. The tribe needed these furs to trade to the Hudson's Bay Company, an economic alliance that, in turn, tied the Blackfeet to the Canadians, who certainly did not relish competition with the Americans. Thus in direct and indirect ways, Native American trading patterns and alliances shaped the early fur trade.

The creation of the Missouri Fur Company in 1809 marked the beginning of the systematic exploitation of the region's fur-bearing animals. Directed primarily by Manuel Lisa and Benjamin Wilkinson, the company employed three hundred French-Canadian and American trappers to hunt along the Missouri headwaters (near present-day Three Forks, Montana). After the trappers left the company's Fort Remon in June 1809, however, Blackfeet Indians killed several trappers and distracted every hunting effort. The company prepared only thirty packs of beaver skins. The 1809 failure was repeated in following years; the company never had a successful trapping season, and in 1811 it abandoned the Yellowstone's Fort Remon. Manuel Lisa reorganized the Missouri Fur Company in 1812, but the new venture, in which he was president, general manager, and principal owner, fared no better, disbanding two years later. Not only had the Blackfeet discouraged the American trappers, but fur prices were prohibitively low due to the war then raging between the United States and England. Without the active assistance of the Crows, who showed little interest in protecting the Americans, a profitable fur trade based along the Yellowstone River was difficult. The first period of extensive economic exploitation of the Yellowstone ground to a halt.[24]

Manuel Lisa died in 1820, but his dream of a western fur empire lived on with others, such as Joshua Pilcher, who assumed leadership of the reorganized Missouri Fur Company. Pilcher's first expedition included Robert Jones, Michael Immell, William H. Vanderburgh, and Andrew Drips, once described as "the ablest band of traders on the Missouri." In 1821, they constructed Fort Benton at the confluence of the Yellowstone and Bighorn rivers, near the site of Fort Remon, and hunted while waiting for the Indians to come trade. But once again, the Crows stayed home, refusing to trap and prepare enough beavers to establish a profitable trade.[25]

In 1822, the company enjoyed its first success. Working on both the Yellowstone and the Missouri, three hundred hunters trapped furs worth twenty-five thousand dollars at the St. Louis markets. But the next hunting season brought disaster. In 1823 Robert Jones and Michael Immell led a party up the Yellowstone to the Three Forks. Although the men spotted a few Blackfeet warriors along the way, nothing happened—until the party headed home. In late May, the Blackfeet ambushed the trappers at a site east of present-day Billings and killed Jones, Immell, and five others. The survivors crossed the Yellowstone and escaped with their lives but had to abandon furs and equipment valued at fifteen thousand dollars. Officials of the Hudson's Bay Company later accepted these purloined furs at Canadian posts, and a minor diplomatic squabble between the United States and England ensued. But diplomatic protests meant little to the financially strapped Missouri Fur Company. The disaster on the Yellowstone cost the company all of its yearly profit and much of its capital, numbering its days as an effective force in the fur trade.[26]

As the Missouri Fur Company skirted with disaster, a new group of

Americans, led by William H. Ashley and Andrew Henry of St. Louis, entered the region's fur trade. Ashley, a St. Louis businessman and the state's lieutenant governor, brought capital to the venture, whereas Henry, a veteran of the Missouri Fur Company, brought experience and expertise. At first, Ashley and Henry followed the traditional American strategy of hunting in the Yellowstone country with company trappers ranging from permanent posts. By October 1822, they had established Fort Henry at the mouth of the Yellowstone. But even with this imposing trading post of picket walls and blockhouses, the new company had little luck in obtaining large amounts of furs.[27]

The following spring's expedition met more serious difficulties: the Arikara Indians refused to allow the party to travel up the Missouri, and army soldiers from Fort Atkinson finally forced passage.[28] This conflict led Ashley to consider transportation options outside the upper Missouri river system. As Henry and his men returned to Fort Henry via the Missouri, Ashley sent a second party, led by Jedediah Smith, overland toward the Rockies. The overland trappers fared well at that winter's Crow camp in the Wind River country of Wyoming. The Crows shared knowledge of trapping techniques, social customs, and locations of more fur-bearing animals to the west. They also protected the vulnerable trappers from the rigors of the climate and the revenge-minded Blackfeet. Perhaps most important, the Crows showed the Americans an easy way to reach those rich lands west of the Continental Divide: the famous South Pass, first used by Americans—Robert Stuart and his Astorians—in 1812. Henry's party, on the other hand, suffered so much from Blackfeet harassment at Fort Henry that the traders moved up the Yellowstone, where that December they constructed a new Fort Henry at the mouth of the Bighorn River.

The success of Smith's roving hunters, compared with the problems encountered at the permanent trading posts, prompted William Ashley to adapt the ancient Indian concept of rendezvous. Every year trappers, free of company supervision, would hunt in the region, then bring their year's catch to a predetermined point each summer. There, at the rendezvous, traders from St. Louis would exchange goods for the furs of trappers and Native American hunters. Ashley eliminated much of the overhead from the fur trade, and since he could also mark up the prices of goods brought to the rendezvous, he made the trade a very profitable business.[29]

Probably by accident more than design, Ashley also created a system of economic exploitation more in tune with the social and economic structure of the plains tribes. The free trappers—now better known as the mountain men—"owed allegiance to no single company. They worked alone, or in small groups, and they sold their furs to the highest bidder."[30] They bonded with Native American tribes, taking Indian wives and joining tribal clans. Because of these close family relationships, the free trappers understood better than most others how the plains tribes valued friendship and family ties in the trading relationship, and the trappers eagerly struck alliances to ensure both their safety and a successful hunt. Typically they shared winter camp with the Native Americans, and by exchanging with their Native American allies new and used goods obtained at the rendezvous, they became part of tribal trade networks. Without the friendship, support, and assistance of the Indians, the mountain men would probably not have met with much success in the demanding environment of the northern plains.

The free trappers, viewed in another way, were rarely romantic outcasts from the mainstream of American society. Some were expectant capitalists, good laissez-faire Jacksonians looking for that main chance to accumulate capital for later eastern ventures in farming or shopkeeping. Others combined their hunting way of life with the market assumptions and demands of mercantile capitalism. However, many lacked the entrepreneurial independence usually associated with the mountain man. They were hard-working company employees, with a life full of drudgery and empty of excitement. Yet in general, good relations existed between the Native Americans and the free trappers. The mountain men were not permanent settlers. They were temporary partners in what the tribes perceived as an Indian trading system. And the trappers knew that it was in their economic self-interest to maintain good relations. Few in numbers, the mountain men, compared with earlier parties of company trappers and the permanent forts, appeared to be a minor threat to the Native American dominance of the northern plains.[31]

Those perceptions began to change when a heavily capitalized company bent on monopolizing the region's fur trade arrived in the Yellowstone country. John Jacob Astor's American Fur Company established a Western Department as early as 1823; four years later, it expanded the department by merging it with Bernard Pratte and Company of St. Louis as well as with the Columbia Fur Company, a Canadian venture that had enjoyed a prosperous trade with the Blackfeet and the Crows since 1825. The American Fur Company reorganized these different companies into the Upper Missouri Outfit, a new division within its Western Department under the direction of Kenneth McKenzie, the former manager of the Columbia company. In the fall of 1829, McKenzie constructed Fort Union at the mouth of the Yellowstone, the first of several company outposts on the river. For the next thirty years, Fort Union would be the center of the upper Missouri fur trade as a succession of traders thoroughly exploited the region's natural resources.[32]

As initially constructed, Fort Union was contained within a log palisade measuring 220 by 240 feet, anchored by two-story stone bastions in the northeast and southwest corners. Company employees shared a long dwelling on the west side, opposite to the storerooms and retail store on the east side. Just off the main gate stood a reception room for visiting Native Americans, a blacksmith shop, and workshops for other tradesmen. The two-story frame dwelling of the bourgeois, or the chief trader's home, was at the north end of the fort, and various minor buildings were scattered throughout the grounds. The fort was the most massive and imposing structure in the Yellowstone country, "an architectural symbol of dominance."[33]

The American Fur Company initially attempted to dominate the upper Missouri trade by relying primarily on the hunting skills of employees based at Fort Union. But again that strategy failed, due to Blackfeet hostility, cutthroat competition from small firms such as the Rocky Mountain Fur Company directed by Jim Bridger from 1830 to 1833, and a decrease in the number of fur-bearing animals. So in 1832, the company reversed course and bought from free traders and Native Americans while expanding the number of its permanent trading posts in Indian country.[34]

The mid-1830s witnessed a bitter fight for survival among the upper Missouri fur companies.[35] In 1834, the competitors divided the fur trade between themselves in a one-year agreement that left the American Fur Company in control of the Crow and Blackfeet trade. Later that same year, competition further cooled when Astor sold the Western Department of the American Fur Company to Pratte, Chouteau, and Company, a group of St. Louis capitalists who retained the company name of the American Fur Company and quickly established control over the Yellowstone's fur business.[36]

No matter what company fur trappers worked for, they knew—or soon found out—that a close, personal relationship with the Crows was an absolute necessity for a profitable trade. The traders, unlike many settlers who later followed in their footsteps, dealt with the Indians directly and developed an understanding of native culture based more on observation and experience than on crude and inaccurate stereotypes. Traders either liked or disliked the Crows, for example, but rarely did they dehumanize the Indians. The Americans, according to the historian Lewis Saum, "never considered the Crows to be killers; in fact, they were felt to be a uniquely humane group. However, the fur men realized that the Crows were probably unexcelled in thieving, robbing, and begging. Traders must have suspected that booty, more than goods received through barter, made the Crows suffer the white man's presence in Absaroka as quietly as they did."[37] Saum fails to give the Crows enough credit. Members of this small tribe also linked themselves to the traders, especially the American Fur Company, for protection against the numerically superior Blackfeet and the advancing eastward threat of the Sioux and Cheyenne Indians. They quietly suffered the traders because the alliance was in their long-term interests and it enabled the Crows to remain in the Yellowstone country, land that had nurtured them for centuries.

As the Crow chief Arapooish observed to Robert Campbell of the Rocky Mountain Fur Company, the Crows deeply loved their homeland for the valuable resources it possessed.

The Crow country is a good country. The Great Spirit has put it exactly in the right place; while you are in it you fare well; when-

20

ever you go out of it, whichever way you travel, you fare worse. . . . The Crow country is exactly in the right place. It has snowy mountains and sunny plains; all kinds of climates and good things for every season. When the summer heats scorch the prairies, you can draw up under the mountains, where the air is sweet and cool, the grass fresh, and the bright streams come tumbling out of the snow-banks. There you can hunt the elk, the deer, and the antelope, when their skins are fit for dressing; there you will find plenty of white bears and mountain sheep.

In the autumn, when your horses are fat and strong from the mountain pastures, you can go down into the plains and hunt the buffalo, or trap beaver on the streams. And when winter comes on, you can take shelter in the woody bottoms along the rivers; there you will find buffalo meat for yourselves, and cotton-wood bark for your horses. . . . Everything good is to be found there. There is no country like the Crow country.[38]

During these years of intense fur trade competition, the Crows were not willing to exchange the Yellowstone's resources cheaply. They refused offers of a keg of spirits because liquor, in their opinion, was a very bad bargain. The Crows expected lavish gifts and hospitality (which the Native Americans perceived as tokens of friendship and alliance). Ceremony was important as well; the Crows came to trade painted in bright colors and dressed in their finest clothes. The trading ritual became almost as significant as the actual exchange of goods. To preserve advantageous economic relations, American traders maintained a post in Crow land until 1860, interacting with the Crows in a complex relationship in which each side believed it had the upper hand. As Edwin T. Denig, a bourgeois at Fort Union, would later observe:

The trade with the Crows never was very profitable. They buy for the horse trade. Their own clothing also, of European manufacture, consists chiefly of blankets, cloths, etc., which, with English guns and brass kettles, do not bear a large advance of price when sold to them. Add to this their interminable practice of beg-

ging and stealing, and the expense and risk in taking goods up the
Yellowstone and peltries down, and but little remains to compensate the trader for his time and trouble.

The Crows looked at Denig's complaints of "begging and stealing" in
another way. According to James Beckwourth, an American trader who
lived with the Crows, they believed that the trading posts were *theirs*.
The forts were "where all their goods were stored beyond the reach of
their enemies, and whence they drew their supplies as often as they
had need of them."[39]

Fort Cass, constructed in 1833 at the confluence of the Yellowstone
and Bighorn rivers, the site of earlier American trading posts, was the
American Fur Company's first permanent Yellowstone post. Before,
the Crows had avoided the inconvenience and danger of traveling to
Fort Union. Until the construction of Fort Cass, they usually had
traded at posts located in the Mandan and Hidatsa villages on the Missouri, retaining the prior aboriginal trade network. Compared with its
predecessors, Fort Cass was a substantial post. Within its tall cottonwood stockade, traders lived year round, exchanging manufactured
products for beaver pelts and other furs and, not incidentally, learning
to understand Crow customs.[40]

The traders at Fort Cass were also much more interested in bison
products than in the past, a change in resource preference that increased their dependence on the Native Americans. Buffalo products
had largely defined Crow material culture for centuries. Now, because
of an aggressive consumer-awareness campaign that touted the
warmth of buffalo coats and the taste of buffalo tongues, Americans
back east also wanted these desired buffalo products, but in much
larger amounts than the Crows ever dreamed of trading at the Missouri
River villages.

Mid-1830s production figures from Fort Cass record the shift from
beaver to bison furs. As buffalo products became the mainstay of the
Yellowstone trade, the Americans built temporary posts near Crow
winter camps to encourage year-round hunting. The Crows, mountain
men, and fur traders entered into a working relationship rarely equaled
in the early history of Montana. The robes were produced, as the geog-

rapher David Wishart has observed, "entirely within the framework of Indian culture and custom."[41] The trade was limited to the number of hides (typically about eighteen to twenty) that a Crow woman could dress during a season. The Native Americans, therefore, indirectly controlled the number of bison killed, since they could prepare only so many hides a year.[42]

Preparation of the buffalo tongues for market, on the other hand, relied on the talents of the American traders. The Indians did most of the hunting, but the traders smoked and salted the tongues for the long trip east to the dinner plates of the well-to-do who possessed a taste for the exotic. Unlike the buffalo robes, which could be best acquired in the winter or early spring, tongues constituted a year-round business, and the trade encouraged the wasteful slaughter of the animals for this single delicacy.[43]

The depression of 1837–39 undermined economic institutions and capital investments throughout the country, including the fur trade of the upper Missouri region. By 1838, Pierre Choteau had emerged as the dominant partner in the American Fur Company, and as recovery returned to the land, he led the firm through a difficult transitional period. To retain control over what was left of the Yellowstone fur trade, Choteau replaced Fort Cass in 1839 with Fort Van Buren, a new post near the confluence of the Tongue and Yellowstone rivers. But this investment never returned many dividends because so few animals were left to hunt in the immediate Yellowstone region.[44] By 1840, the beaver had largely disappeared. Americans, armed with the steel trap, had overexploited the resource rather than allow for a sustained yield. Perhaps just as important was the decrease in bison herds. Valued both for its meat and its fur, the buffalo had been overhunted in the past decade.[45]

A terrible calamity in 1837 had also significantly decreased the region's Native American population. Clothing that had been exposed to the smallpox virus was stowed aboard an American Fur Company steamboat headed up the Missouri. Once the disease reached Fort Union, it took only a few weeks to infect all the tribes of the area. The ethnohistorian John Ewers has estimated that the disease killed almost two-thirds of the Blackfeet. The totals for other tribes were just as

23

ghastly. The Crows, however, fared better than most. Heeding urgent warnings to stay away from Fort Cass, they were spared the worst of the epidemic, although their losses were in the thousands.[46]

During the early 1840s, the American traders and Crows tried to rebuild the fur business. In 1842, the American Fur Company's Charles Larpenteur, after burning Fort Van Buren, constructed Fort Alexander on the Yellowstone's north bank, about twenty miles above the abandoned post. The Union Fur Company opened a trading house near the mouth of the Little Bighorn the following year, but by 1845 it sold out to the American Fur Company. In the late 1840s, traversing the Yellowstone by mackinaw boats, using the river largely for transportation, Harvey, Primeau, and Company also tapped the Crow trade.[47]

During the 1850s several companies remained in the fur trade business, although profits continued to shrink. To shore up the declining fortunes of the American Fur Company, Alexander Culbertson moved the Crow trading post once again, establishing Fort Sarpy I on the north bank of the Yellowstone just below the mouth of the Rosebud River. The economic prospects of Culbertson's company showed little improvement until Congress approved the Fort Laramie treaty in 1854. The United States placed the Crows on a huge "reservation" embracing much of the tribe's traditional territory. The agreement did not take away tribal land, but in principle it prohibited Indian war parties from attacking whites traveling west. In exchange, the tribe received fifty thousand dollars annually for the next ten years. The American Fur Company received the federal contract to distribute the annuity, and its last posts stayed in operation largely for that reason. In May 1855, the company destroyed Fort Sarpy I, and two years later it assembled a final Yellowstone post, Fort Sarpy II, upriver toward the mouth of the Bighorn River. The distribution of the annuity continued to generate some income for the company, and the fur trade lingered on at Fort Union until 1865, when the owners ceased operations altogether and sold the fort to the North Western Fur Company.[48]

Just as the fur trade changed the landscape of the Yellowstone Valley, it also changed the lives of the people it touched. The story of Robert Meldrum, an American Fur Company employee, demonstrates how mutual economic concerns bound whites and the Crow Indians. A native of Kentucky, Meldrum lived among the Crows for twenty years. Named "Round Iron" by the tribe, he married a Crow woman and was an expert in the language and customs of the tribe. By the 1850s, he had moved up the company's ranks to the position of bourgeois, or chief trader, at Fort Sarpy I.[49]

Meldrum's acculturation to Crow culture shocked newcomers to the Yellowstone region. Full of their stereotypical ideas of what Indians were like, and how they should be treated, visitors and new employees dismissed Meldrum as a lazy good-for-nothing who let the Indians do whatever they wished. James Chambers, who arrived at Fort Sarpy in 1855, expressed "disgust for both the unseemly generosity and the indecorous conduct of his superior." Meldrum, in Chambers's opinion, was a poor trader and was inattentive to the company's interests because he was too concerned about Crow needs and desires, an observation echoed by Captain William Raynolds during his visit to Fort Sarpy II in 1859. One visitor to Fort Sarpy I remarked that Meldrum's "prodigal liberality" with the Crow set a bad precedent for future Indian-white relations.[50]

These newcomers did not appreciate Meldrum's understanding of the Crow world. He grasped, for example, the importance of gift giving in native culture. To the Crows, his "prodigal liberality" demonstrated Meldrum's desire for friendly trade relations while maintaining his own favored tribal position. His hospitality kept the alliance between the company and the Indians secure. Without Crow support, Meldrum realized, Sioux and Blackfeet war parties could overrun his post at any time. He accepted the Crows as an equal partner in the economic world of the fur trade, and he behaved accordingly.

One event in particular provides an interesting perspective on Meldrum's understanding of Crow culture. On March 9, 1855, a group of Crow warriors arrived at Fort Sarpy I after killing some Blackfeet warriors. As Chambers noted in his journal, Meldrum told the Crows "that the Blackfeet were dogs his heart was good when he heard of their being kill'd &co &co After he was through he presented a squaw with a dress & ninety strands of Beads." Chambers added, "Old Fellow thinks I goods are scarce & you might have saved them & traded for robes." But Meldrum knew that rewarding the Crow for killing the "common enemy" was just as important to the company's fortunes as was the trade for a few more buffalo robes.[51]

Unfortunately, the military commanders who surveyed the Yellowstone country during the 1850s failed to build on the positive Indian relationships established by Meldrum and other fur traders.[52] In 1859 Captain William F. Raynolds of the army's Corps of Topographical Engineers, undertaking a two-year exploration of the upper Yellowstone, quickly found himself involved in the process of economic exchange on the northern plains. On August 17, 1859, the expedition encountered its first Crow visitors, and two days later, a camp of thirty to forty Crows joined the soldiers, with their leader, Two-Face, taking up residence in Raynolds's own tent. By August 22, large numbers of Crows had camped near the expedition. Assuming that the army carried trade and annuity goods, the Crows treated the soldiers as if they were traders for the American Fur Company.

The soldiers were happy that the Crows were friendly, but soon the demands of Crow amity became too much for Raynolds and his men to bear. The captain could no longer hide his displeasure. "Like All Indians," Raynolds jotted in his journal on August 22, "they are importunate beggars, and about camp they take constant and the most disagreeable liberties, throunging into our tents, rolling their filthy bodies up in our blankets, and prying into everything accessible." Yet even more upsetting to Captain Raynolds (a very religious man who refused to march his men on Sundays) was the relationship between the Crow husband and wife. The "women are the mere slaves of the men," he reported, "doing all the menial service." One incident in particular aggravated the captain. "A young Indian, almost a mere lad, with a stout and fine looking squaw wife, has pitched his lodge a short distance from camp. . . . In all their visits to camp the wife carries her liege-lord upon her shoulders through the water with most obsequious devotion."[53]

Raynolds's lack of experience with plains culture meant that he largely understood Crow culture in stereotypical terms. The Crows had the same problem. Accustomed to dealing only with fur traders, they assumed that this large body of whites was just another group of traders heading toward Fort Sarpy II—and so the Crows acted accordingly. Their lack of deference for the soldiers combined with their overt friendliness to unnerve Raynolds and his men.

Things only got worse a week later when the expedition reached Fort Sarpy II. The company agent, Robert Meldrum, initially ignored the soldiers in favor of his Crow friends. Raynolds sarcastically reported that Meldrum "promptly commenced traffic with the savages, considerately allowing our matters to take care of themselves." The following day, Raynolds wanted to council with a Crow chief, but this was delayed until the Crows could locate the chief's missing horse. The delay upset the captain, and he found the meeting even more unsatisfactory—the Crow leader wanted to speak only about "secondary" topics, such as relations between the Crows and President James Buchanan.[54]

By early September, Raynolds had concluded that the Crows would only hinder the successful completion of his expedition. A large group of warriors, who could provide directions and protection, wanted to continue with the soldiers once they left Fort Sarpy II. Raynolds said no. "This is decidedly overdoing the matter of amicable relations," he wrote in his journal. "A single guide would be of invaluable service, but the continual company of 500 savages of all ages and both sexes, devoid of any strict ideas of property, expecting to be allowed free access to our stores, and with a general friendship for our portable articles rather than for our persons, can hardly be esteemed one of the leading advantages to be derived from amity with [the Crows]."[55]

The army explorers never trusted the Crows, concluding they were "greedy savages" from the very first contact. The soldiers' envy, distrust, and suspicion of the Crows—rather than the traders' cordial relations and mutual dependency—were attitudes later shared by many of the settlers who followed the hoofprints of the soldiers' horses.

By 1861, the soldiers had left the Yellowstone Valley—they were now needed back east to smother the fires of insurrection and civil war. The fur trade had largely ended as well. Indeed, by middecade, mighty Fort Union at the confluence of the Yellowstone and the Missouri would be dismantled and transformed into an army post, Fort Buford. But for a few years yet it would be difficult to dismantle the patterns of exchange that had characterized Indian-white trade for well over sixty years. The Crows, although greatly decreased in number by economic warfare with the Blackfeet and Sioux and by killer diseases brought unknowingly by other Indians, traders, and missionaries, dominated the relationship to its last days. They provided food, protection, wives, and families and took the time to hunt and then prepare buffalo products and other pelts for trade. Without their assistance, the fur trade would never have achieved the success it enjoyed during these years.

What did they receive in return? Obviously the Crows thought they were getting their pelt's worth. Their alliance with the traders ended their dependence on the goods available at the Missouri River villages. It gave them a measure of protection from their enemies to the north and, increasingly, from the east. The trade also provided new materials and goods, which represented a remarkable increase in their standard of living. But in exchange the Crows had paid a stiff price. The buffalo, the key component of Crow material culture, had been overexploited. The Crows had new consumer demands that traditional native technology could not answer. More to the point, they were engaged in an economic relationship where they had long-term disadvantages. As Wishart has argued, the Americans possessed "a license for unconstrained exploration that was untenable for a people who were totally dependent on the ecosystem." Thus when the fur regions "had been stripped of their furs the trappers and traders simply turned to other resources and to other areas. The impact of this exploitation was destructive to the physical environment and to the native inhabitants alike. Perhaps it is through this dark lens, rather than through the rosy lens of frontier romanticism, that the fur trade of the West should be viewed."[56]

CHAPTER 2

Early Settlements,
1864–1877

Ω

The settling of the Clark's Fork Bottom was part of a wider population movement that reshaped the Yellowstone Valley during the last third of the nineteenth century. From 1864 to 1877, in the first phase of that movement, Americans attempted to plant several permanent settlements at different places throughout the upper Yellowstone region. Because of the region's isolation, the lack of a Yellowstone transportation base, and the hostility of the Sioux and Northern Cheyenne Indians, however, these individual initiatives never took root. The federal government's victory in the Great Sioux War of 1876–77, and the subsequent establishment of Forts Keogh and Custer, created possibilities for a new future. By the summer of 1877, the first settlers had arrived in the heart of the Yellowstone Valley, the Clark's Fork Bottom, determined to establish a permanent transportation base along the banks of the Yellowstone River.

The mid-1860s was a time of transition in the Yellowstone Valley. Political boundaries changed in 1863. Almost the entire length of the Yellowstone, from the current northern boundary of the national park to the confluence of the river with the Missouri, was now part of Idaho Territory; the next year it would become part of Montana Territory.

Americans also changed their preferences. The few remaining fur-bearing animals along the Yellowstone no longer interested large capitalized companies, although individuals and entrepreneurs remained in the trade for another two decades. The new resource of choice was gold, which already had been discovered in the western mountains of Idaho and Montana territories. In 1864, gold rush fever reached the Yellowstone.

The fever first touched Thomas Curry, an Irish miner who was one of thousands of prospectors at the diggings of southwestern Montana Territory, where more and more miners arrived each day to find less and less gold. The gold camps of Bannack and Virginia City were exciting places, but Curry was in Montana to find his fortune, not to court prostitutes and get rip-roaring drunk every night. In 1864, he decided to try his luck elsewhere; perhaps fortune and glory lay in the mountains to the east. At Emigrant Peak, soaring over the Yellowstone Valley near present-day Pray, Curry found that place—or so he thought—and he promptly established Yellowstone City along Emigrant Gulch (not far from today's Chico Hot Springs). Soon his "city" was overflowing with miners of all shapes, sizes, and descriptions, as well as seventy-five dwellings of the most ramshackle sort: log cabins, boarded tents, tipis, and the like.

The first winter at Yellowstone City was difficult. "The ground was very deep and hard to work," the early Yellowstone historian E. S. Topping recorded, "and many of those who had claims did not get them properly opened." Abundant wild game, and Crow indifference to the prospectors' presence, allowed the mining camp to survive. Auguste Archambeau and Frank Cin Cin, two French-Canadian trappers, opened a trading post to supply some of the comforts of life, especially watered-down booze for those cold winter days. Despite the cold weather, bad whiskey, and poor pickings, one miner recalled that residents "enjoyed life to the utmost. Balls and parties were frequent and well attended, the most cordial good fellowship prevailing."[1]

Isolated at first, Yellowstone City was soon connected to the outside world. The territorial legislature of 1864 granted Sam Word, N. P. Langford, and others a charter for the Broad Gauge Company, a stage and telegraph line that connected Virginia City to Yellowstone City and then continued down the valley to old Fort Union at the Yellowstone's confluence with the Missouri. It was the region's first "hightech" connection to the East. The company began construction the following spring, supplied with lumber from John J. Tomlinson's new sawmill, which was about nine miles downriver from Yellowstone City. Tomlinson and his wife, Margaret, had arrived in Yellowstone City on August 27, 1864, after leaving their home in Iowa and traveling the Great Platte River Road, then the Bozeman Trail, to Montana. The company hired W. J. Davies to take Tomlinson's lumber and build three ferry boats for crossings at Yellowstone City, at the mouth of the Bighorn (about where the American Fur Company had abandoned its Fort Sarpy II), and at the Clark's Fork River (a Bozeman Trail crossing). A crew of three men and a pony operated the ferries. Once he finished that work, Davies built several mackinaws to float goods—and hopefully the gold to come—down the Yellowstone.[2]

When spring came to the Yellowstone in 1865, little beehives of activity dotted the valley. New immigrants were busy building homes, light industries, and an overland transportation network. In addition, an increasing tide of immigrants crossed the Yellowstone Valley headed for the goldfields via the Bozeman Trail. This sudden flurry of activity, especially the wagonloads of new settlers who trudged along the Bozeman Trail, did not sit well with the newest residents of the area, the Sioux and Cheyenne Indians.[3] Already forced to abandon their eastern homelands, neither tribe wanted to lose additional land and resources to the increasing number of white settlers pushing into the northern plains. To scare away the immigrants, bands of Sioux and Cheyenne warriors regularly attacked travelers. On August 24, 1866, for example, a party of unknown tribal affiliation killed William K. Thomas, his son, and his wagon driver along the Yellowstone in present-day Sweet Grass County. The Indians took almost everything but Thomas's diary, which somehow survived to document his ill-fated trek.

To protect its intrusion into Indian territory, the federal government established Fort Ellis near the town of Bozeman and Fort C. F. Smith along the Bighorn River. The Crows welcomed the new forts as a sign that the Americans were renewing their old political and commercial alliance. They visited the posts on a regular basis, providing information about the Sioux's whereabouts, serving as scouts and soldiers, and supplying the soldiers with food in the harsh winter months. Loyal and effective allies, the Crows warned the army of the Sioux and Cheyennes' planned joint assault on three of the Bozeman Trail forts in 1867; unfortunately, the army paid no heed and suffered accordingly. This success spurred even more intense Sioux and Cheyenne hostility toward the settlement and development of the Yellowstone region. By 1868, the army had withdrawn from Fort C. F. Smith, which the Sioux quickly torched, and wise travelers had abandoned the Bozeman Trail. The Fort Laramie treaty of 1868 underscored the Sioux and Cheyenne domination of the region. It officially closed the Bozeman Trail and reserved the Native Americans' seasonal hunting rights throughout the Powder, Tongue, and Bighorn drainages.[4]

The closing of the Bozeman Trail halted further settlement along the Yellowstone. The once promising placer mines at Emigrant Gulch had panned out two years earlier, and now the ferries and Fort C. F. Smith were destroyed. What the Crows thought about this turn of events is difficult to say. They had allowed the Americans into their land as a means of protecting their territory, and according to the Fort Laramie treaty, much of the land south of the Yellowstone remained theirs. Yet, outnumbered and outgunned as they were by the Sioux and Cheyennes, the Crows held a tenuous position. And now the Americans—their allies—apparently had left again.

This time the absence lasted only a few months. In the spring of 1869, the Americans returned to construct Fort Parker, the first official Crow Indian agency, near where Mission Creek emptied into the Yellowstone River, twelve miles east of present-day Livingston. Largely completed by late November, the post consisted of a ten-foot stockade, with a pair of two-story blockhouses, which enclosed several dwellings and associated work buildings. An accidental fire claimed this first fort in the spring of 1870, and the army built anew with adobe brick. Both forts looked much like the earlier trading posts of the American Fur Company, and the Crows, for the most part, treated the agent, Fellows D. Pease, and his employees as they had treated the fur traders ten years earlier. In the Crows' way of thinking, Fort Parker was their property, built by the Americans to protect their goods. Actually, this assumption was close to the mark. The economic relationship at Fort Parker involved an exchange of land and services for a yearly annuity and other gifts from the federal government—thus, the goods at the fort had already been "purchased."[5]

As in the fur trade, the Crows and Americans forged close ties. Agency employees soon became enamoured of the Crow way of life; they married Crow women and moved their families into the post. The well-known story of Thomas H. Leforge and his Crow wife, Cherry, is a good example of what attracted agency employees to Crow culture. As Leforge later observed:

> Oh, it was a great life. I had a good wife who made for me fine buckskin clothing, kept my hair in the best of order, kept me scented with sweet-grass, had my bed and my entire lodge always in neat condition, prepared for me the sweat-bath lodge whenever I wanted to use it, did everything that a woman can do to make a man comfortable and happy. I alternated at hunting and doing duty at the agency or in the military service, each a congenial employment and each bringing in plenty of funds to sustain us. At all times I had ample leisure for lazy loafing and dreaming and visiting. In the summer I wore nothing but breech-cloth and moccasins when out in the camps away from the agency or the fort. As I idled and smoked, my wife sat by my side and did sewing or beadwork.

The Crows became frequent visitors to the agency, and some took up semipermanent residency. In 1873, the closeness of this relationship infuriated an Interior Department inspector, who ordered the Crows out of the fort and forced employees to either legally marry Crow women or leave them.[6]

Reformers at the Interior Department hoped that Indian agencies like Fort Parker could teach the plains tribes how to be like whites, not vice versa. They wanted the friendly, peaceful Crows to become settled, prosperous farmers. To that end, Agent Pease had his men construct three miles of fences and two miles of irrigation ditches while planting one hundred acres of good bottomland by the summer of 1871. These actions marked the beginning of the valley's agricultural cultivation. Yet the fur trade still dominated economic activity at the agency. Thomas Leforge's memoirs include a detailed description of the agency's trading practices, a description that closely follows the trading routines of the former fur trade posts. "Gifts," according to Leforge, "always inaugurated the procedure of trading." Generally children received candy, women were given handkerchiefs and beads, and men "got knives or other suitable articles." At other times, the Crows received "calico, ammunition, sashes, skeins of thread . . . and all sorts of trivial things that the old-time Indians used to prize so highly."[7]

Once this generosity had established "good feeling," the "exchange selling of goods began," with the women first, followed by the children and men. The items the Crows received included "saddles, bridles, ropes, blankets, calico, sugar, coffee, knives, guns, ammunition, tweezers for pulling stray beard hairs, canned foods, beads in large and small quantities, pins and needles, cheap jewelry made of glass and brass, beans, rice, [and] dried apples." To encourage the Crows' consumer habits, the agency would sell on credit, as long as the debt was cleared from the next hunt. Leforge "never knew of any failure to collect bills of this kind."[8]

A more open-market version of the fur trade also beckoned at a tiny settlement of crudely built log cabins just north of the agency near the confluence of the Shields and Yellowstone rivers. In 1868, William Lee had established a ferry here to provide transportation across the Yellowstone for travelers from Fort Ellis and Bozeman to the Crow Agency at Mission Creek. In 1869, Frank "Buckskin" Williams had built a cabin to house a saloon and trading post. This place became the "headquarters and main resort of the trappers, miners and frontiersmen of the upper river. Here the trappers brought their furs and here the traders came to buy." When, as Thomas Leforge recalled, "the traders gave dances and feasts to attract the Indians," the Crows came also to trade buffalo skins. By this time, the Crows had a strong consumer taste for the materials of capitalist America. Pretty Shield remembered, "We dressed many robes to trade for the things we wanted." And according to Two Leggings's memoirs, Crow warriors at this time were willing to exchange fifty buffalo robes for a single repeating rifle and another robe for every twenty cartridges.[9]

In 1873, the location became known as Benson's Landing after Amos Benson and Dan Naileigh built a log-house saloon, where illegal liquor sales to the Native Americans and army soldiers took place. Benson's Landing became a stop for stage traffic and had its own post office. Hugo J. Hoppe opened another saloon–trading post–hotel in 1873–74 to serve the increasing number of travelers between Bozeman and the agency.

The year 1874 marked the end of the first decade of settlement activity along the Yellowstone. There was little to show for all the efforts. Although the federal government officially owned Fort Parker, it seemed that the Crows controlled it. Benson's Landing was a sorry excuse for a "town," totally dependent as it was on the presence of the agency and the patronage of Crow Indians who still wished to exchange pelts. When the gold rush had ended along Emigrant Gulch, everyone had packed their belongings and abandoned Yellowstone City.

Nor did Sioux and Cheyenne antagonism toward development of the Yellowstone area show any signs of abating. When the Northern Pacific Railroad sent survey parties, under military protection, into the valley in 1872, a large force of Sioux warriors attacked the command of Captain Eugene Baker at a site about four miles northeast of present-day Billings. Baker successfully repelled the assault, but the engagement served as another disincentive to settlement. The only true permanent development in the valley was the establishment of Dr. Andrew Jackson Hunter at Springdale, just downriver from Benson's Landing. Here, in 1870, Hunter built the Yellowstone's first "resort," constructing covered-log bathhouses three years later. According to Thomas Leforge, Hunter was a die-hard Confederate who named his children Elizabeth Longstreet, Mary Lee, Davis Beauregard, and, of course, Stonewall Jackson. Pompous in bearing, the good doctor "was portly and dignified, was incessantly chewing tobacco, wore full whiskers, kept his iron-gray hair bobbed at the neck, and his head was always topped by a silk stovepipe hat." At this time, the Indians ignored Hunter's venture because it was too isolated and small to pose any real threat to their hegemony. (Later, after the development of the Northern Pacific Railroad, "Hunter's Hot Springs" would become a major Yellowstone tourist attraction.) With Hunter's business and nearby Benson's Landing as the only functioning private enterprises, the permanent settlement of the valley appeared to be years away.[10]

The year 1874 was also a bleak time in the more settled Bozeman area of the Gallatin River valley to the west. Entrepreneurs had quickly established Bozeman as southeastern Montana's leading trade center. The Bozeman Trail initially served as the settlement's primary eastern transportation link, but the treaty of 1868 made any movement on this once popular road extremely hazardous, if not impossible. Freighters could move goods north to Fort Benton, the head of navigation on the Missouri River, for a steamboat ride eastward. But river transportation was expensive and had its own dangers as well. At one time, most eastern Montanans had looked to the oncoming Northern Pacific Railroad, then crossing the Dakota plains, as their transportation savior. In 1874, however, Jay Cooke's great venture stood still in Bismarck, Dakota Territory, with the company left almost bankrupt in the wake of the economic panic of 1873–74. A direct transportation link to the East—which seemed to be an absolute necessity for future growth and prosperity—still eluded the residents of the Gallatin Valley.[11]

Yet, not every voice on the streets of Bozeman spoke of doom and gloom. J. L. Vernon, a former surveyor for the Northern Pacific Railroad, was optimistic about the future. Arriving in Bozeman at the end of the 1873 survey season, he bragged about several rich gold mines he had located along the Yellowstone Valley, particularly near the mouth of the Tongue River, deep in the heart of Sioux country. Whereas Vernon's grandiose scheme to prospect along the Yellowstone captured the attention of many local businessmen, others pushed a more conservative proposal. A group of Bozeman citizens organized the "Yellowstone Wagon-road Association," hoping to survey and build a road connecting the hub of the Gallatin Valley to the head of navigation on the Yellowstone River, which they assumed to be the mouth of the Bighorn River. The wagon road would have the immediate benefit of freeing local merchants from the expensive prices of the traders and freighters at Helena and Fort Benton and would provide, in addition, a direct route for transporting produce and cattle from the Gallatin Valley. Where to invest? Which expedition had the most promise? These questions were raised in many Bozeman homes. The temptation of quick riches from Vernon's expedition initially overshadowed the plans of the wagon-road association. But on January 20, 1874, Vernon abandoned his expedition, leaving the wagon road as the only available option.[12]

The idea of a wagon road to a Yellowstone port involved more than idle chatter. In 1863, General Alfred J. Sully had used steamboats in his campaign against the Indians, with the crafts reaching the Bighorn River. Ten years later, an army experiment with steamboat navigation on the Yellowstone had produced further interesting results. To supply and protect surveyors for the Northern Pacific Railroad, the army had contracted with Sanford B. Coulson, head of the Missouri River Transportation Company of Yankton, Dakota Territory, to send a steamboat up the Yellowstone. Coulson chose the *Key West* and its pilot, Grant Marsh, for the assignment. Marsh in turn hired Luther S. "Yellowstone" Kelly, a young New Yorker who had spent the past five years hunting throughout the Missouri River country, to serve as a guide. Captain Marsh piloted the steamer as far as the river's Wolf Rapids, just below the mouth of the Powder River, and later in the season he took the *Josephine* over the Wolf Rapids with ease. With navigation of the river possible, Bozeman business leaders knew that a route to the East was now more than mere conjecture.[13]

Three days after Vernon abandoned his plans, broadsides plastered throughout Bozeman announced the creation of the "Yellowstone Wagon Road and Prospecting Expedition." The name, representing a good bit of marketing by the wagon-road supporters, was designed to retain the original backers while it attracted those excited about Vernon's calls for a Yellowstone gold rush. Many leading businessmen in Bozeman, including T. C. Burns, Nelson Story, and H. N. Maguire, contributed five thousand dollars to the venture. The broadside pleaded for more funds and noted, "This enterprise will do much to develop the various resources of the lower country, induce immigration and encourage railroad and steamboat approaches." It took less than a month to organize 150 men for the push down the Yellowstone. Rather than finding their fortunes or establishing a navigation base, however, they encountered a spirited Sioux and Cheyenne defense. The Bozeman men beat a quick retreat home. The expedition was a disaster, but its historian expressed confidence about the future. "In time," Addison M. Quivey predicted, a "great throughfare to the east" would connect Bozeman to the Yellowstone River.[14]

The following year, in 1875, another group would leave Bozeman in search of quick riches in the Yellowstone Valley. The organizers of the "Fort Pease" expedition—the merchants Paul McCormick, Zed Daniels, and Fellows D. Pease, the former agent of the Crow reservation—had reacted to two bits of interesting news. First, the federal government was moving the Crow agency from near Benson's Landing to a new site off the Stillwater River about 20 miles south of present-day Columbus. What was left of the fur and illegal whiskey trade, in other words, had to shift eastward. Next, it was common knowledge that Grant Marsh would be piloting the *Josephine* up the Yellowstone that summer, and many assumed that this voyage was destined to establish the river's future head of navigation. Based on the prior army experiments in 1863 and 1873, Pease and McCormick guessed that the mouth of the Bighorn would be where the *Josephine* stopped, and they wanted to grab a spot for a trading post as soon as possible. But they guessed wrong. As they made plans to float to the Bighorn, Grant Marsh was already carving "Josephine, June 7, 1875" on a cottonwood tree a few miles west of the future site of Billings. That was how far steamboats could move up the Yellowstone in the summer of 1875.[15]

Meanwhile the Fort Pease expedition reached the Bighorn and Yellowstone confluence, the site of several earlier fur trading posts, and assembled a fort one hundred feet square, with two corner bastions and log dwellings for the post employees. Here the arrangement of space inside and outside the fort was quite similar to what the fur trade companies had constructed at such outposts as Forts Union, Cass, and Sarpy. The bastions served as guardhouses and gave the Bozeman traders a view of the landscape and the dangers hidden therein. The stockade provided protection from expected Sioux and Cheyenne attacks. Inside the fort, the emphasis was on shared space for the employees; there were no single-family homes, for no families resided here.

Although Fort Pease looked like the old fur trading posts, its ultimate economic goal was different. Paul McCormick, second-in-command of the expedition, looked at Fort Pease not as a seasonal trading post where traders would renew past patterns of exchange with the Crows but as the Yellowstone's first permanent settlement, a place he confidently named Big Horn City. McCormick and the other major investors looked forward to a thriving fur trade with the Crows, but more important, they believed that they had snatched the Yellowstone's primary steamboat base. In their dreams, Big Horn City would soon become the Fort Benton of southeastern Montana. And when Paul McCormick spoke of a city, he thought of something quite different from a trading post. Fur traders, like their Native American allies, typically looked at the landscape as one seamless whole, an ecosystem to be exploited, certainly, but one where survey lines, townships, and street lines meant nothing. Instead McCormick envisioned plat maps, geometrically defined town lots, aligned streets, single-family dwellings, and cast-iron fences.[16]

What did the Crows think of the plans of the Bozeman merchants? Certainly they were interested in renewing past trading practices. To their eyes, Fort Pease appeared to be the resurrection of the American Fur Company posts, where they had enjoyed such good relations with traders like Robert Meldrum. But things had changed in the last twenty years. In the past, American reliance on the Crows for labor in preparing the pelts and robes as well as for protection against Blackfeet attack meant that the Crows had enjoyed the upper hand in the trading relationship. Now new fur-processing technologies at eastern factories greatly diminished the traditional reliance on Crow women to carefully prepare buffalo robes for exchange. Nor could the Crows protect Fort Pease from the Sioux Indians. They now had little to offer the traders but the furs; their economic role was more subservient than at any time in the past. Paul McCormick, although he maintained friendships with Plenty Coups and Medicine-raven, enjoyed a much more dominant position in the trade than Robert Meldrum had ever possessed.[17]

During the winter of 1875–76, the ferocity of attacks from Sioux and Cheyenne warriors increased to such an extent that, by February 1876, Pease and McCormick demanded that the U.S. Army rescue their men. In due time, a group of soldiers from Fort Ellis escorted the traders to

Bozeman. The Sioux and Cheyennes stopped Big Horn City from becoming a permanent transportation base for the farmers, trappers, and merchants of eastern Montana.

A successful American trader had to tread a fine line of distinction between Crow and Sioux territory in the Yellowstone Valley. By establishing their post too far away from the Crow agency, Pease and McCormick had ignored that line and failed. Horace Countryman and Hugo Hoppe paid attention and succeeded. Both had been traders at Benson's Landing, heavily dependent on the Crow trade. When the government moved the agency, Countryman and Hoppe moved as well, building a new trading post at the confluence of the Stillwater and Yellowstone rivers (near present-day Columbus). Their new post—even with illegal whiskey flowing freely—never matched the rather paltry size of Benson's Landing. Countryman's ranch, as contemporary accounts often called it, was too close to the Sioux danger and too far away from the agency headquarters to ever become more than a frontier outpost. The new Crow agency stood about twenty miles south of the Yellowstone River, deep in Indian territory, and in this much more isolated setting, government officials were determined to do their best to "civilize" the Crow Indians.[18]

The second Crow Agency was a physical symbol of that new determination. Built of adobe brick, the agency formed three sides of a square, or a modified U-shape. It was fortified with a cannon, and the buildings formed an effective stockade against Sioux or Cheyenne attack. Policies at the new agency would prove to be quite different from those the Crows had enjoyed at Fort Parker, where relationships had been much more relaxed, perhaps reflecting the norms of Indian culture more than those of Victorian society. The new agency would not allow the lack of discipline, the Indian-white cohabitation, and all the rest that the federal inspector had found so distasteful in 1873. A new breeze was blowing in Washington, one that wanted to sweep out the corruption rampant in the Interior Department. Reformers called for peace, assimilation, and education for the nation's Native American population.[19]

Dexter Clapp, the reservation agent, was the government's minister of reform on the Yellowstone. He first gave the Crows wagons and farm implements to encourage agriculture. The semi-nomadic Crows—who preferred hunting, horses, and travois—puzzled about these items until realizing their utility as trade items. The Indians felt the same about beef rations (buffalo was more plentiful and tasted better), bacon (although the grease was good for tanning skins), and the white man's clothing (scratchy, uncomfortable, and too hot in the summer). Bagged flour was another matter: the flour itself was good for trading, and those colorful bags made handsome tipi decorations and were handy for clothes as well. The Crows' ablility to take the products of the Industrial Revolution and use them in creative ways included more than flour bags. Today, examples of their material culture from the 1860s to 1880 are in the collections of the Montana Historical Society in Helena; these items not only underscore the Crows' ability to adapt European goods to native traditions but also document the increasing reliance of the Crows on American goods. The society's collections include leather belts decorated with brass tacks and glass seed beads, bags of black cotton and red wool trade cloth, and dazzling dresses of red wool trade cloth, blue felt, glass beads, and checked cotton cloth lining.[20]

The Crows' increasing reliance on American manufactured goods pleased Agent Clapp, except for the trade of whiskey, an item the Crows had once scorned. He complained in the spring of 1876 that whiskey left behind by the Fort Pease expedition had turned the reservation into "almost a pandemonium of drunkeness and brawling" for two weeks. Thomas Leforge, however, remembered that throughout the 1870s, the Crows remained stoutly opposed to liquor consumption. He noted, "Often I have seen drunken Crows hog-tied by the dog-soldiers and their whisky bottles smashed."[21]

Clapp may have exaggerated the whiskey problem to strengthen his case for an extension of the reservation's northern boundary. The Crows had signed their first treaty with the United States in 1825 following tremendous losses from a combined Sioux-Cheyenne attack in 1822. (One scholar estimated the Crow losses at five thousand, an extraordinary number for plains warfare.) Through this alliance with the Americans, the Crows hoped to receive protection from further attacks. The military built no forts as promised, but the Indians probably considered the fur trading posts constructed throughout the Yellowstone region from the late 1820s into the 1850s as maintaining the alliance. In 1854, Congress ratified the 1851 Fort Laramie treaty, which strengthened the alliance by giving the Crows an annuity of fifty thousand dollars for ten years in exchange for establishing formal boundaries for a Crow reservation. The area set aside most of the traditional tribal hunting grounds, including the west bank of the Powder River drainage, all of the Bighorn, Stillwater, and Boulder rivers, the land south of the Musselshell River, and all of the Yellowstone from its headwaters to its confluence with the Powder. The reservation totaled 38.5 million acres.[22]

However, the Fort Laramie treaty of 1868 reduced tribal land to a mere 8 million acres, confining the tribe to land south of the Yellowstone from its headwaters to east of the Bighorn River. In 1873, the government again opened negotiations with the tribe, hoping to exchange worthless prairies further east for imagined mineral riches in the mountains of the reservation's western boundary. This time the negotiations became very complicated and lasted several years. The Americans wanted to move both the Mountain and the River Crows north of the Yellowstone to the land watered by the Musselshell River—traditional Crow hunting territory—and proposed a rather unequal exchange: give up the Yellowstone Valley for the Judith Basin. The tribe agreed to move north, but not to exchange the land. "This is our country," Chief Blackfoot observed, "and what we give is worth more than all the other side of the River. You want to give us a hole, we want a big country."[23]

In the fall of 1875, President Ulysses Grant became involved in the negotiations. Officials in his Interior Department had argued that the Crows needed relief from whiskey traders like Horace Countryman. How could the Crows be taught the values of white civilization if the dregs of that same civilization continued to poison their minds and bodies? If the land on both sides of the Yellowstone belonged to the Indians, Agent Dexter Clapp insisted, no one would be close enough even to attempt trading with the Crows. Grant agreed that here was a solution to the diplomatic impasse. An executive order on October 25, 1875, set aside land north of the Yellowstone from the Great Bend to east of the mouth of the Bighorn as an addition to the Crow reservation.[24]

This insulation of the Crow agency lasted only four months. Cattlemen in the Judith Basin, merchants in Bozeman, and politicians in Helena, the territorial capital of Montana, cried foul. They wanted that land back. Facing a new presidential election, the Republican administration forgot about reform and caved in to the demands of Montana businessmen and officials. On March 8, 1876, Grant revoked his order—Washington's centennial gift to its loyal Crow allies.[25]

If the Crow alliance meant nothing to Washington that March, attitudes changed days later with the opening shots of the Great Sioux War of 1876. At first the Crows had "mixed feelings" about getting involved. Crow warriors had served the army well as scouts and auxiliaries in earlier conflicts. But 1876 was a different matter. Their reservation had once again been reduced in size. The Crows lacked confidence in the army's claims that it would defeat the Sioux—the bluecoat soldiers had bragged about that for years. Yet the U.S. military, reasoned Crow chiefs, was still the tribe's best bet. As Chief Blackfoot explained to Colonel John Gibbon, "We want our reservation to be large, we want to go on eating buffalo, and so we hold fast to the whites." The consensus among the tribal leaders extended to individual warriors. Two Leggings believed that the military alliance was the only alternative. "We helped the white man so we could own our land in peace." The Crows would fight.[26]

The first battle in the Yellowstone country took place southeast of the Crow reservation along the Powder River valley. There, on March 17, Colonel J. J. Reynolds of the command of General George Crook smashed into a combined Sioux-Cheyenne camp. But Reynolds failed to destroy the village, and extremely cold weather chased the soldiers back to the warmth and safety of Fort Fetterman in Wyoming. Hostilities cooled until the hot months of summer, and during this lull, the army received the welcomed, and essential, assistance of the Crows and Shoshonis. On June 17, along the Rosebud River, Crazy Horse and his Sioux and Cheyenne warriors almost trapped Crook's command in a canyon. Assisted by 250 Crow and Shoshoni auxiliaries, the besieged soldiers fought back. Six hours of determined fighting left Crook and his troops bruised, bloody, and a bit shaken. The Sioux and Cheyennes were confident that the next fight would bring victory.[27]

Just eight days later, that battle took place on the Little Bighorn River. The combined Sioux-Cheyenne forces decisively whipped General George Custer, who lost one-half of the Seventh Cavalry in one of the most lopsided defeats in American military history. News of the "Custer Massacre" shocked the nation in general, and eastern Montana in particular. Yet for the Sioux and Cheyennes, their success on the Little Bighorn had few lasting benefits: it was a classic example of winning the battle but losing the war. The defeat left the U.S. military momentarily reeling, but the army renewed the war with much greater determination that fall and winter, led by Colonel Nelson "Bear's Coat" Miles. By the spring of 1877, even Crazy Horse had surrendered. The war was over.[28]

Determination alone did not spell success for the army's 1876–77 winter campaign. Another contributing factor lay in its decision to build two supply posts, or cantonments, in the Yellowstone country.[29] The posts at the confluence of the Yellowstone and Tongue rivers and on the Little Bighorn River, together with a steamboat base called Terry's Landing located one mile southwest of the present-day town of Terry, provided essential logistical support for the soldiers as they chased the Indians. And once the shooting was over, the federal decision to expand the two cantonments into full military posts directly influenced the permanent settlement of the Yellowstone Valley.

The first, and most important, post belonged to Colonel Miles and his Fifth Infantry. Miles claimed a Yellowstone supply post as early as August 28, 1876, when he dispatched two companies to the mouth of the Tongue River. Two weeks later, he formally established his headquarters there. Military correspondence usually referred to the post as the "Cantonment on the Tongue River."[30]

Soon after construction of the post, white settlers arrived to live within its safety. As G. M. Miles noted in his diary: "Quite a settlers store was started by Mat Carrol who came in from west part of State. The Settlers store sold too much whiskey [and] Gen'l Miles said the Whiskey caused him more trouble than the Indians." Miles would close Carroll's saloon the next spring. Another early merchant was C. W. Savage, who opened a trading post.[31]

Assuming the name of Miles Town, this small settlement of high-risk businessmen and whiskey traders continued to grow in 1877. Maurice Conn and the Bassinski brothers opened stores. John Carter, a bartender, bought out Mat Carroll's closed whiskey business and started a new saloon. Dance halls and other places of amusement for the soldiers were also constructed. On June 14, 1877—almost a year after the Sioux-Cheyenne victory at the Little Bighorn—the territorial government organized Custer County and named Miles Town as the county seat. The settlement's permanence was, more or less, assured.[32]

The following month, General William T. Sherman arrived at the Tongue River cantonment to review the construction of the post's permanent fortifications, later named Fort Keogh in honor of Captain Myles Keogh, who had fallen at the Battle of the Little Bighorn. There he proclaimed, "The Sioux Indians can never again regain this country." The new fort symbolized the army's victory in the 1876–77 war, solidified American control of the Yellowstone Valley, and opened the doors to white settlement all along the river. As General James S. Brisbin remarked, "Prior to 1877, I would say there was no safety for either life or property along the Yellowstone." [33] For several years after the coming of the Northern Pacific Railroad, Miles Town—later Miles City—would be the Yellowstone's biggest town, largely due to the commanding presence of its neighbor, Fort Keogh, and its excellent access to the steamboat trade along the Yellowstone River.

The effect of the second Yellowstone post—Fort Custer at the confluence of the Bighorn and Little Bighorn rivers—was less immediate and more indirect. Lieutenant Colonel George P. Buell and the Eleventh Infantry established the post on May 10, 1877, and construction of a permanent fort started soon thereafter. Like its sister fort to the northeast, Fort Custer—named for General George A. Custer—received its official name on November 8, 1877.[34] Ever since the abandonment of Fort C. F. Smith along the Bozeman Trail, the Crows had wanted another military post to strengthen their alliance with the

Americans. With Fort Custer squarely within the reservation's borders, the Crows finally had achieved their objective.

The presence of Fort Custer encouraged the establishment of a second town on the Yellowstone River, at its confluence with the Little Bighorn River. Steamboats sometimes turned here to take their goods and supplies down the Little Bighorn to the new fort. If the water was too low, the boats unloaded their cargo at the confluence so that freight teams could move it overland to the army post. By July 25, 1877, Paul McCormick had returned to the mouth of the Bighorn and attempted to resurrect his former settlement of Big Horn City. "Here a ferry had been established," Colonel O. M. Poe reported, "a town laid out (called Big Horn City) and the ferrymen have built a log-hut as the legitimate beginnings of the prospective metropolis of the region." The soldiers made camp that evening "near the only building in the 'city', upon ground which had been made muddy and sticky by the rain of the afternoon, as only the soil of an alkali plain can be." In time, this settlement became known as Junction City, roughly sixty miles from Miles Town to the east and sixty miles from the Clark's Fork Bottom to the west.[35]

In 1877 General William T. Sherman inspected the new Yellowstone forts. In his report to George W. McCrary, the secretary of war, Sherman said nothing about the Yellowstone's early settlements west of Fort Keogh, but he did note, "There is a strongly-marked wagon-trail, but no bridges or cuts; a purely natural road, with steep ascents and descents, and frequent gullies, about as much as wagons could pass." Over this rough, many times impassable, road would come the first settlers of the future Yellowstone County. They settled in an area they called the Clark's Fork Bottom, which was located at the heart of the Yellowstone Valley along the river's northern bank, roughly from present-day Billings to Park City. A Bozeman *Avant Courier* reporter described this region as "an expanse of level alluvial land extending from the Yellowstone River to the boundary foot hills, forty miles in length, by an average of nine in width. At various points it is sixteen miles wide, and must contain 150,000 acres of excellent soil and grassland" along with thick stands of cottonwood trees. The correspondent added, "Experts pronounce it wheat and oat and vegetable land, par excellance." The Clark's Fork Bottom does contain rich soil, but it also has a dry climate.

46

Any land beyond the immediate river bottomland must be irrigated for successful horticulture. On the other hand, its natural grasses, irrigated or not, are ideal for raising stock. Visiting the Bottom in 1880, Granville Stuart remarked that the land was "well grassed"; in fact, he had "seen no country yet where I would like to trust more than a few thousand cattle." In choosing the Bottom as their new home, settlers appeared to be following a rule of thumb observed by the historian Timothy Mahoney in the earlier settlement of the upper Mississippi. They wanted land that had market access, good quality, and traffic flow. In the Yellowstone frontier of 1877, the Clark's Fork Bottom was one of the few places that had all three advantages.[36]

In time, this section of the Yellowstone Valley became home to three separate settlements: in the center stood Canyon Creek, nearby present-day Laurel; the western gateway was Young's Point, a few miles upriver from present-day Park City; and Coulson, a village on the Yellowstone River, served as the eastern point of the Clark's Fork Bottom. From 1877 to early 1882, those who settled this land, together with newspaper reporters in Bozeman and Miles City, most often described these three places as if they composed a larger whole, the "community" of the Clark's Fork Bottom.[37]

The first permanent settlers of the Clark's Fork Bottom arrived in the spring of 1877. Most were from Bozeman; some came from as far west as Deer Lodge and Virginia City, and one settler, Ed Carpenter, was newly arrived from New York. Once the homestead plat books arrived in Bozeman, the settlers moved quickly to legitimize their claims. Joseph M. V. Cochran was lucky. He happened to be in Bozeman when the books arrived, and filing under the Homestead Act of 1862, he claimed land along the Yellowstone where Grant Marsh had ended the voyage of the *Josephine* in 1875. Perhaps Cochran believed he had grabbed the river's head of navigation—a choice piece of property indeed. Bela B. Brockway and Ed Forrest, two hunters who had noticed the potential of the land during their eastern travels to hunt in the Black Hills and later as members of the Fort Pease expedition, returned to make their homes along Canyon Creek. They were the Bottom's first actual settlers. After helping to construct Fort Custer, John R. King decided to stay in the valley. His first business was building mackinaws for the river trade down the Yellowstone, an occupation that earned him the nickname of "Commodore." Alonzo Young and his son Forrest built cabins at Young's Point along the Yellowstone at the Bottom's western gateway. In time, their home included a stage stop, post office, and tavern. Another stage station was operated by H. H. Stone and Elliot Rouse near Canyon Creek, two miles upriver from Brockway's ranch.[38]

Through the existing homesteading laws and the presence of the region's two military posts, the federal government already had given settlers incentives to move into the Clark's Fork Bottom. In the summer of 1878, it added new inducements by awarding S. S. Huntley of Bozeman a mail contract for the area between Bozeman and the Tongue River cantonment. Huntley established a Yellowstone ferry crossing near the mouth of Pryor's Creek, and soon the small settlement of Huntley surrounded his enterprise. The federal contract also meant that a reliable stage road had to be constructed, replacing the rugged wagon-trail General Sherman had noted that summer. Once again, federal patronage and money directly spurred the settlement of the Yellowstone Valley.[39]

The needs of the federal government also brought the potential of the Clark's Fork Bottom to the attention of Perry W. McAdow of the McAdow Bros. Wholesale Company of Bozeman. Perry and his brother William won the 1877 contract to supply the Crow Agency with cattle and flour. In fulfilling this obligation, McAdow came to know the country well and would soon become its leading entrepreneur. A resident of Montana Territory since 1861, McAdow had been born in Mason County, Kentucky, in 1838. His family moved to Missouri the following year, and Perry spent most of his early childhood on the family farm at Platt Purchase. At the age of eleven, Perry accompanied his father, who practiced medicine, and his maternal uncle on a trek to the gold fields of California. Arriving too late to make much money from the boom, the three Missourians decided to come home. Unfortunately, Perry's father died during the return trip, which turned what had been an exciting jaunt into a family disaster. Perry had to go home and operate the family farm. He later entered the local masonic college but abandoned his studies when the West beckoned again in 1858.

McAdow, then only twenty years old, moved to Salt Lake City, where he worked as a salesman for the firm of Gilbert and Gervish. In the summer of 1860, he returned to Missouri for the last time. When the spring thaw opened the Missouri River to traffic, he promptly boarded a St. Louis steamboat headed to Fort Benton.

Disaster again struck as McAdow entered Montana Territory, for at the Poplar River, the boat exploded and sank. Perry escaped any physical injury, but he lost everything he owned and had to walk the remaining 350 miles to Fort Benton. This accident began a pattern that ran throughout McAdow's life in Montana. Sudden reversals would leave Perry a broke, but never a broken, man. Like many western entrepreneurs, he had the knack of dusting himself off and starting over once again.

In 1862, McAdow—or "Bud" as his Montana friends always called him—got lucky. One of the first prospectors at Gold Creek and Pioneer Gulch, Bud had panned one thousand dollars by the summer of 1862, and with this sizable grubstake, he searched for more gold at Bannack and Alder Gulch, later known as Virginia City. It appears that McAdow and his partner, A. S. Blake, did well at both locations, but by 1864 Bud had either tired of the miner's life or, more likely, had eyed a better way of making money. His experiences at the California and early Montana mines had taught him that perhaps storekeeping and outfitting, rather than prospecting, was the best way to strike it rich at a mining camp. In 1864, Bud abandoned the mines to operate a steam-powered sawmill on Granite Creek and a lumberyard in Virginia City. Then he sold the mill, and with the profits he established a ranch and sawmill, then a flour mill, in the Gallatin Valley. The Gallatin River, and the booming town of Bozeman, became the center of his entrepreneurial empire for the next fifteen years, culminating in the wholesale business he operated with his brother William.

Yet not everything had been successful for Bud since that boiler explosion on the Missouri River. In the spring of 1863, McAdow, his partner, and a few other hardy souls had floated down the Yellowstone to trap and prospect near the Bighorn River. Soon after they arrived, however, a party of warriors (probably Sioux) attacked the prospectors, killing two and wounding several others. Without the timely intervention of a group of Crow warriors, McAdow and all his friends would have died. This fiasco kept McAdow away from the Yellowstone for many years, but he obviously never forgot the country's potential. Once the military had secured the valley, McAdow returned as one of the upper Yellowstone's first capital investors.[40]

Perry McAdow's initial interest in the Yellowstone focused on how to produce and transport the 1877 provisions for the Crow agency. To keep transportation costs from eating away his profits, he looked for a cheaper way of ferrying the Yellowstone than the service currently provided by S. S. Huntley at the region's first ferry crossing. So in July, he announced plans to build a sawmill in the eastern end of the Bottom, a place soon known as "McAdow's Mill." Bud located the mill near a natural ford in the Yellowstone, one often used by bison and Native Americans. With John Shock as a partner and resident operator, McAdow took some of the lumber from his sawmill and constructed a ferry, made of steel-wire and rope, as an alternative way of crossing the Yellowstone. McAdow, and other travelers, could now escape the dictates of the Huntley ferry.

Next, McAdow wanted more land on which he could raise the crops and cattle specified in the agency contracts. Using the newly approved Desert Land Act, he grabbed squatter title (formally filing in 1879) to 450 acres of prime Clark's Fork Bottom property. The Desert Land Act granted up to 640 acres of "desert" land for eight hundred dollars to anyone who would improve the land by irrigation in a three-year period. On this land, McAdow could cultivate several different types of grain, fulfilling his agency contracts plus, perhaps, trading crops to hungry soldiers at the newly created Fort Custer, since a road between Fort Custer and Bozeman crossed the Yellowstone by way of his ferry.

Supplying the military posts certainly was an economic opportunity not to be ignored. McAdow, along with several other Bozeman entrepreneurs, had previously floated mackinaw boats from Bozeman downriver to the forts, supplying the soldiers with vegetables, butter, and eggs. Their profits had been substantial. By locating himself on the eastern tip of the Clark's Fork Bottom, McAdow believed he could dominate the mackinaw boat trade while establishing a settlement that had the potential of evolving, at least, into the supply point for Fort

Custer or, at best, into the head of navigation on the Yellowstone River. He, not Paul McCormick at Big Horn City or S. S. Huntley at the Huntley ferry, would have the "Fort Benton" of the Yellowstone River.[41]

Perry W. McAdow understood that transportation was the key to the settlement and development of the valley. The potential traffic on the Yellowstone River was too significant to ignore. From his home in Bozeman in the spring of 1877, he had written Martin Maginnis, the Montana territorial delegate to the U.S. Congress: "We must make an effort to save our Territory from being depopulated. I am satisfyed that unless we get a R. R.—that in a few years there will not be enough of us left to make a corporals guard." McAdow, in other words, invested in the Clark's Fork Bottom not only because of the potential of the country but also because he believed that a transportation link to the East had to be secured or his Bozeman operations would be threatened.[42]

McAdow's first venture into the Yellowstone as a young man had ended in disaster, and in September 1877 it appeared that history had repeated itself. Throughout the summer, White Bird, Looking Glass, and Chief Joseph had led a group of nontreaty Nez Percé Indians away from the clutches of the U.S. Army in perhaps the most famous freedom trek in American history. They had traveled from Oregon through Idaho and into Yellowstone National Park, trying to find a safe haven. Turning into the Yellowstone Valley, the Nez Percés hoped that their old allies, the Crows, would provide sanctuary. Unwilling to risk their valuable alliance with the Americans, the Crows said no, and their warriors took immediate delight in stealing as many horses from the Nez Percés as possible.

On September 13, the Nez Percés entered the Clark's Fork Bottom, where they burned the stage station of Stone and Rouse. Both men fled for Bela Brockway's cabin two miles away. Here, bolstered by the timely arrival of a stagecoach with a driver and three passengers, the settlers determined to fight it out—until they saw the number of Nez Percés. They exchanged a few shots then hightailed it to the brush around the river.

The Indians torched Brockway's cabin and haystacks and proceeded to have fun with the abandoned stagecoach. Donning a shipment of black stovepipe hats they found inside, they took turns riding the coach. Then, nattily attired in breechcloths, formal hats, and war paint, the Indians rode on to Joseph Cochran's place. Here the only bloodshed of the day occurred. Cochran, luckily, was out cutting timber with a gang of workers down by the Yellowstone near McAdow's Mill. But his house guests, Clinton Dills and Milton Summer, were surprised at dinner and murdered.[43]

With stovepipe hats riding high, the Nez Percés next approached the mill. There the settlers had enough warning to throw together some breastworks. "Every scattered store and cabin and group of wagons," Alice Shock later recorded, "was an improvised fort." Their actions saved them and the mill from attack, but the Indians burned the local combination store and saloon (apparently owned by McAdow and operated by John Shock) before riding off. It had been quite a scare, and that night the mill workers threw a big party to celebrate the fact that their scalps were still firmly on their heads.[44]

That was about all they could celebrate, for their meager homesteads were in ruins and the saloon was destroyed. When news of the destruction reached Bud McAdow in Bozeman he must have wondered if bad luck had again destroyed his dreams for the Yellowstone. Two months later, he wrote his Helena bankers that he was going to the Yellowstone to survey his investments. What he found—the homesteaders rebuilding, the mill still working—was encouraging. Even better news came from back East, where the newly reorganized Northern Pacific Railroad had decided to resume construction. This time, a single Indian raid was not enough to discourage McAdow from further developing his Yellowstone empire.[45]

CHAPTER 3

The Emergence of Coulson,
1877–1879

Ọ

P. W. "Bud" McAdow stood on the banks of the Yellowstone, surveying his fledgling operations in the Clark's Fork Bottom. In the few
weeks before winter, McAdow had an important decision to make.
Should he cut his losses and get out of the Yellowstone region? Richer
and more powerful businessmen than he had failed here before; why
should he take any chances? Yet, despite the potential of future Indian
raids, the depleted fur resources, and the lack of known mineral resources, McAdow still believed in the future of the Yellowstone. Bud
chose to roll the dice, betting that his future in the Clark's Fork Bottom
would surpass his past experiences in Montana.

His first task was to repair the damage left by the Nez Percé Indians.
Rebuilding his store and saloon, McAdow renamed the settlement
"Coulson" in honor of S. B. Coulson, the general manager of the Coulson Line steamboat company, which owned the *Josephine* and several
other boats. By naming his "town" after the man who then controlled
the transportation destiny of the Yellowstone, McAdow hoped for a return favor: that the town of Coulson, not the competing Huntley,
would become the river's head of navigation. S. B. Coulson's steam-

boats were the only eastern transportation link in the region, and Bud desperately wanted a steamboat base for his property.[1]

Although the town now had a proper name, it still lacked a post office, and no place could claim to be a town without one. Bud put his political contacts to work, and by early December he had a post office located at his store, with his storekeeper, Sam Alexander, as postmaster. Bud took advantage of the Bottom's need for local governmental services as well. With the formal organization of Custer County—Miles Town was the county seat, almost 150 miles distant—county officials appointed Sam Alexander as the Bottom's first justice of the peace and Bela B. Brockway as the local constable. With Sam Alexander in charge, McAdow's combination store and saloon at Coulson became the de facto governmental center of the Clark's Fork Bottom.[2]

From his home in Bozeman in early 1878, Perry W. McAdow wrote his friend Martin Maginnis, the territorial congressional delegate, "When you come down into the Yellowstone Country you will be surprised to see how fast we are settling it up." Indeed, the settlements of the Clark's Fork Bottom made a rapid recovery from the Nez Percé raid of the previous September. McAdow did his part by persuading Harry and Alice Reed to move from their ranch near Countryman's stage station at the mouth of the Stillwater River and live at Coulson. Harry would operate McAdow's sawmill and later his ferry.[3]

In general, these early months of settlement at Coulson match the pattern noted by the geographer John Hudson in his study of town evolution on the North Dakota plains in the early twentieth century. First came some type of general merchandise store, which typically relied heavily on the fur trade, followed by the the establishment of a small manufacturing venture (such as McAdow's sawmill), a blacksmith, and finally a post office. Hudson concluded that of these four components, the post office was the crucial acquisition. "It paid money, drew customers, and provided a regular link with the outside."[4]

In addition to establishing the general store, the sawmill, and the ferry, McAdow also hired William Heffner, John J. Alderson, and M. N. Sanders to go to Coulson and construct ferryboats and mackinaws. Nothing further is known about M. N. Sanders, but William Heffner and John J. Alderson became two of the Bottom's most famous pioneers. Born in Breden, Germany, in 1838, Heffner worked at the army sawmill at Fort Ellis before accepting McAdow's commission. After building the boats, he returned to his job in Bozeman, where an accident later cost him three fingers. Heffner eventually moved to Coulson, taking on odd jobs before operating a local rock quarry which provided the stone for many Billings buildings in the 1880s and 1890s, including what would later become the Western Heritage Center. Heffner brought valuable craft skills to Coulson, a necessity for a growing community.

John J. Alderson, born in Arkendale, Yorkshire, England, on October 2, 1840, came to Coulson as a man rapidly approaching middle age and still in search of fame and fortune. When he had immigrated to the states twenty years earlier, Alderson landed in Minnesota. Little is known about these years except that young Alderson joined the Union cause in the American Civil War, serving with the First Minnesota Volunteer Infantry until he heard of gold strikes in an isolated territory called Montana. In 1863 Alderson left the army and headed for Virginia City. Like many, he panned nothing but gravel; Alderson abandoned his dreams of gold to become a resident of the Gallatin Valley. Soon he was a moderately successful farmer. In 1876, he was a grain merchant in Bozeman, where he came under the watchful eye of the McAdow brothers. The following year Bud picked Alderson to watch over his Yellowstone operations at Coulson, and the Englishman was a permanent resident by the summer of 1878. His wife, Ellen, a spry thirty-one-year-old Illinois native who moved to Coulson with her husband in 1878, and Alice Reed, the wife of the stagecoach operator Harry Reed, were the first female residents of Coulson.[5]

John and Ellen Alderson were part of a much larger movement of settlers to the Clark's Fork Bottom during the spring and summer of 1878. Several Gallatin County families, some who had filed claims in Bozeman the previous year and others who planned to claim squatter rights, left the Gallatin Valley that spring for new homes along the Yellowstone. The settlement at Young's Point, a stage stop with a saloon and restaurant about three miles upriver from present-day Park City, received formal recognition in July 1878, when Alonzo J. Young was named postmaster. Around the Young ranch in 1878 settled his son Forrest and the families of Bill Mitchell, John Kinney, and Edward Alling.[6]

Other eastern Montana residents selected ranches near the town of Coulson. Most important to our story is the arrival of the Orson Nickerson Newman family in the spring of 1878. Newman had been born in Orleans County, New York, in 1830; the next year, his parents moved to Michigan, where Orson grew up. He lived at home, working the family farm, until he was twenty-eight years old. He married in 1858, and he and his wife, Elizabeth, immediately left to try their luck on the Great Plains, moving first to the frontier of western Nebraska, where they farmed for four years, and then to Colorado in the fall of 1863. The Newmans stayed there for only a couple of weeks before striking out for the Montana frontier. Joining a party carried by seventy-five bull-driven wagons, they headed for the placers at Bannack. Lady luck, unfortunately, eluded their grasp, and in the spring of 1864 Orson and Elizabeth took what money they had and established a small ranch in the Madison Valley.

The family's first Montana adventure never found success. Orson even tried the Alder Gulch mines before abandoning Montana that fall to head for new gold strikes in Nevada. Heavy snows delayed their journey, so the Newmans detoured to San Diego and later Riverside, California. Newman remembered Riverside as "the garden spot of the world," yet it still wasn't enough. In 1873 the family was on the move again. Why they left the California "garden" is difficult to understand, but the severe nationwide recession of 1873 may have forced the family to leave. Whatever the reason, they "put the yoke on the cattle," as Newman recalled, "and started north, passing through Portland, Barrow [Barlow] Pass and the Palouse country, and got back to Virginia City, Mont., in 1875." The second stay in Madison County proved to be more fruitful than the first; Orson even became a local justice of the peace. His twenty years of western travels give meaning to the historian Patricia Limerick's observation that "to many Americans, the West promised so much that the promise was almost sure to be broken."[7]

Three years later, in 1878, Newman uprooted his family one last time, and with thirty-five head of cattle, three yoke of oxen, and three teams of horses, they moved to the Clark's Fork Bottom, arriving on March 16, 1878. They selected a Yellowstone River homestead on the grounds of an old Crow camp, where the "Indians used to bury their dead in the hollow of an old tree stump." One of the first things the family did, according to a daughter, Mary Newman Scott, was "to dig out the dead bodies and rob them of their mocassins and leggings."[8]

Traveling with the Newmans were the families of Aaron Ford, who left no account of his life and pioneer days, and Richard W. and Davidella Clarke, who both wrote about their days on the Yellowstone. Born in Pennsylvania in 1842, Dick Clarke first tasted western life as an employee of the Indian agency at Fort Leavenworth, Kansas, in the early 1860s. Hearing the tales told by all the soldiers, fur traders, and Native Americans passing that way, Clarke soon hankered to find his own fortune. In 1866, he headed for Montana via the Bozeman Trail to try his luck in the western mines. But two years of hard work yielded little. In 1869, Clarke abandoned mining, bought a Gallatin Valley ranch, and then traveled all the way to Topeka, Kansas, to marry the sixteen-year-old Davidella.

For the next nine years, the Clarkes scratched out a living while the family grew by leaps and bounds, with a new baby arriving about every other year. By 1878, Dick and Davidella had five children to feed, a tough if not impossible task on their small wheat ranch. That spring, when their friends the Newmans and the Fords suggested moving together to the Yellowstone, Dick and Davidella agreed. Of the three families, the Clarkes were certainly the poorest. While the Newmans brought lots of livestock and built a huge two-room, thirty-foot-long log cabin when they arrived, the Clarkes got by with a crude dwelling made of logs and tent canvas. Its condition frankly embarrassed Bud McAdow, who vowed, "I'll find lumber enough to see that the kids won't have to be on the bare dirt if I have to take the roof off my saw mill." Even Bozeman creditors took pity. Before leaving the Gallatin Valley, Clarke stopped in Bozeman to discuss a $200 debt owed Dr. Achilles Lamme. The good doctor predicted that the Indians would murder Clarke, and he tore up the note. "It is paid now," he stated. Later that year, when Lamme took the first commercial steamboat on the Yellowstone, he stopped at Clarke's home and was appalled that it lacked a stove. The entire family could freeze that winter. "You come over to the landing and get a stove," Lamme ordered Clarke. "Those children need one." The stove and other merchandise totaled $125, but Lamme told Clarke to pay when he could. Farming proved to be so profitable that initial season at the Clark's Fork Bottom that Clarke repaid this substantial debt, plus the earlier $200, the very next year.[9]

Another important early resident of the Coulson area was John R. "Commodore" King. Born in Michigan in about 1849, King first settled at Deer Lodge, Montana Territory, in 1870. He stayed there for a year before moving to Helena and working odd jobs. By 1872, King was a hunter and trapper in the Judith Basin and Musselshell Valley of central Montana. Here he learned to live and trade, mostly with the Crow Indians, who introduced him to the unlimited hunting of the Yellowstone Valley in 1873 and 1874. The next year, King abandoned his trapping to assist in the construction of the new Crow agency along the Stillwater River. Not until the outbreak of the Great Sioux War of 1876 did King earn his nickname of "Commodore." During the summer conflict, King operated mackinaw boats to carry supplies from Benson's Landing to Terry's Landing, and in December he floated the river to deliver a message from Fort Ellis to the new cantonment on the Tongue River. Once established in the mackinaw business, King continued to move freight down the Yellowstone in 1877 and 1878. He became a Coulson resident in 1878, working at McAdow's sawmill and rafting lumber down to the booming settlement of Miles City before turning to the operation of his own ranch by the spring of 1879.[10]

Other settlers in 1878 included Alfred Wolverton, who lived near Bela Brockway and would soon be appointed the area's second justice of the peace, John W. Shock, John Hogan, and the four Salisbury brothers from Ohio—tall, lanky chaps known collectively as "24 feet of Salisbury." Everyone arrived in time to prepare for winter and to harvest the first crops of the Bottom. J. V. Bogert, a correspondent for the Bozeman *Avant Courier*, recorded the agricultural diversity of the valley in this account of a "country dinner" hosted by Wolverton and Brockway:

> corn, 10 to 12 inches long in the ear; the finest peach-blow and
> Goodrich potatos; enormous tomatos; cucumbers half an arm in

length; pickles made "on the spot" this season, and watermelons—long ones, round ones, big ones, and all luscious as a peach. As we looked on, surfeited, so to speak, before a mouthful, Brockway said if we could wait he'd get up some squashes and cauliflowers from the garden, and then he said he had turnips and onions and beets and carrots, which he'd cook for us if we thought there was not variety enough in sight. [11]

In one sense, the pioneers who built the little rural community documented by the Bozeman reporter in 1878 were the same type of person: white, overwhelmingly male, and willing to take on the challenge of frontier life to build a better future. But by looking at the roles they occupied in the region's emerging economy, it is clear that the pioneers who occupied the Bottom in 1877–78 consisted of an entrepreneur, a small group of his employees, and a much larger group of homesteaders. The interactions between these groups, and with the neighboring Crow Indians, would largely define the Bottom's economic relationships until the coming of the Northern Pacific Railroad in 1882.

As the region's initial entrepreneur, that is, the person whose market contacts extended beyond the Clark's Fork Bottom and who had adequate amounts of capital for speculative investments both in and out of the Bottom, Perry W. McAdow was the most important actor in the Bottom's early history, even though he was not a resident. In 1877–78, McAdow, it is important to remember, was still a Bozeman wholesale commission merchant. Lured by the potential of government contracts to supply Fort Custer and the Crow Indian agency, he was carefully extending his trade networks eastward so as not to risk all his capital in a new venture. Coulson—as the crossroads for overland trade between Bismarck, Dakota Territory, and Walla Walla in Washington and as the stage crossing for Fort Custer—was to be the center of his operations. The bottomland surrounding the tiny hamlet was also valuable to McAdow. The new Desert Land Act allowed him to claim hundreds of acres very cheaply to grow agricultural commodities. The business of the settlers of the Bottom and an ideal river base for trade between his operations in Bozeman and Fort Keogh belonged to McAdow as well.

Table 1: Residents of the Clark's Fork Bottom Listed in 1877
Custer County Tax List (spelling in original)

Name	Value of Property	Assessment	Total Tax Paid
John Alderson	$ 350.00	$ 350.00	$ 9.16
Bela B. Brockway	150.00	150.00	7.70
Edward Forrest	100.00	100.00	6.80
P. W. McAdow	2500.00	2500.00	47.00
Total number of taxpayers: 112			

Source: Tax List, 1877, Custer County, Montana Historical Society, Helena

Cold, hard numbers taken from the Custer County tax lists confirm McAdow's position as the entrepreneur of the region. As table 1 indicates, his property was worth from seven to twenty-five times that of the other three Bottom residents paying taxes in 1877. When the tax rates are adjusted to uncover the value of property owned by the truly typical Custer County pioneer (by dropping from our calculations the taxes of the top five taxpayers in Custer County, who were all residents of Miles City and owned 51.7 percent of the taxable wealth in the county), McAdow paid more than three times the adjusted average of taxes paid by residents in all of Custer County. In the context of the Yellowstone frontier economy, Bud McAdow was certainly a rich man.[12]

The tax list also uncovers the very different economic position of such early Bottom settlers as Ed Forrest and Bela B. Brockway. As homesteaders, Brockway and Forrest made their living from hunting and trapping and supplemented their diets by garden produce. They traded furs in Bozeman to supply their other material needs. In fact, none of the homesteaders who arrived in the Bottom at this time became truly self-sufficient farmers. Hunting and trade with the Indians further supported their agrarian pursuits. In this frontier "borrowing system," they traded with the Crows for much of their clothing, bartered with the local merchant for foodstuffs and other supplies, swapped their labor with each other, and offered their labor to those who

Table 2: Residents of the Clark's Fork Bottom Listed in 1878
Custer County Tax List (spelling in original)

Name	Value of Property	Assessment	Total Tax Paid
Joseph Cochran	$ 180.00	not given	$ 8.24
David Currier	420.00	"	12.65
John Horr	125.00	"	7.25
Edward Johnson	250.00	"	9.50
Daniel Lehey	275.00	"	9.95
Daniel Lavalley	240.00	"	9.32
Archie McMurdie	200.00	"	8.60
Perry W. McAdow	6690.00	"	125.42
A. J. Young	538.00	"	14.68 4/10
Total number of taxpayers: 236			

Source: Tax List, 1878, Custer County, Montana Historical Society, Helena

could afford it, while also selling vegetables and grains to travelers, the military, and the Indians.[13]

The employees of P. W. McAdow compose still another group of economic actors. These men were hired hands, engaged by McAdow to work at his Yellowstone operations. The 1877 Custer County Tax List (table 1) shows that John Alderson, who supervised McAdow's businesses, owned far less property than his boss, but what he had was worth more than twice the ranches of Brockway or Forrest. In 1878 (see table 2), another McAdow employee, the sawmill worker David Currier, was the third-wealthiest man taxed in the Bottom, but his property was worth far, far less than the holdings of McAdow. Currier's wealth was closer in line with that of Alonzo Young, the Bottom's second-wealthiest man, who operated a stage stop and ranch. Some of the difference in property valuation between employees and homesteaders is due to the location of the property. Employees lived in the town of Coulson, and their holdings, accordingly, were considered to be more valuable than the scattered ranches of the valley. But in reality, the differences in economic status between employees of McAdow and the homesteaders scattered throughout the Bottom were mostly statistical. Since McAdow's economic resources were so vast and varied compared with the property of both the settlers and his own employees, it is better to conclude that two groups of economic actors participated in the early development of the Clark's Fork Bottom: McAdow, the entrepreneur, and the actual settlers, be they employees or homesteaders.

The tax lists for the late 1870s support this conclusion. For all of Custer County in 1878, the average tax paid was $34.49. If we once again eliminate the top taxpayers to adjust for their great wealth (these ten, composing 4.2 percent of the taxable population, owned 54.5 percent of the taxable wealth), the average tax paid by the truly typical settler was $16.38. As shown in table 2, of the Clark's Fork Bottom residents who paid taxes, only Perry McAdow paid more than this adjusted county average, and he paid over seven times that amount. Indeed, McAdow belonged to that elite class of ten men who owned over half the taxable wealth of Custer County. Also in 1878, the Bozeman *Avant Courier* listed Perry and William McAdow as among the "heavy" taxpayers of neighboring Gallatin County (the newspaper defined "heavy" taxpayers as those who paid more than $100). McAdow was now one of the wealthiest men in southeastern Montana.[14]

The tax list for 1879 reveals that although several settlers in the Bottom had achieved economic gains, no one came close to narrowing the wealth gap between the settlers and McAdow. A total of 323 taxpayers were assessed $9,023.78, with an average tax of $27.94. If the top fifteen taxpayers (4.6 percent of those taxed, owning 56.5 percent of all taxable wealth) are eliminated to get a better idea of the property value of the truly typical settler, the adjusted average tax in Custer County becomes $12.76. In the Clark's Fork Bottom, as indicated in table 3, a majority of the taxpayers paid more than the adjusted average for the first time. But once again, Perry W. McAdow was the region's biggest taxpayer. His property was valued at $6,000, more than seven times that of the next-highest resident, and McAdow paid $137.60 in taxes, more than six times the amount paid by the second-highest person on the list. The same basic relationship appears in the 1880 Custer County Tax List, with P. W. McAdow paying taxes six times the amount paid by the Bottom's second-highest taxpayer. But in 1880, a majority of Bot-

Table 3: Residents of the Clark's Fork Bottom Listed in 1879
Custer County Tax List (spelling in original)

Name	Value of Property	Assessment	Total Tax Paid
J. R. Anderson	$ 50.00	not given	$ 5.89
Jn. Alderson	400.00	"	15.80
B. B. Brockway	175.00	"	8.85
H. Caldwell	150.00	"	8.00
R. W. Clark	620.00	"	18.64
Isaac Danford	420.00	"	14.24
S. H. Erwin	410.00	"	14.02
Edwd Forest	173.00	"	8.85
A. L. Ford	40.00	"	5.89
John Horr	225.00	"	9.95
David Currier (estate)	780.00	"	22.04
J. B. Kinney	476.00	"	15.45
Archie McMurdy	200.00	"	8.24
P. W. McAdow	6000.00	"	137.60
O. N. Newman	794.00	"	22.07
W. D. Olmstead	585.00	"	17.84
Racek Bros.	180.00	"	8.96
A. J. Young	494.00	"	15.43
S. Stallcup	200.00	"	10.54
Total number of taxpayers: 323			

Source: Tax List, 1879, Custer County, Montana Historical Society, Helena

tom residents were assessed less than the adjusted average tax paid in Custer County. This downturn probably reflects the damage of an 1879 hail storm that destroyed the crops of several area ranchers and damaged properties in Coulson.[15]

A brief look at the homesteading records of the Coulson vicinity further underscores Bud McAdow's economic dominance. Table 4 documents homestead holdings of the Bottom's early settlers. McAdow,

Table 4: Homesteaders Filing in the Clark's Fork Bottom, 1879–1880
(spelling in original)

Name	Date Filed	Acres	Date of Final Proof
P. W. McAdow	3/18/1879	457.86	10/24/1881
Aaron F. Ford	5/17/1879	160.00	6/10/1887
Henry Colvell	5/9/1879	155.76	7/18/1884
O. N. Newman	5/17/1879	143.60	after 5/2/1896
J. M. V. Cochrane	5/8/1879	79.34	cancel–9/2/80
James. O. O'Brien	11/28/1879	160.00	cancel–8/31/81
John Hogan	9/24/1880	160.00	7/8/1886
John Alderson	3/15/1879	176.36	9/10/1880
Michael O'Connell	5/13/1879	160.00	3/16/1886
William A. Allen	5/10/1880	40.00	cancel–6/12/82

Source: Homestead Tract Books of the General Land Office, 1879–80, Yellowstone County, Montana, National Records Center, Suitland, Maryland

who had enough capital to file a desert land claim, was the largest landowner. His 450-acre claim dwarfed the others. His employee John Alderson had the second-largest homesteading claim in the area, but he owned only 16 acres more than the typical 160-acre homestead claim.

These differences in wealth also took physical shape in the type of homes built. McAdow had the best house in the Bottom, a balloon-frame dwelling covered with clapboard and built in 1880. No photographs of the house exist today, but surviving descriptions emphasize its spaciousness and beauty and speak of its frame construction. It wasn't much according to the Victorian standards then popular in Bozeman, Helena, and Montana's other major cities, but it was Coulson's finest by far. And if McAdow's cheap frame dwelling was the best Coulson could offer, we can fairly assume that the other homes of the Bottom must have been quite plain indeed.

From settlers' accounts in the homestead records filed with the U.S. Land Office, we know that many homes were single-pen or double-pen log cabins. Andrew Jackson Hunter's residence at Springdale, documented by a print in Michael Leeson's 1885 history of Montana, had a low pitch roof and consisted of three connected rooms, two for his family and one for a post office. Documented by camera in 1948, Alonzo Young's house near Park City, which some claim to be the first cabin in the Bottom, was a classic single-pen cabin, made of hand-hewn logs, with a steep roof creating an upstairs loft. Historic photographs at the Western Heritage Center document O. N. Newman's dwelling, one of the Bottom's largest according to contemporary accounts. His sawn-log house measured about thirty feet in length, large enough to house his family of ten and to serve the community as a social center for dances and other gatherings.

But Hunter, Young, and Newman were among the Yellowstone's wealthiest ranchers. Their neighbors lived in smaller cabins or even dugouts. William A. Allen, the blacksmith at Canyon Creek and later a self-trained dentist and local historian in Billings, recalled that his 1879 cabin was the first at Canyon Creek to have a shingle roof. His neighbors used sod or dirt to keep out the rain. Others, such as Richard and Davidella Clarke, resided in jerry-rigged combinations of logs and canvas. Timothy Reardon, newly arrived from Boston, built on a more grandiose vernacular scale. Fearful of Indian attack, he built a "complete stockade" around his cabin and stables, adding foot-wide slabs of sod to the stockade walls. These variations in the built environment of the Clark's Fork Bottom—dwellings ranging from dugouts to a comfortable frame home—graphically depict the economic differences separating settlers of the region.[16]

For McAdow's Coulson to be a viable trade center, he needed the settlers—and the potential trade they represented. Coulson in the summer of 1878 offered a general store, a post office, a sawmill, a ferry, and a justice of peace. But few settlers would have ventured into the Clark's Fork Bottom if not for the continued direct and indirect assistance of the federal government. The federal presence at Forts Custer and Keogh had made it safe for settlers to pull up stakes and move eastward. And once they had established ranches, they discovered that the army posts provided a market for crops and for trophies from the hunt, along with other indirect economic incentives. Quartermaster records from Fort Custer allow for a reconstruction of the official trade between the post and the settlers. As table 5 indicates, the military supplied the residents of the region an average of $441 annually in exchange for lodging, food, and supplies and in 1880–81 paid for the lodging and salary of Valentine Wickersham, the operator of the telegraph at Alderson's Hotel in Coulson. The $564.59 paid to Wickersham for salary and expenses indirectly aided the local economy, since he had to turn over a substantial amount of that total to Alderson for food and lodging. Indeed, compared with the residents of the other settlements around Young's Point and Canyon Creek, Coulson-area residents in general received more of the benefits of the military's business, a further indication of the economic supremacy of the settlement within the Bottom.

It is more difficult to document the unofficial trade between the settlers and the soliders at Fort Custer. According to one account, Richard W. Clarke and Aaron Ford took wagonloads of produce to the fort where, in exchange, they received "extra army rations, bacon, sugar, coffee and other necessities." Other settlers probably participated in this barter trade as well, for soldiers at these isolated posts were known to do almost anything to supplement and add variety to their basic army diet.[17]

Far more important than the trade with the military at Fort Custer was the economic activity between the settlers and the Crow Indians. Indeed, the value of the Crow trade was so significant that it encouraged many settlers to maintain friendly relations with their Native American neighbors even when the whites considered themselves morally, culturally, and racially superior. However, only in a few isolated cases did the Crow-settler relationship ever match the closeness and mutual dependency sometimes found in the fur trade era.

It was a good thing that the settlers forged a trading relationship with the Crows, because the settlers would receive few direct benefits from the Crow agency itself. Bud McAdow won the 1877 agency contracts for beef and flour, but his delay in fulfilling the flour contract and the poor quality of the beef he supplied infuriated agency officials. The next year H. C. Bulis complained to his Washington superiors about McAdow's ferry across the Yellowstone at Coulson. McAdow had lacked official permission to build the ferry landing on the southern bank of the river (which was reservation territory), Bulis reported, nor

Table 5: Payments by Fort Custer Quartermaster to Residents of the Clark's Fork Bottom, 1879–1881

1879

Recipient	Number of Payments	Amount
John J. Alderson	3	$156.75
McAdow & Shock	2	112.00
P. W. McAdow	2	97.11
Canyon Creek residents	2	12.94
Young's Point residents	3	43.48
Total	12	422.28

1880

Recipient	Number of Payments	Amount
John J. Alderson	3	$ 90.60
Valentine Wickersham[a]	7	361.04
McAdow & Shock	3	89.00
Other Coulson residents	2	31.22
Young's Point residents	2	40.76
Canyon Creek residents	3	99.39
Total[b]	13	350.97

1881

Recipient	Number of Payments	Amount
John J. Alderson	6	$229.37
Valentine Wickersham[a]	8	203.55
Other Coulson residents	5	148.27
Canyon Creek residents	10	196.09
Young's Point residents	7	65.78
Aug. Wagner	2	57.35
Total[b]	30	696.86

[a]Wickersham is paid solely for his salary and expenses as telegraph operator.
[b]Wickersham's totals are not included.

Source: Correspondence of the Quartermaster, Fort Custer, Montana Territory, 1878–82, National Archives, Washington, D.C.

had he gained permission to then grade a new road connecting his ferry to the southern bank of the Huntley ferry. McAdow's actions poisoned relations with agency officials, who looked to Bozeman merchants such as L. M. Black, T. J. Dawes, Harvey Rea, and Lester E. Willson, to Horace Countryman at the mouth of the Stillwater River, and to the capitalists T. C. Power of Fort Benton and John Murphy of Helena for the grain, beef, and goods to fill future contracts.[18]

Although the official trade of the Crow agency would not flow toward the Clark's Fork Bottom, settlers took full advantage of the unofficial and, in most cases, illegal trade with the Crows. According to the correspondence of agency officials, trade between Crows and settlers was so pervasive that it threatened the discipline of the reservation. "It is of the upmost importance that the Indians should trade at the agency. If they go off it makes a bad impression on their minds," reported David Kern in 1878, "& they become dissatisfied with the agency." Augustus R. Keller was much more direct in his criticism. He told Captain E. C. Gilbreath in late 1879, "Traders must cease their interference with the management of the Indians." Later in an August 2, 1880, letter to his superior R. E. Trowbridge in Washington, Keller said that the Crows had "had an abundance of supplies when they left the agency to have lasted them until they reached the buffalo" for their annual hunt. But once they crossed the Yellowstone, they began trading with the residents. Keller concluded:

> There is no greater impediment to the civilization of the Crows, and no greater obstacle in their government, and no cause so fruitful of trouble and annoyance, as this question of barter and trade. The Yellowstone river is lined with traders, many of who suceed in getting their emissaries into the Indian camp, and by bribing the chiefs, and persuasion and misrepresentation, and fraud, suceed [*sic*] in inducing them to go to such points as the traders interests may require.

Keller believed that continued trade with these "lawless" Yellowstone settlements—Junction City, Huntley, Coulson, and Miles City— would soon impoverish the Crows.[19]

Agency concerns about the "effect" of the Indian trade certainly did not worry the settlers—the trade was too lucrative to ignore the Crows' offers. And the federal government's shift in attitude about trading with whites must have puzzled the Crows. For decades, federal officials had encouraged the Indians to exchange animal skins for the goods of white traders. Indeed, complaining that the Crows did not hunt enough, fur traders had sought to develop a consumer ethic among the tribe. Under the guise of reform and assimilation, those policies were stopped. Agency officials of the late 1870s no longer encouraged a direct Crow-settler trading relationship because it undermined policies to keep the Native Americans isolated from white influence. Only after the agency professionals had taught the Crows the ways of white "civilization" in the unpolluted environment of the isolated reservation, reformers sincerely believed, could the Indians be freed to encounter the all-too-different reality of white "civilization." It is no wonder the Crows were frustrated with life on the reservation.

To ensure the proper isolated setting where acculturation could take place, Crow agency officials routinely ejected non-Indians from the reservation. Keller, for example, threw out a black cowboy named Tex for the unspecified trouble he caused. Officials worried as well about new gold-rush stampedes incited by press reports of gold on the reservation. Epidemic diseases, such as scarlet fever and measles, still ran rampant through the reservation. Since only thirty-four hundred Crows lived at the reservation in 1878, agency officials believed that if immediate steps were not taken to keep the Crows isolated, the tribe could disappear.

To Agent A. R. Keller, the obvious way to reverse the Crows' population decline was to step up the pace of assimilation. As early as 1875, the Crows had received tools, seeds, and implements for farming; by 1878, agency employees had planted corn on the reservation. Keller wanted to do much more. In 1879 he ordered McGuffey readers for the Crow schools, and the next year he made plans to reorganize the buildings on the reservation, giving better physical examples of the "civilized" way to live.[20]

In February 1880, he begged his superiors in Washington for more funds to build farms. As he explained to E. A. Hayt in Washington, the Crows knew "nothing of building," but they wanted to farm their own lots. "With proper encouragement," concluded Keller, "I can put these people on the high road to civilization in a comparatively short time." Soon the agent was asking for garden seeds, a new "irrigating ditch," and money for constructing homes for prominent chiefs. At first, Keller estimated the houses would cost $150 each, then $200 each; he later settled on an amount of $3,000 for fifty houses, with the Indians supplying the labor and with the raw materials coming from the reservation. In time, twelve "chief" houses would be built, the first "model homes" of the Yellowstone Valley.[21]

Keller's assumption that the Crows would abandon their tipis for log cabins represented a case of cultural blindness. The tipi was a dwelling perfectly suited for the plains way of life; it was made of local materials, was easy to construct, and was portable. Another advantage was its flexibility. The tipi could be expanded in size; flaps could be raised to allow in cool breezes in the summer or could be closed tightly to prevent drafts in the winter. By comparison, the log house had few advantages. It was a stationary dwelling that lacked the flexibility needed for the demanding climate of the northern plains. But cabins did fix their residents at one spot, and of course, that is what Agent Keller wanted: to make the Indians farmers.

Model homes were only the beginning of Keller's construction plans. The agent asked for funds to construct a sawmill, a seed house, and a children's boarding house for the school. The mill would provide lumber for the other projects, and the seed house was necessary for large-scale agricultural production. Keller's plans for the boarding house were more ambitious. The dwelling would further isolate Crow children from the alleged bad influence of their families in the already "isolated" reservation. That way, the children's assimilation into white civilization could be sped along. The floor plan for the boarding school had a decided Victorian cast: the first floor had a large "parlor" and dining room, kitchen, pantry, separate girls' and boys' bathrooms, and the "matron's bedroom"; the second floor had two separate dorms for the boys and the girls. Keller hoped that his new Indian village of private dwellings, industrial buildings, and a boarding house would lay the foundation for a nation of farmers. Its designed appearance would match the many company towns then appearing on the American landscape. The Crows, however, never showed an interest in Keller's plans. Indeed, the only people pleased with his call for bids up to six thousand dollars were potential contractors along the Yellowstone. Horace Countryman, for one, thought he could make good money at that price and asked Samuel T. Hauser, the Helena banker, to stand security for his bid.[22]

Try as they might, Keller and the other reformers failed to persuade the Crows to abandon their traditions. Continuing to swap furs and government items with their neighbors across the river, the Crows followed old tribal ways, especially the custom of exchanging goods only with those who were friendly and who shared similar friends and enemies. To stay in the tribe's good graces, some settlers went as far as did William A. Allen and Bela Brockway: in 1880, the two accompanied a Crow war party chasing Blackfeet Indians who had stolen horses belonging to the Crows and settlers. Allen, Brockway, and the warriors defeated the ancient Crow enemies, retrieved the horses, and returned home singing Indian victory songs. Other settlers offered the hand of friendship by adjusting to Crow notions of hospitality. It was a tribal tradition, according to Joe Medicine Crow, for the table of a Crow family to be "open to all comers at any time"; a visitor should never leave hungry. The Newmans were active traders who often shared their table with the Crows, but their friendship was tested when a band of warriors visited the Newman ranch shortly after killing some Sioux horse thiefs. The Crows arrived with their coup sticks adorned by Sioux scalps. Mary Newman Scott recalled: "They paraded around the buildings, whooping and war dancing. Finally they put down their poles [coup sticks] and came into the house for something to eat." In the tradition of Crow hospitality, the Newmans fed the warriors all the family had. Afterward, "nearly all night they kept up their dancing and whooping out in the bunk house where they stayed. The third day they went on their way and no one was sorry to see them gone."[23]

Although annoyed by the length of the Crow visit, the Newmans continued to share their table with future Native American visitors. John B. Kinney, who lived near Young's Point, was not so unselfish, and he paid the consequences. A group of warriors visited Kinney, but this settler saw the Crows only as a nuisance and ordered them to leave.

The Indians were insulted, and "one of them made an insolent reply," which Kinney answered by shoving the warrior out of the cabin, adding humiliation to the earlier insult. The Crows reacted predictably. That night they shot three of Kinney's mules and chased off the rest of his stock. The Indians never returned to the ranch again.[24]

Kinney perhaps later regretted his rash behavior because he was eliminated from a trade that reaped considerable benefits for many of his neighbors. The Newmans, for instance, received their "Sunday-best" dress shirts in exchange for foodstuffs. "The dress shirt of that time," reported Mary Newman Scott, "was a denim shirt of blue and white that was furnished by the government to the Indians. The Indians would not wear them but traded them to the whites." The Newmans were not alone; one visitor to the Bottom observed that everyone was wearing the government-issued clothing. The Crow agent, Augustus R. Keller, also noted the Indians' preference for their own clothing. "My object in decreasing the estimate for clothing," he reported to his superiors in early 1880, "was to prevent a great waste of those articles [since] the Indians are in the habit of giving them in large quantities, to white men along the Yellowstone." Later he observed that if blankets and heavy clothing were distributed in the spring, when the climate did not require such items, the Crows would trade the goods "north of the Yellowstone and the approach of winter" would find "the Indians very scantily provided with" those items. The Crows would not use the government clothing until the disappearance of the buffalo forced them to do so. Other important items of trade included the rations the government gave the Crows. The Indians would save the beans, trading the accumulation to the settlers. The Crows also usually swapped their bacon and flour. In hard times, they were known to offer a buffalo robe or horse for three cups of sugar, but some settlers refused the deal due to the scarcity and high price of sugar.[25]

William A. Allen, who had served as a blacksmith at Fort Custer before moving to Canyon Creek in 1879, left a vivid record of the trading relationships that bonded the Crows and the settlers. In his *Blankets and Moccasins: Plenty Coups and His People, the Crows* (1933), Allen told of one 1879 trading session at Hoskins and McGirl's store, downriver from Coulson at the competing settlement of Huntley. Here the

Crows usually exchanged horses and buffalo and elk hides for other horses, "coffee and calico and beads and sugar—much sugar." The fraternity at the store was like that of the old fur-trading days—a place where the Native Americans mixed with grizzled free trappers and local residents. The trade began with "a feast of barbecued buffalo meat, ending up with buffalo tongues, washed down by much whiskey, of which all partook." Then everyone gambled for the rest of the day, betting on poker, horseshoes, best-shot competitions, and horse races. The Crows especially loved horse racing.[26]

The Indian-white trade in the Clark's Fork Bottom also had its lucrative side in the furs the Crows prepared for exchange. In 1880, Agent Keller reported that the Crows had traded sixty-five hundred buffalo robes worth about twenty-six thousand dollars, along with thirty thousand pounds of other pelts worth about six thousand dollars. An undetermined amount of these furs went to Perry W. McAdow's wholesale business in Coulson, where he advertised himself as an Indian and fur trader. Thus, the value of the Indian trade touched any resident who wanted to participate, from Perry McAdow to the poorest ranchers of the Bottom.[27]

The Crow trade, Fort Custer trade, and military protection contributed significantly to the opening of the Clark's Fork Bottom from 1877 to 1879. In turn, the emergence of Coulson, in addition to Junction City and Miles City, as viable Yellowstone trade centers further encouraged new immigration to the valley. "There is an unquestionable current of immigration hitherward, and I am glad to say, a better class of people are prospecting for homes in the Yellowstone Valley, than the original element of 'wood hawks' saloon keepers and refugees who have usually predominated," reported Thomson P. McElrath, the editor of the Miles City *Yellowstone Journal*, to a Northern Pacific Railroad official in September 1879.[28]

McElrath was on the mark; 1879 would be a key year of growth and stabilization for the new communities of the Yellowstone region. Many of the new immigrants to the Clark's Fork Bottom were family farmers, planning to take up permanent residence. The newcomers at Canyon Creek included Frank L. Summers, W. A. Allen, John Reardon, and Joe Danford. One of Joe Danford's sons, who arrived at Canyon

Creek on the sixth of July, later recalled: "It was the most desolate place I had ever seen. The country was hot and there wasn't a blade of grass or a single tree. The grasshoppers had ravaged everything and nothing but a brown aspect greeted our eyes." But the Danfords, along with the other new homesteaders, soon "had lovely gardens and raised much grain." Indeed, each of the ranches settled in 1878 and 1879 was located near the river or Canyon Creek, since the newcomers believed that the lower benches had the best land. The soil was sandy and light and could be irrigated easily and cheaply.[29]

In the summer of 1879, Sidney H. Erwin opened the Bottom's second general store at Canyon Creek. With William Allen, the blacksmith, located nearby, Canyon Creek developed as a minor economic competitor to Coulson. Erwin was a native of New York and had lived in Minnesota, where he had served as an army scout during that state's Sioux War of 1861. He moved to Montana during the gold rush era and prospected in the Black Hills before moving to the Bottom in July 1879. Erwin's Canyon Creek soon added a post office to its general store and blacksmith shop. But Canyon Creek lacked the necessary transportation infrastructure to threaten McAdow's Coulson enterprise as the trade center of the Clark's Fork Bottom. It could make no claims for the head of navigation, it lacked a ferry, and it served no major crossroads. But even though Sidney Erwin never posed a serious economic challenge to McAdow's predominance in the Clark's Fork Bottom, his die-hard Republicanism later provided plenty of political competition for McAdow's Democratic party activism.[30]

In 1879, business opportunities expanded significantly at Coulson. Louis Allard came to work for McAdow and later for the Newmans. Joseph Cochran was likewise employed, freighting goods from McAdow's Bozeman operations to Coulson and other area settlements in hopes of saving enough to open his own store. McAdow was making changes as well, leasing his mill in December 1878 to two Bozeman residents, Greenwood and Day, while considering new investments. In January 1879, the mill foreman, John Alderson, begged Bud to invest more at Coulson. "There is one thing more we should try to do," he commented, "and that *is* get some one in here with a good stock of goods. I feel certain that a House of that kind would pay at the Present time, and of course would be getting better all the time." Alderson was convinced that McAdow was the right man and asserted, "It would benefit more than any one thing else you could do." He also reminded McAdow that failure to build a major commercial business might spell doom for McAdow's plans on the Yellowstone River. "I think this comeing season will settle our destiny in regard to wheather we have the Town [the commercial hub of the river trade] or Some other Point gets the start." He added, "We will have to work with a will."[31]

McAdow did not react immediately to Alderson's pleas, but later actions suggest that he gave his employee the green light to further develop Coulson, not with a new general store but with a large hotel. A hotel could take advantage of the increasing number of travelers on the Yellowstone area roads as well as serve as a symbol of the town's determination to succeed. Alderson and McAdow's plans called for control of squatter's land claimed by another former McAdow employee, David Currier. Negotiations went nowhere; Alderson and Currier violently argued about ownership of the land. Currier came to Alderson's home, brandishing a gun. Alderson then shot and killed David Currier, rode off to Bozeman, and filed a formal claim. (Later that spring a jury ruled that Alderson had fired in self-defense.) By July, the first substantial structure in the Clark's Fork Bottom, a two-story log hotel owned and operated by John Alderson, was in operation. Alderson's advertisements boasted of "neat and comfortable beds and a good 'square' meal at a reasonable price," cooked by his wife, Ellen. The hotel symbolized McAdow and Alderson's hopes for the settlement. Compared with the unimpressive general store and post office, it assured passersby that Coulson was more than a dot on the map; the town was a well-established and prosperous community, a leading Yellowstone Valley trade center.[32]

Other changes were in store for Coulson. During the summer, McAdow sold his Coulson sawmill to Day and Hunter, who moved it to the Bull Mountains. Bud reinvested his profits in a new general merchandise store, which doubled as his base in the fur and Indian trade. The new store and hotel gave physical meaning to McAdow's and Alderson's claims for Coulson as a major Yellowstone trade center. A frontier outpost for modern capitalism, Coulson was meant to be to the Yellowstone River what Fort Benton was to the Missouri River, a central transportation base where McAdow could be the leading wholesale merchant, fur trader, and outfitter for the upper Yellowstone, exchanging raw materials of the region for finished products and goods, even for fine foods such as oysters, hams, and other delicacies.[33]

Clearly the local economy was in a preliminary stage of development. The human relationships involved in this level of economic exchange were close, even exceedingly personal. Barter was commonplace in the Clark's Fork Bottom in these early years. John Summers often received meat and produce in exchange for his labor as a blacksmith, cobbler, and casket maker. In January 1879, Alderson had experienced employee revolt at the mill when he had refused to pay David Currier and John Horr in whiskey. Currier and Horr wanted whiskey because in the Crow trade, whiskey was a much better medium of exchange than dollar bills. What little money there was at Coulson was often in the hands of Alice Reed Shock, a widow who was trusted by workers to safeguard their belongings. Muggins Taylor, an early resident and later deputy sheriff, called her the "First National Bank of Coulson."[34]

The geographic net of the market economy was limited in scope. By way of freighters and the steamboats, the settlers could obtain goods from almost every corner of the United States, but most trade took place between McAdow at Coulson, Erwin at Canyon Creek, and Thomas McGirl at Huntley, between the settlers and the army forts, between the Bottom communities and the surrounding urban centers (such as Bozeman), and between the settlers and the Crow Indians.

But by 1879, cash exchanges were playing a more important role in the local economy. Men traded their labor to neighbors to accumulate cash. Orson N. Newman, one of the wealthiest ranchers, worked for about a week in August and September 1879 for John R. King at Coulson. In exchange, Newman received six dollars a day, needed hard cash in a year when a July hail storm almost totally destroyed his crops, along with those of Aaron Ford, William Olmstead, and Joseph Cochran. Other settlers, of course, had no choice—lacking property, they worked for their neighbors to raise enough money to start their own ranch. Van Jackson Salisbury worked for Alonzo Young as a stage horse tender, and during the fall he assisted buffalo hunters. His three brothers took similar jobs. When Joe Danford arrived in the summer of 1879, he earned his seed money by helping his neighbors at Canyon Creek. In Coulson, Alice Reed Shock earned twenty-five cents a wash, doing the laundry for the employees of Perry McAdow.[35]

The inner workings of this frontier economy are well documented in the diary of Orson N. Newman for 1879. He details selling potatoes, onions, and some garden produce to Alderson's hotel and to several travelers heading down the Yellowstone from Bozeman. The soliders at Fort Custer and the agency employees on the Crow reservation were always willing customers for fresh, locally grown produce, milk products, and meats.[36]

Hunting remained an important supplement to incomes and diets in the Clark's Fork Bottom. Every family that left a written recollection remembered hunting deer, buffalo, elk, and antelope. One account claimed that every fall "all the ranches turn[ed] out . . . and hunted the buffalo." The families would keep enough skins for their purposes, then trade additional buffalo robes to the fur traders along the Yellowstone. The Newman family also marketed game meat. Every season they brought in wild game meat by the wagonload and sold it throughout the area.[37]

Mired in the thick of these patterns of economic exchange was Perry W. McAdow, the entrepreneur. By hiring workers to move to Coulson, he gave the community much needed labor, skills, and, perhaps most important, cash in the form of workers' wages. His 1879 general store was the center of the region's market economy. Here is where the Bottom residents came to trade their products for "store-bought" goods, where the Indians could exchange their pelts, and where a grubstake might be lent to a promising farmer. Alice Reed Shock once remembered McAdow as "the chief factor in most of the early Coulson enterprises."[38] Her choice of the word *factor*—a term used in the nineteeth century to describe the manager of a fur trade post—is very appropriate. As head of the Indian fur trade, provider of imported goods, and chief employer, McAdow was like a miniature American Fur Company. Coulson was his town, and his decisions would control its destiny.

The economic relationship between McAdow and the settlers can be seen in his role as employer and provider. Bud hired the residents of the Bottom on a seasonal and full-time basis. Lucius and Wilder Nutting, who lived with their father on a homestead near present-day Laurel, are two examples of McAdow's part-time employees. They built a barn for his farming operations, which Lucius remembered as "an immense one, the posts being 12 inches square and the frame being built like a quartz mill." John J. Alderson is a different example because he was a full-time employee, supervising John Horr, John R. King, David Currier, and others at McAdow's sawmill. He also built ferry boats and mackinaws for McAdow. Even after the construction of his own hotel, Alderson continued as a part-time employee. In March 1881, he built and oversaw "the running of several flatboats from Benson's Landing to Coulson" for McAdow's wholesale company in Bozeman. Also enjoying a salary from McAdow were Coulson residents such as John Shock, John R. King, David Currier, and Joseph Cochran.[39]

The amount of trade detailed in the diaries of O. N. Newman for 1879–80 between his family and McAdow's general store in Coulson indicates how dependent the settlers were on the essential commodities the business offered. At the store, the Newmans bought axes, bacon, oats, forks, boots, overalls, shoes, and candles while, at times, having their plows sharpened. McAdow also owned the only thresher in the region. "It was very big," Lucius Nutting remembered, "and took four yoke of oxen to pull the engine, two yoke to pull the separator besides bull wackers for each one." Since no one in the Bottom, except McAdow, produced more than five hundred bushels of grain, Bud probably purchased such a large machine anticipating the day when bountiful farms would populate the region. The machine was a good employer as well, requiring six men at all times to operate it.[40]

As both an employer and a provider, McAdow often found himself in close contact with the residents of the Bottom. He usually spent the summer months on the Yellowstone, checking on his operations and strengthening the bonds of familiarity and common purpose he shared with the settlers. From 1877 to 1879, the settlement reflected several characteristics of a frontier company town, but no surviving accounts mention any discontent directed by the settlers toward McAdow.

Rather, there is universal admiration for Bud. He too had been intimately and personally involved in the settlement of Coulson; his economic power had created and helped to maintain the community. He was one of them.

So by 1880, the beginning of a new decade, a new trade center had been established on the upper Yellowstone. In an economic sense, Coulson was a transitional community, having several ties to past patterns of exchange, especially the settlers' trade with the Crow Indians, but also possessing a sound enough physical and demographic base to ensure its immediate survival. When John Alderson and Bud McAdow walked up the stairs to the second story of the Coulson hotel and gazed out its windows down the Yellowstone, they must have dreamed of things to come and the key role they would play in the future of Coulson.

The "Progressive Development of Civilization" in the Clark's Fork Bottom, 1880–1881

Ó

By 1880, the recent settlement growth of the Yellowstone Valley was obvious to all residents. Thomson McElrath, the editor of the Miles City *Yellowstone Journal*, proudly boasted, "In no part of the earth is the interesting spectacle of the progressive development of civilization exhibited so openly, and so accessibly to the transient observer, as is now the case in the Yellowstone Valley." Here, "the whole process of social growth unfolds itself before his eyes like the successive revelations of a panorama. Another generation will not be accorded such a privilege of observation and study."[1]

The new immigration and the economic development of the past two years had changed the settlement landscape. Compare, for example, the impressions of Colgate Hoyt, a future western railroad investor and company officer who traveled through the Yellowstone in 1878, with McElrath's account of the valley in 1880. Hoyt's accounts of the early settlements were none too flattering. With the exception of Miles City, he found a few scattered shacks and dugouts masquerading as towns and settlements, with the valley residents hopelessly isolated from civilization.[2]

McElrath's 1880 book *The Yellowstone Valley*, though full of the booster rhetoric typical of publicity publications, recorded a very different landscape. He counted twenty-one settlements between Miles City and Bozeman. "Some of these are simply isolated ranches, while others are represented by little communities." Coulson was one of these places "where besides a post office, there are a telegraph office, store, saloon, saw mill, ferry and a local anomaly in the shape of a large two-story hotel." The town had 50 residents; in the larger upper Yellowstone region, 588 settlers, composed of 215 male ranch owners, 73 women, 142 children, and 158 hired laborers, lived between Benson's Landing and Fort Keogh at Miles City. Many of the ranchers were squatters—McElrath counted only thirty preemption claims, seventy-four homestead claims, and five desert land act claims between Fort Keogh and Benson's Landing, a stretch along the river valley of about 250 miles. If any skeptics needed more numbers to document the region's progress, McElrath had the figures ready at hand from the 1880 census: there were 429 buildings, 1,713 acres under cultivation (Bud McAdow owned about one-fourth of this land), and 23,435 head of cattle, 645 horses, and 8,201 sheep roaming the prairie.[3]

The next two years would have their difficult times, such as the terrible winter of 1879–80 that brought flakes "as big as popcorn" and temperatures of forty degrees below zero.[4] In general, however, the time was one of continued expansion as four events escalated the process of economic change: a major land cession by the Crows, the beginning of mining in the Judith Mountains to the north, the immigration of additional settlers, and the impending arrival of the Northern Pacific Railroad. Looking at each of these developments in detail provides an opportunity to see how T. P. McElrath's "interesting spectacle of the progressive development of civilization" shaped the Clark's Fork Bottom at this pivotal period in its history.

Greed for gold and silver was the impetus behind the new treaty with the Crows. In the late 1870s, prospectors discovered rich mineral deposits in the high country of the Crow reservation surrounding the headwaters of the Clark's Fork and Stillwater rivers (roughly the present-day Cooke City area). The Indian agent dutifully complained about the miners' encroachment on the reservation, but his words stopped no one from going to Cooke City. By late February 1880, the

Bozeman press called for new land cessions by the Crows. The government soon caved in to these demands and opened negotiations with the tribe.

The initial discussions among the Crow chiefs, Agent Augustus R. Keller, and Special Agent C. H. Barstow reached no agreement. To increase the pressure on the Crows to sign, the federal agents decided to take six Crow chiefs to Washington. There the chiefs could talk directly to President Rutherford B. Hayes, visit Mount Vernon, and in general be awed by the might and glory of American civilization. This strategy failed to make much of an impression, except in an indirect and delayed manner. In the twentieth century, Plenty Coups, who had been so impressed by the Mount Vernon idea of a museum to the "father" of the whites, decided to donate his Pryor home and ranch to the state government for use as a historical park.[5]

Local residents were very interested in the Washington negotiations. In May 1880, P. W. McAdow had written Martin Maginnis, the territory congressional delegate, "If there is a Treaty made with the Crows insist upon a road for the public travel from Coulson to Ft. McKinney via Ft. Custer, we cannot possibly get along without this road." An improved public road cutting through the reservation and crossing the Yellowstone at Coulson certainly would help McAdow's investments because it added another valuable transportation link to the town. But Maginnis and the other federal officials in Washington understood that a road through the heart of the reservation would antagonize the Crows. The federal government wanted the Cooke City area at all costs. Ignoring McAdow's plea, its negotiators bothered with little else in drafting the treaty.[6]

On June 12, 1880, the six Crow chiefs met with the tribe to secure approval of the treaty. Opening the council with a brief statement, Agent Barstow promised that if the tribe approved the new treaty, the government would not "permit a railroad or telegraph line to be built across the Reservation" because "it would only help to bring white men into your country." He even gave the solemn promise of "the Great Father" to keep "the Railroad and telegraph off of your land." Barstow lied; federal officials were well aware that the Northern Pacific was already headed straight for the heart of the Yellowstone Valley, and they planned to do nothing to stop it or to keep it on the northern bank of the Yellowstone River and off the reservation.[7]

The assembled Crows knew nothing of Barstow's duplicity, but many did not like the treaty. Yet rejecting the agreement, as Pretty Eagle admitted, was dangerous. He repeated the warning of President Hayes: "if we did not give it up, it might be bad for us that they might put us in some other place." Iron Bull took the vote, and almost everyone present voted in favor. Spotted Horse remained skeptical. "I don't want to let any land go east of Clarke's Fork," Spotted Horse proclaimed, "and I want you [the agent] to make the white man get off of the eastern end of our Reservation." The federal agents promised to do so immediately.[8]

The promises proved to be empty ones. Federal officials did not remove illegal encroachments—like McAdow's ferry landing on the southern bank of the Yellowstone—from the reservation borders, nor did they keep their promise to bar the Northern Pacific Railroad from Crow country. In fact, nothing happened immediately because Congress would not ratify the treaty. In Washington, there was a split between reformers who questioned the wisdom of reducing the reservation and protreaty supporters who believed that the agreement did not open enough land. That August, federal negotiators returned, this time asking for a four-hundred-foot-wide swath along the southern bank of the Yellowstone River for the railroad right-of-way. A treaty was signed on August 22, but again Congress refused to vote on its ratification.[9]

The failure of Congress to act on either treaty upset the Yellowstone settlers. In late October, Samuel T. Hauser, a leader of the Montana Democratic party, heard troubling news from the Yellowstone country:

There has been false reports circulated through the remote precincts of the county and especially the Yellowstone in regard to Maginnis. Keller the agent of the Crows had been quietly at work through parties he can controll on the Yellowstone circulating stories that Maginnis was opposed to the pending Crow Treaty, that he opposed it last winter in Washington and that he is . . . entirely lukewarm to the interests of Eastern Montana. They have got the people on the Yellowstone to such a point that the success of the pending Crow Treaty is the question at issue with them.

To counteract the rumors, Maginnis forwarded six petitions to Washington demanding ratification of the treaty before the year was out. But his petitions, pressure from other Montana politicians, and cries for more land from Yellowstone settlers could not budge Congress into action. Not until July 1882 would both treaties be formally ratified.[10]

Despite this delay, the treaties of 1880 gave settlers in the Bottom new hope for the future—for the Northern Pacific was certainly coming their way, and the Crow obstacle to the railroad had been neutralized. Both whites and Native Americans behaved as if the treaties were in force. The land south of the Yellowstone was still legally Crow territory, but more miners moved to Cooke City, and the Northern Pacific began to build into the valley during the fall of 1881, with the tracks reaching Billings only a month after Congress formally approved the railroad right-of-way treaty. The Crows offered no obstacles to either the miners or the railroad workers.

Nor did the Crows stop trading with the settlers north of the Yellowstone. In the fall of 1880, Orson Newman twice noted in his diary that Crows spent the night at his ranch. The Indians recognized Bud McAdow as the "leading factor" of the area and regularly stayed overnight at his wholesale store in Coulson, treating it like past fur trading posts where the Crows would visit and stay if they liked. At the more isolated settlements of the region, according to Henry A. Frith, "pelts furnished a satisfactory medium of exchange for the commodities of life" as late as 1881. Economic behavior rooted in the fur trade era continued in the Clark's Fork Bottom.[11]

The discovery of gold in the Judith Mountains, which stood roughly 110 miles to the north, was the second event that influenced the economic maturation of the Clark's Fork Bottom. In 1879, Joseph R. Anderson—better known as "Skookum Joe"—along with C. C. Snow, Eugene Ervin, Pony McPartland, and David Jones, left Junction City in search of gold and silver in the Judith Mountains. Winter cut short this first trip, but the five prospectors returned the following spring, and this time, Anderson struck pay dirt at Virgin Gulch and at Alpine

84

Gulch. With the assistance of several métis, who lived in the Judith Basin, Anderson made sluice boxes for placer mining and quickly developed his property into the best in the district. His partner, David Jones, also panned some nuggets at the head of Warm Spring Canyon. News about the gold strikes spread fast. By May, the mining camp of Maiden had been established—almost overnight it seemed—deep in the Judith Mountains.[12]

The Judith gold rush excited everyone in the Clark's Fork Bottom. On May 5, 1880, Bud McAdow wrote Martin Maginnis:

> The mines struck in the Judith Basin—are proving to be good— the valleys are immense—equal in extent to four times the size of Gallatin. The Judith Country is destined to be the granary of Montana a second *Red River.* There is now about one thousand people in that country and room for thousands more. I have moved my saw-mill to the Yogo Mines. Will go over myself in about ten days. We are trying to get a mail rout [*sic*] from Martinsdale [a small cattle town in Meagher County] to Yogo to connect with the mail from Martinsdale to Coulson.[13]

As this letter to Maginnis documents, Bud McAdow never forgot his early mining experiences: as much money could be made supplying the miners as could be made from actually mining the ore. McAdow promptly cashed in on the building frenzy by moving his Bozeman sawmill to Maiden. Then he attempted to connect his Coulson trade center, by means of a government-supported stagecoach, to the new mines so that his store would become a major outfitter for prospectors headed for the Judith Basin.

Visiting Maiden for the first time in May 1880, McAdow staked Skookum Joe and Davy Jones the necessary capital to develop their newly discovered Black Bull quartz mine while he also invested in the War Eagle mine, with Anderson, Jones, and Ben Dexter as partners. In McAdow's Judith operations, Ben Dexter would play a role similar to that of John Alderson at Coulson. Dexter watched over McAdow's investments and ran a store and sawmill for his employer at a place called Andersonville. Compared with the reliable Alderson, however, Dexter proved to be an untrustworthy partner. McAdow constantly had difficulties with Dexter's "drinking up" the firm's profits. Despite this personnel problem, McAdow made money at his Judith properties. The success of the War Eagle encouraged McAdow the following year to invest in another Anderson-Jones venture: the legendary Spotted Horse mine.

Well pleased with the progress of his Judith investments, Bud returned to Coulson during the summer of 1880. He expanded his stock of mining equipment at the Coulson store, advertising the business as the perfect outfitter for prospective Judith miners. And he talked incessantly of the promise of Judith. One Canyon Creek resident recalled that Bud "spent most of his time seated in the cool dining room of the [Coulson] hotel" where "the conversation generally drifted to the 'Spotted Horse.' He was very enthusiastic over the Judith country and its mines. People would smile at him and think he was visionary."[14]

Lured by the gold strikes to the north and the promise of new land cessions by the Crows, immigrants to the Clark's Fork Bottom took advantage of an especially good season of weather to establish their ranches and businesses. "The summer of 1880 was made especially attractive by its frequent and abundant showers. Everything flourished," recorded Helen Braum, who resided near Canyon Creek. "The grass grew tall enough for hay all over the valley. The streams were bordered by bushes loaded with wild fruits." The arrival of new settlers in 1880 was an important third contribution to the economic development of the Clark's Fork Bottom.[15]

Among the newcomers came merchants to compete with Bud McAdow at Coulson. Throughout the spring and summer, small businesses throughout the region grew in number. The Bozeman *Avant Courier* reported: "As far as the eye can reach up and down the valley, new buildings can be seen. Work on Canyon [Creek] City is looming up. Quite a number of persons at present are camping in the willow thickets in the vicinity waiting for new buildings to be put up so they can move their tents from the brush and not have their places of business so secluded." To meet the demand for building materials, McAdow located a sawmill at Canyon Creek and began filling orders. Sidney Erwin promptly took advantage by adding a sixteen-by-forty foot tavern and twenty-two-by-fifty foot L-addition to his store. His expanded operation became the center of the Canyon Creek "business community," which, of course, was a business community in only the frontier sense of those words. Canyon Creek was never more than a collection of log structures housing a general store, two blacksmiths, and a couple of taverns. Although it was a minor "inland"-town competitor to Coulson, the village served as a second important focal point of settlement in the Clark's Fork Bottom.[16]

The new immigrants also included skilled laborers, who further contributed to the local economic maturation. At Coulson, Valentine Wickersham became the telegraph operator at Alderson's Hotel, giving the town a high-tech connection to the rest of the country. Two other welcome newcomers were John H. Peck, a mechanic from New York, and Edward Johnson, a carpenter from Norway. At Canyon Creek, the blacksmiths J. W. Danford and John Summers both opened shops, and Summers worked as a cobbler and casket maker as well.[17]

Besides the chance to practice one's trade in a new town, other opportunities also lured settlers. Some came solely to hunt the herds of buffalo, elk, and antelope. Hunting had always been a part of the local economy; Bela Brockway could still kill six "fine" buffalo during a trip from Fort Custer in 1880. The traditional family hunt brought in winter provisions for almost every ranch.[18]

But other hunters, more professional and systematic, came to participate in the ghastly buffalo slaughter of the early 1880s, which eliminated the bison from the Yellowstone Valley. The development of a tanning process that made it profitable to transform buffalo hides into leather sparked renewed interest in bison furs among eastern clothing markets. Crow women or fur trappers skilled in the time-consuming methods of hide preparation were no longer necessary; factories could process as many furs as hunters could ship back East. Adding to the slaughter was a desire among many Americans to exterminate the bison. Its disappearance, they assumed, would force the Native Americans to change their lives and become "settled" and "civilized."

Using Sharp .50-caliber rifles, the hunters worked in teams based on a division of labor in which one man shot the animals and another skinned them. Since the buffalo lacked the instinct to run when a hunter began his kill in the herd, the teams could kill and skin sixty-five bison a day, leaving the skins to dry in the hot summer sun. Later they rolled up the hides and hauled them to the banks of the Yellowstone River, where the hides were pressed into packs for shipping to the eastern tanning factories.

The carnage left behind covered the valley. In 1880, Granville Stuart observed that the bottoms of the lower Yellowstone were "literally sprinkled with carcasses of dead buffalo. In many places they lie thick on the ground, fat and the meat not yet spoiled, all murdered for their hides which are piled like cordwood all along the way." This deliberate waste disgusted him. "'Tis an awful sight," Stuart added, "probably 10,000 buffalo have been killed in the vicinity this winter." Traveling north of the Yellowstone, Pretty Shield found the same wasteful slaughter.

> Ahh, my heart fell down when I began to see dead buffalo scattered all over our beautiful country, killed and skinned, and left to rot by white men, many, many hundreds of buffalo. The first I saw of this was in the Judith basin. The whole country there smelled of rotting meat. Even the flowers could not put down the bad smell. Our hearts were like stones. And yet nobody believed, even then, that the white men could kill *all* the buffalo.[19]

Most of the slaughter was confined to the valley east of Miles City, but the upper Yellowstone had its share as well. John Danford had thirteen hides at his cabin, and neighboring ranchers, like Ed Forrest, Bela Brockway, Tim Reardon, Mike O'Connell, and John Walk, hunted regularly. "From these men," recalled John Dover, "[I] learned that one had to have other things than a gun with which to hunt buffalo. One had to have a four horse team and a wagon and men to help skin, if one intended to make money at it." Despite the added expense of the additional workers, the hunt was worthwhile, for the hides brought from $2.25 to $2.50 apiece. From 1879 to 1882, 250,000 bison skins were sold in the Yellowstone Valley, with the peak coming in 1881–82, when 100,000 skins were sold.[20]

Smoked buffalo meat also brought good prices, but it was a costly, dirty, and time-consuming job. Ed Lee was one Bottom resident who smoked and dried tons of buffalo meat for the eastern market. Helen Braum has left a graphic portrait of his operations:

> His smoke houses were quite unique in their way, but no[t] especially inviting in appearance. They were teepees, constructed of raw buffalo hides, driping with blood and extremely odorous. The chunks of meat were hung in there and a little fire kept smudging in the center. On approaching this strange looking camp it did not look like a human habitation but upon hallooing, the gory proprietor would emerge, or more accurately speaking, would crawl out. His clothes, his hands and face were smeared with blood and grease, well mixed with smoke and common dirt, until he presented a most horrible illustration of what various kinds of dirt can do for a man when they are all applied at once.[21]

Settlers also hunted antelope in large numbers, slaughtering most of the herds native to the Clark's Fork Bottom. Billy Mitchell at Park City used a pack of greyhounds to kill six or seven antelope at one run. It took little effort to hunt these passive animals. "They passed the settlers cabins, and often would stop and look with gentle, questioning eyes, at the invaders of their homeland," wrote Helen Braum. "They were occasionally shot from the cabin door." The antelope hunt was lucrative enough. A skin brought from sixty-two cents to a dollar, and the animal could be skinned in five minutes. In Canyon Creek during the winter of 1880–81, William Rogers killed about three hundred, and Bela Brockway, Forrest Young, and John Kinney slaughtered six hundred in the rimrocks north of present-day Laurel.[22]

The agricultural potential of the Clark's Fork Bottom also attracted new settlers. "The drawing card for settlers to Montana," according to the Canyon Creek resident Frank Summers, "was the report of the wonderful climate . . . and the beautiful Clarks Fork Bottom of the Yellowstone." Table 6 documents the number of homesteaders who crowded into the valley in 1881. Several of the filings involved formal claims to squatter land. Bela Brockway and Ed Forrest, for example, had been among the first settlers in the Bottom. Perhaps they feared that the increasing number of newcomers might threaten their title and

Table 6: Homesteaders Filing in the Clark's Fork Bottom, 1881
(spelling in original)

Name	Date Filed	Acres	Date of Final Proof
W. D. Olmstead	11/9/81	160	cancel–4/24/82
George H. Wilson	12/14/81	160	cancel–9/19/82
W. H. Stutts	5/19/81	160	cancel–4/3/82
John H. Koltes	11/19/81	160	cash–5/15/83
J. M. V. Cochrane	3/15/81	160	4/2/86
C. H. Newman	12/16/81	80	n/a
Ben H. Hogan	10/24/81	147.52	12/21/87
E. T. Bishop	10/25/81	160	cancel–4/25/82
E. T. Bishop	3/8/81	125.99	cancel–4/25/82
N. B. Givens	4/22/81	160	cancel–4/4/82
John Summers	6/1/81	160	cancel–6/3/82
B. B. Brockway	11/6/81	159.27	8/3/83
George L. Danford	10/3/81	160	9/10/88
Samuel R. Salsbury	6/23/81	160	cancel–8/1/85
Jackson Salsbury	6/23/81	160	2/8/88
Winfred S. Salsbury	5/30/81	160	5/23/87
Edward Forrest	6/27/81	160	10/30/86

Source: Homestead Tract Books of the General Land Office, 1881, Yellowstone County, Montana, National Records Center, Suitland, Maryland

they decided to confirm their preemption rights. More likely, the rush to file came with the creation of the land office at Miles City on October 9, 1880, ending the long trek to Bozeman, over the Bozeman Pass, that earlier homesteaders had faced. Homesteaders certainly didn't need to have their ranch built before filing—they needed only a foundation. Ben Hogan in 1881 took "out four cottonwood logs and laid them down in a square" before starting out to file his claim for 147.5 acres.[23]

Newcomers soon learned that farming the virgin soil of the Clark's Fork Bottom had its rewards—they had seen Alderson's huge watermelon patch at Coulson when they arrived—but it demanded hard work. Henry Colwell, who settled along the banks of the Yellowstone near Coulson, concisely summarized the work week: "I am a farmer by traid that toils for his daily Bread till early morn till the sun goes down. then to the house for supper. to get that is the fait of a poor old Batch." Even days off were stressful for Colwell. He recalled: "Sunday is the day of Rest. not for the poor old Batch for the first thing he does is to clean up the house and then to the washtube he goes up to his head in Suds. that is the fait of poor old me."[24]

Orson N. Newman's diary for 1880 presents a comprehensive picture of a rancher's typical year.[25] January was a month for hunting. His sons killed nine deer on the fifteenth, and six days later Orson joined them to hunt deer and antelope. This time the family brought back twenty-three carcasses, but it had been "very cold and everyone suffered from it." Orson added, "I froze my toes." The weather stopped no one, and on the very next day, the Newmans killed twenty more animals.

February was the time to thresh the winter oats and to begin preparations for spring planting. On the thirteenth, Orson sent ten dollars to Bozeman for garden seeds. In March the family continued its preparations for the spring. Cold weather kept everyone indoors the first two weeks, but new garden seeds from St. Paul arrived on the fifteenth, and by the twenty-fifth Orson was seeding his first oats of the year. The oat crop kept him busy for a week or so, but in April two weeks of cold, snowy weather delayed the Newmans' spring planting schedule. At the end of the month, they planted potatoes, followed by broom corn on May 7. Newman's May entries also underscore the fact that he lacked agricultural self-sufficiency. On May 25, for example, he went to Sidney Erwin's store at Canyon Creek and "got some sweet potatoes," and four days later he went to Coulson to purchase "a sack of flour for $6.50."

Planting crops continued into June; on the twelfth, the Newman boys set out five hundred cabbage plants. July was the time to cut the season's first hay, rich grass free for the taking on the benches overlooking the Yellowstone. A week after the Fourth of July, the family was working in the truck garden, and on the thirteenth Orson bought "a mower machine" from McAdow's store at Coulson to speed up the hay production. "All hands making hay," he recorded on July 15. "Put up 20 tons in all." In late July the Newmans, following a Native American tradition, searched the valley for wild berries. On the twenty-fourth Orson noted, "We had good luck picking wild berries." And on August 1 he wrote, "All hands [were] after berries on Alkali Creek."

The Newmans picked their first green corn of the season on August 1, along with harvesting the first of the oat crop, an activity that took until the seventeenth to finish. By the end of August, harvesting all types of produce was well under way. On the twenty-seventh the family was "pulling beans," and the first melons were ready two days later. Early September was hectic—crops had to be picked before the winter's first frost. On the first Newman noted: "Threshing oats and beans for neighbors and gathering garden truck. Got a barrel of pickles." The melons were picked by the eleventh, just in time to miss a "big frost" that very night. Two days later the Newmans picked their pumpkins and started to prepare their corn for market. The harvest was over by the end of September; the family husked their corn on the twentieth, then dug up the potato crop on the twenty-third.

October was the time to market the results of the labor, and Newman's diary indicates the extensive trade involved in the market economy of the region. On October 1, Newman made "up a load of vegetables and grain to take to Bozeman and sell." He left three days later "with a load of 1,354 pounds." Trading his first products at Sweet Grass, he sold "onions and pickles at Hunters Hot Springs" on the sixth. Throughout the journey, Newman was able to sell his pickles to settlers and travelers along the "trail." By October 9, Newman was in Bozeman, where he "sold balance of load" then "stayed at Brick Hotel there," which had 150 horses in its stable. He enjoyed several days in Bozeman, relaxing and taking care of business. On the eleventh, he had his corn ground at the mill and "went out in the country to look at some cows." Two days later he returned to Bozeman and "collected $68. Paid for the flour and began to load for the trip back." Before leaving on the fourteenth, he bought twenty-three dollars' worth of clothes and then headed home in the cold and snow.

Newman was home by October 20, but his work was not yet over. The "next morning [he] started digging turnips and other garden truck." Within a week he was at Coulson "with cabbage and onions," and "for the next few days [he was] marketing truck in Coulson" while a "freighter bought some [vegetables] at farm for $28." Now Orson was ready to sell the rest of his oats. On October 31, he "sold 2,000 pounds of oats to [Harry] Reed for $1.99 a bushel," and he "hauled two loads of oats to Coulson, 4,411 pounds," two weeks later. His diary for November 22 noted that it was time to prepare for winter, and on the twenty-eighth Newman recorded the end of his marketing season by writing that he "spent balance of month hauling oats to Coulson," for which he would receive $260 by December 15.

Although 1880 had been a good year for the Newmans, other Bottom residents were not so lucky. Three Coulson residents—H. Caldwell, Timothy Reardon, and S. Stallcup—lost their homes to pay back taxes. Lillie C. Young, the wife of Alonzo Young, abandoned farm and family, forcing her spouse to announce that he would no longer be responsible for her debts. She moved to Coulson and would later remarry there. Then those who had prospered that summer lost many of their gains during another harsh winter in 1880–81. "The winter of 1881," recalled George Danford of Canyon Creek, "was the hardest winter that Montana has ever experienced since white man first came here." The depth of the snow varied from two to five feet, but Helen Braum remembered, "It was deep enough everywhere to render travel slavish for man and beast." Settlers jerry-rigged snowshoes to hunt animals trapped in the deep drifts, keeping the isolated ranches in meat at least. The difficulties of the winter were compounded by an epidemic of scab disease, which destroyed many herds of livestock. The Newmans, for example, lost 90 percent of their sheep.[26]

The spring of 1881 brought welcome relief from the cold and snow, but warm temperatures melted the heavy snow so quickly that floods threatened to wash away every Yellowstone settlement. Coulson, Canyon Creek, and Young's Point escaped the worst of the floodwaters, but downriver at Miles City, residents were not so lucky. Days of high water ruined many businesses and forced residents to use boats merely to paddle from one end of town to the other. To ease the local food shortage, John Alderson and Perry McAdow rushed to their sister city's rescue, and padded their own pocketbooks in the process. Alderson floated down the Yellowstone with two thousand sacks of Gallatin County flour from the McAdow brothers' mill in Bozeman to sell at Miles City.[27]

Once the water receded, the settlers returned to business as usual, but during the late spring and summer of 1881 the weather turned unusually hot and dry. The specter of drought soon stalked the land. McAdow and Alderson, because of their access to a small irrigation ditch built to satisfy the requirements of the Desert Land Act, had no worries about the drought. But everyone else was desperate for water, and some ranchers lost their seed to the extremely dry, hot weather and were forced to become freighters. Then a prairie fire in August 1881 destroyed much of the winter feed for the settlers' livestock. Debts at McAdow's and Erwin's stores were "immense," and what goods remained at both stores were of a decidedly inferior quality until the steamers could come up the Yellowstone and replenish store stocks. Helen Braum remarked, "It was either feast or famine, but most of the time it was famine, so far as anything good to eat was concerned." She remembered that "French toast was a standard dish" and that one settler "expressed well the general feeling by saying he could stand forty or fifty meals of it, but he did not like it for a steady diet." The local diet would not improve until much later: T. C. Power and Company, a major freighter and steamboat company in Fort Benton, mishandled and ruined McAdow's shipment of goods in the fall of 1881. Bud's bitter complaint to Power gives an idea of what the settlers had missed:

> Hams and cheese . . . are completely ruined by being soaked in water and mud. Nearly all my matches are wet and spoilt and a large proportion of can good boxes being wet and exposed to the hot sun have swelled and burst. If a Steam Boat Company has the privalidge of discharging a Cargo on the bank of the River and not be responsible for its destruction just as soon as I find that out to be the fact I will quit doing business. I don't want to *belly ake* but the Company have treated me shabily and I will not be imposed on any longer.[28]

At the same time that McAdow griped to Power, however, the future prospects of Coulson brightened as the tracks of the Northern Pacific

Railroad approached the Clark's Fork Bottom. The impending arrival of the railroad would boom the region's economy more than any other event in the early 1880s. Local businessmen, especially McAdow and Alderson, eagerly awaited the same economic transformation that had just occurred down the valley at Glendive and Miles City.

On the Fourth of July, 1881, the first Northern Pacific train had appeared in Glendive. Whereas the population of the town the previous year had been about 150, now 1,200 to 1,500 people lived there. The town had two lumberyards, a post office, and a theater as well as general merchandise stores, dance halls, and some twenty-one saloons. One hundred town lots had been sold, and the construction of Northern Pacific offices and machine shops was under way. Throughout the summer, Coulson residents heard of the continued boom at Glendive. By October, a hotel and 100 wood or wood-and-canvas dwellings and businesses stood in Glendive, increasing to 150 buildings by November 30, 1881. Walter Cameron, a railroad construction worker, remembered the Glendive of December 1881 as "a wild frontier town, mostly board shacks and log cabins." On arriving there, he and other new railroad employees "who had money enough to buy liquor got gloriously soused and gun plays and fist fights were common."[29]

The story was much the same at the Northern Pacific's next major stop, Miles City. Once it was confirmed that the railroad would be built through the town, speculators and local residents assembled saloons, dance halls, and other places of amusement for rail workers as quickly as possible. By the time the railroad arrived in November 1881, the appearance of the town had undergone major alterations. Its population totaled 1,000, with three merchants doing an annual business of $300,000. The influx of money from railroad workers temporarily sent prices skyrocketing. But as the freight traffic from the railroad lowered the cost of importing goods into Miles City, the cost of living in this eastern Montana town quickly decreased. The editor of the Miles City *Yellowstone Journal* observed, "The railroad brought the community at once in touch with the more concise and narrower life of 'The States,' [and] the 'nickel' displaced the 'quarter' as the smallest coin in use, and prices shrunk accordingly."[30]

One way of measuring the immediate impact of the railroad is to read Walter A. Cameron's reminiscence of his days in Miles City. Cameron arrived in Miles City in December 1881. He considered the town to be "a collection of log and board cabins" with a "floating population" of about 3,000, "mostly men of rough and tough variety. A few merchants had drifted in and started up some merchandizing businesses. . . . And in these places could be seen doctors, merchants, lawyers, and other varieties of professional men as well as the common laboring men jostling and crowding each other in their efforts to see what was going on in the place." His first night in the town was spent at a hotel built "from some lumber salvaged from steamboats that had been wrecked on the nearby Yellowstone River years previously." Strolling through the town, Cameron "found plenty of eating accomodations . . . and *drinking* places" but discovered that the prices were too high. For example, an egg, a piece of bacon, a biscuit, and a cup of coffee cost one dollar![31]

From Miles City, the railroad crossed the river, traveling along the southern bank of the Yellowstone toward the Coulson ferry. This route bypassed Junction City, which stood on the northern bank across from the Bighorn confluence, and that town immediately suffered an economic decline as rail traffic eclipsed river transportation. The fate of Junction City might have given McAdow and Alderson a reason to pause and reconsider the future of Coulson, but they had no doubts of their impending good fortune. Since the railroad entered its narrow right-of-way through the Crow reservation after leaving Miles City, common sense seemed to dictate that the Northern Pacific would have to build another major rail stop once it emerged from the reservation and crossed the river, before building again along the northern riverbank. In July and early August, Northern Pacific surveyors were making their final marks in the Clark's Fork Bottom—the tracks, it seemed, would cross the Yellowstone River at the Coulson ferry and head straight into town! As one contemporary later wrote, the Clark's Fork Bottom "was very much out of the world, having no connection with the throbbing heart of commerce save by the dusty jerky road or precanious [sic] steamboat, but a radical change was approaching." Grading for the line between Miles City and Coulson began in October, with sawmill operators, contractors, and graders serving "as the advance guard of the construction army."[32]

These activities directly affected Coulson and the Clark's Fork Bottom in two ways. First, the demand for ties, piling, and bridge supports created a new industry of timber production. "Many who spent the former winter on the plains hunting the shagy bufalo [*sic*]," recalled Helen Braum, "now laid aside the rifle for the axe and the hunter of '80 became a wood-chopper." Settlers thus seriously depleted yet another Yellowstone resource because they could make "fair wages" providing wood. Second, by mid-October 1881, Alderson and McAdow decided to put their plans for Coulson, the railroad town, into action. At the Custer County Courthouse in Miles City, Alderson filed an elaborate town plan, turning, at least on paper, what had been a haphazardly arranged grouping of log cabins, shacks, frame dwellings, stores, and the two-story Alderson's Hotel into a formally designed town of seventeen full and partial blocks and seven streets neatly organized in a symmetrical fashion facing the Yellowstone River. With over 250 individual lots, plenty of room existed for residences and businesses alike, and Alderson immediately began to sell options on his properties.[33]

The mere anticipation of the Northern Pacific Railroad had turned the bad times of the summer of 1881 into the boom of the winter of 1881–82. McAdow and Alderson were certain of success, and local residents followed their lead. According to one observer: "The leading citizens, voicing the sentiments of the principal land owners, McAdow and Alderson, were unalterably of the opinion that no power on earth could cheat Coulson of its ultimate greatness. It was the only place on the bottom where a city could be built. It had water, it had drainage, it was the logical, the only location." In December 1881—Coulson's fourth birthday—it must have seemed that all the hard work had finally paid off. Coulson was now a "real" town, a place of lots, grid lines, and streets. In their wildest dreams, the settlers would never have imagined that the town had less than a year to live.[34]

CHAPTER 5

Bonds of Community,
1877–1881

◻

In earlier chapters, we have explored the settlement and development of the Clark's Fork Bottom in largely economic terms. Why did
the entrepreneurs and settlers come—and stay? What were their occupations? What was the nature of their economic relationships within
the community and within the larger market economy of eastern Montana? We discovered that the economic life of the Clark's Fork Bottom
was, more often than not, composed of exceedingly close and personal
exchanges of goods and services involving both the settlers and the Native Americans. Since a mere two hundred settlers lived in the Bottom's thousands of acres in 1880, it took a great deal of effort to build a
successful local economy. These bonds of exchange carried over into
the community's social life, combining to give the settlers a sense of
place and shared purpose.[1]

During the first months of white settlement in 1877, formal, organized social events were very few in the Clark's Fork Bottom. Men
were too busy building stockades, raising cabins, scratching out dugouts, and keeping an eye out for the Indians to plan community dances
and parties. Nor were there any white women about. The men who survived the September Nez Percé raid at McAdow's Mill held a big drink-

ing bash afterward—something had to be done with all that booze from the burned-out tavern—but this celebration was the only big party recorded in the first months of settlement in the Bottom.

Visiting was more common, with plenty of drinking and card playing in the time-honored frontier pattern of male bonding.[2] Another exchange of fellowship occurred when the pioneers helped each other raise their ranch buildings. Work provided an additional chance to enjoy the company of others, be it cutting wood for McAdow's mill or going out on hunting parties deep into the countryside. Trading with the neighboring Indians also had its social aspects in the drinking, gift giving, gambling, and horse racing that accompanied the actual exchanges between the Native Americans and the white traders.

The rhythm of life in those days had a slow, unchanging pace. The work week was so demanding and repetitious that some early ranchers totally lost track of time. During travels in the Yellowstone Valley in 1878, Colgate Hoyt encountered a rancher who admitted he didn't keep time well but argued that he only needed to know the seasons to keep his ranch operating. Hoyt pried further, asking whether the man and his neighbors observed Sunday. "Oh yes they always kept one day in seven, though sometimes they got a little off the Track." To illustrate his point, the rancher told of a recent visit to two neighbors, whom he found dressed in their Sunday best, sitting on the front porch smoking their pipes. He asked why the men were resting. It was Sunday, they answered. "'Sunday' says he 'why boys dont you know Sunday has passed three days ago & this is *Wednesday* man.'"[3]

The paucity of social life did not change until the first single white women arrived in the Clark's Fork Bottom. When the Newmans immigrated to the valley in March 1878, their oldest daughter, Sarah, was fourteen and the only young woman available for marriage in the area. To the amazement—and perhaps envy—of her twelve-year-old sister Mary, "soon all the old bachelors began to put on their best clothes and white collars and came visiting." Sarah found none to her liking and remained single for several more years. The great disparity between the numbers of men and women noted by Mary Newman Scott never changed much. Two years later, according to the 1880 census, there were two males for every female in the Clark's Fork Bottom and only eight single women above the age of fifteen for the horde of single men in the community. As the Northern Pacific Railroad approached in 1881 and 1882, bringing hundreds of rail workers, contractors, and storekeepers, this ratio became additionally skewed, even though the railroad also brought new families and some female cooks, along with prostitutes.[4]

The lack of female companionship added to the burdens faced on a daily basis by the women of the Clark's Fork Bottom. As the historian Glenda Riley has stressed, women on the plains frontier experienced "crushing work loads, frequent births, illnesses and deaths, recurring depression, loneliness, homesickness, and fear." Yet, most women found ways of "creating rich and varied social lives out of limited or seemingly non-existent materials and opportunities." This appears to have been the case in the Clark's Fork Bottom. Whenever possible, the women, whether they lived on isolated ranches or in the small hamlets of Coulson and Canyon Creek, sought each other's assistance in doing their daily work. Good-natured ribbing of the macho males of the frontier also was common. Ellen Alderson and Alice Shock constantly poked fun at Muggins Taylor, a former army scout who had brought the first news of the Custer fight to the eastern Montana communities. To quiet this braggart, Ellen and Alice secretly took bullets out of his pistol; Muggins did not care for this joke at all and severely reprimanded the women for their insensitivity to the tools of the male domain.[5]

The men who had resided at earlier American outposts in the Yellowstone region—the fur trade forts, the military outposts, and the reservation agencies—had also lacked white female companionship. To compensate, many men took Crow Indian brides in common-law marriage or as concubines. Indeed, the Crows often offered their daughters to the traders as a way of strengthening economic ties and alliances, and the traders accepted the women with that understanding. But there is no evidence that any Bottom settler took a Crow wife or lover. Undoubtedly, some sexual relations between the Crows and the settlers took place (considering Victorian cultural norms and the racism of the period, it was not something a settler would leave a permanent record about), but probably nothing occurred on the scale or the frequency witnessed during the fur trade. The settlers of the late 1870s wanted to trade with the Crows—and did so on a regular basis—but they did not join Crow families to facilitate the exchange, as white traders had done in the past.

During 1879, community dances and parties became more frequent. Orson Newman's diary for that year mentions many different types of community gatherings. At the barn and cabin raisings for Aaron Ford and William Olmstead, the bonds of community took actual physical form in the shape of log buildings. The Newmans hosted several dances; their daughters Sarah and Mary Newman, fifteen and thirteen years old respectively, were the primary attractions. Orson also recorded his attendance at several school meetings held at various places in the Bottom. Indeed, the establishment of a local school in 1879 was a great catalyst for community events.[6]

The Bottom's first school was at Ed Newman's homestead, where his family had donated a building. Nat Givens (or Givins), a well-educated rancher from Sedalia, Missouri, and a widower with six daughters, volunteered to teach the children on a three-month subscription term. That way he could instruct his own daughters along with the other children and get paid for his trouble as well. In its appearance, this private school wasn't much. The tongue-and-groove log building "was by no means a pleasant place as when the wind blew, the smoke went down the chimney and when the doors were opened to let out the smoke, the children and their teacher were nearly frozen by the wintry blasts." There were no desks or blackboards, only cottonwood benches and slates. The pupils who attended this school along with five of the teacher's daughters—Marie, Rose, Fluta, Louisa, and Bessie—were the five Newman children—Sarah, Asa, Mary, Albert, and A. R.—the four daughters of Richard and Davidella Clarke—Rose, Laura, Florence, and Alice—and Rose Bishop, Ellen Reardon, and Dan Sullivan.[7]

Givens taught only one session before resigning his post to accept a more lucrative job at McAdow's sawmill. He had difficulty coping with the life of a single parent, and later accounts mention his heavy drinking. His replacement, Annie Alling, a twenty-two-year-old former schoolteacher from Kansas, was far more successful, remembered fondly by both students and parents. Hired at thirty-five dollars a

month, she began in early November 1879, with some students traveling eight miles to attend the school. Alling taught the basics of reading,
writing, and arithmetic, and the students made such good progress that
she decided to end the school session in late January with an "exhibi-
tion," where her students could demonstrate their new talents. According to the Bozeman newspaper, this "grand festival" impressed
everyone. The following night, Alling hosted a party for the adults at
McAdow's newly completed Coulson home. The supper was judged as
"excellent," and the dancing lasted till dawn, with Valentine Wickersham, the army telegraph operator at Alderson's Hotel, being
"obliged to play [his fiddle] continously [*sic*]."[8]

McAdow's big party in Coulson capped a year of parties and entertainment. The Newmans had hosted a Fourth of July party, where gai-
ety mixed with somber patriotic orations. Orson even composed his
own poem—the "Tree of Liberty"—for the occasion. A document of
the community's inherent patriotism, the poem is also a reminder that
the isolation of the frontier did not keep the settlers from practicing a
few of the more refined aspects of Victorian culture:

> Glorious tree of Liberty
> We hail thee, emblem of the free
> Let thy branches ever spread
> Till all may rest beneath thy shade.
>
> Planted by our patriotic sires
> That withstood old England's battle fires.
> We hail thee with glad hearts and true
> And pray that all may cherish you.
>
> May our children learn to tell
> The tales of thee, we love so well
> And of the hands that sealed their fame
> With thy great and sacred name.
>
> Our Washington that noble son
> That led them on to victorys won.
> May thy name emblazoned be
> Upon the crest of liberty.

May thy virtues and thy grace
Be ever sacred to our race.
May we all remember well
The hands that broke the tyrants spell.

Waving banner not unfurled
Be at peace with all the world.
Let all our noble sons agree
To protect the glorous tree.

Let no Monarch of the Crown
E'er attempt to pull thee down.
Let it e'er remain on earth
Bright emblem of our home and hearth.[9]

The parties continued that winter. As a Canyon Creek resident reported in the Bozeman *Avant Courier* of December 18, 1879, "The bachelors in the neighborhood now spruce up and rustle around pretty lively, as there has lately been an increase in the female population." The Newmans threw a Christmas party; a New Year's Day celebration took place at Coulson; and Joe Danford hosted another dance a week later. According to the *Courier* of January 15, 1880, when James Mossburg and Joseph Dennison of Canyon Creek finished building their dwelling and tavern, the two "invited the young folks to call evenings and bring their pipes and knitting with them."[10]

Mossburg and Dennison's invitation makes clear that visiting between the scattered ranches and settlements remained important. Orson Newman's diaries for 1879–80, for example, document a regular pattern of visits among the Newmans, the Dennisons, and the Danfords. John Alderson's hotel at Coulson, the stage stop and tavern of Alonzo Young at Young's Point, and Sidney Erwin's store and tavern at Canyon Creek were active places of social exchange where settlers would come to visit with the travelers passing through the Yellowstone region and learn the latest news from the East. In addition, settlers would take meals at Alderson's Hotel; for Orson Newman, a meal away from home allowed him to get away from the family table and break the monotony of the dinner routine.[11]

Table 7: Age Distribution in the Clark's Fork Bottom, 1880

Age Range (in years)	Percentage of Population
0–10	19.5
10–19	15.0
20–29	29.5
30–39	18.5
40–49	10.0
50–59	6.5
60–69	1.0

n = 200

Source: 1880 Census, Custer County, Montana Territory, National Archives, Washington, D. C.

Certainly the long winter months in the Clark's Fork Bottom left the settlers bored and restless. No one enjoyed the opportunity to relax and get together more than the many young people residing in the region. Nineteenth-century American society was decidedly youthful, and the Bottom was no exception to this general rule. According to the 1880 census, the average age in the Bottom was twenty-five years, and as table 7 details, almost two-thirds of the population was under the age of thirty. Few older settlers lived there: only one in six settlers was over the age of forty.

But the parties did more than give the young people a chance to stretch their limbs, court the opposite sex, and burn off excess energy. They gave everyone a chance to escape, temporarily at least, from the isolation and rigors of the farm. Here they could enjoy the fellowship of their neighbors as they listened to the fiddler's call, drank their fill, and shared stories of gains made—and misfortunes better left forgotten—as they built a new life on the frontier. The women of the Bottom were the active organizers of these events and took great pride in the special dishes they concocted for the community gatherings.[12]

Perhaps the biggest bash in the early history of the Clark's Fork Bottom took place at Billy Mitchell's ranch, near present-day Park City, on the Fourth of July, 1880. The Mitchells sent invitations to everyone in the valley, and some families came from as far as thirty miles away. After enjoying an excellent dinner, the settlers listened to a dramatic reading of the Declaration of Independence before singing "My Country 'tis of Thee" twice. "We wanted to be patriotic," recalled Helen Braum, but "we knew no other songs." In the following year, no one's diary or memoir recorded another grand Fourth of July celebration. The harsh winter, blistering summer, and hard times in general left only bread and ice water that July, and "such fare was more conducive to anarchy than to patriotism."[13]

No matter how poor the fare might be, the contemporary accounts of social gatherings were always chatty and positive. Later reminiscences also favorably recalled the old dances. Old-fashioned hospitality, plenty of booze, and the natural instinct toward nostalgia help to explain many of these fond memories. But another important influence was the lack of ethnic, racial, or regional divisions among the settlers. The Clark's Fork Bottom in 1880 was a remarkably homogeneous community. As documented in table 8, most of the settlers were Yankees, with 46 percent coming from midwestern birthplaces. A mere 1.5 percent, on the other hand, were born in the South. A slightly higher number—9 percent—were foreign-born, but most of these came from England, Ireland, Scotland, and Canada, countries that had some cultural similarities with America. The community had two immigrants apiece from Norway and Germany. No records mention any hostility toward these four men; perhaps this was due to the needed skills—carpentry and masonry—three of the four brought to the Bottom rather than to any tradition of ethnic tolerance. The percentage of foreign-born residents of the Clark's Fork Bottom was significantly lower than in other, more settled western urban centers. A column submitted to the Bozeman *Avant Courier* reveals a degree of bigotry in the community. The item noted the arrival of a Chinese male in the Bottom in early 1880 and bluntly expressed the hope that he would start his settlement elsewhere. The unnamed Chinese soon left the area.[14]

Further adding to the homogeneity of the Clark's Fork Bottom was the fact that most settlers pursued the same occupation—farming. As table 9 shows, nearly half of the settlers were farmers. The next largest

Table 8: Birthplaces of the Clark's Fork Bottom Residents, 1880

Birthplace	Percentage of Population
New York	13.0
Ohio	12.5
Missouri	9.0
Montana	8.5
Illinois	7.0
Iowa	5.0
Massachusetts	4.5
Kansas	4.0
Pennsylvania	4.0
England	3.5
Other	29.0
n = 200	

Source: 1880 Census, Custer County, Montana Territory, National Archives, Washington, D. C.

category was housekeepers, yet most of these women lived on family farms where their labor, and that of their children, both inside and outside the house involved the welfare of the farm operation.[15] Although male farm reformers of the era frowned on women working in the fields, such sexual distinctions in farm labor were often nonexistent in frontier communities. If we consider the farmers, housekeepers, and stockmen together as one occupational category, about 70 percent of the Bottom residents were engaged in agricultural work. The town of Coulson was really the only place of occupational diversity, with the residents engaged in such jobs as ferryman, stage driver, mechanic, retail dealer, and telegraph operator. Only three males in Coulson listed themselves as farmers, although John J. Alderson listed himself as a hotel operator and farmer.[16]

Parties and dances were not the only diversions in the early years of the Clark's Fork Bottom. Many settlers were voracious readers. Orson Newman's diary, for example, records a trip to Coulson in the dead of winter to buy newspapers. "Papers and magazines were passed around

Table 9: Occupations in the Clark's Fork Bottom, 1880

Occupation	Percentage of Population
Farmers	46.3
Housekeepers	19.5
Laborers	6.5
Merchants	3.3
Mail carriers	2.4
Stock raisers	2.4
Clerk	1.6
Stage drivers	1.6
Ferrymen	1.6
Stock dealers	1.6
Carpenters	1.6
Miners	1.6
Others	10.0
n = 123	

Source: 1880 Census, Custer County, Montana Territory, National Archives, Washington, D. C.

until they were worn out," remembered Alice Reed Shock. Every time Richard Clarke went to Coulson to deliver milk and butter, he stopped at Shock's house to read the latest stories in popular magazines. Mrs. Shock also recorded that traveling theater companies from Bozeman would perform at McAdow's store in Coulson. When Ellen Banks of Bozeman arrived to perform a "Chinese" musical, Bud helped to clear out the store and arrange the scenery for the production. The play was such a success that the community put on a few amateur plays of its own. Unfortunately, no one left records of either the titles of these plays or the names of the actors.[17]

Due to a lack of single women, few weddings took place in the Bottom. The first recorded wedding was on April 27, 1881, when the widow Alice Reed married the ferryman, John Shock. In July, Lillie C. Young, who had left her husband Alonzo two years earlier, remarried, this time to a new Coulson resident, Caleb Rich, who had recently moved from Bozeman. William D. Olmstead, the local justice of peace, performed both ceremonies at Alderson's Hotel, since there was no church in the Clark's Fork Bottom.[18]

Our common mythology about frontier communities has the settlers raising their school and church almost as quickly as their own cabins. But in the Clark's Fork Bottom, the pioneers did not get around to building a schoolhouse until two years after the initial settlement of the region. A church was not constructed in the region until the coming of the Northern Pacific Railroad, five years after the first settlers had arrived.

What do these delays tell us? The delay in the construction of the school is not surprising because until 1879, few children lived in the Bottom, and without students, there is little point in having a school. The lack of a church, however, is one of the most striking facts of the region's early history. The Bottom thus differed markedly from the early-nineteenth-century rural community of Sugar Creek, Illinois, where churches, according to the historian John Faragher, "sustained the association of households and helped to provide a communal consensus." Religious observances must have taken place in the Bottom, but John Summers's diaries offer the only evidence of religious activity, and that did not begin until the summer of 1881 when he began to attend "Sunday school" at the local Canyon Creek schoolhouse and "preaching at Danfords." Before then, Summers observed Sunday as did most other Bottom residents—as a day of rest and relaxation. On Sunday August 1, 1880, for example, he took the day off to write letters, have a bath, and change clothes, a day very similar to the one observed by the ranchers that Colgate Hoyt documented in 1878.[19]

Why did this pattern of behavior change in 1881? There is no clear answer. As immigration increased, perhaps a highly motivated religious person moved into the valley and took matters into his or her own hand. Perhaps not until 1881 was there a large enough population to support religious activity. Finally, the hard times of the summer of 1881 might have led Summers and others to look to religion for solace and support.

Funerals were a time for more somber religious ceremonies. Because of the harsh nature of life on the frontier, the Clark's Fork Bottom had its share of deaths. During the twentieth century, a story grew about "Boothill" cemetery in the northern rimrocks overlooking Billings and about the many Coulson settlers buried there who had "died with their boots on" in wild shoot-outs, Indian attacks, or some other violent means. But from 1877 to 1881, Coulson rarely took on the character of the romanticized "Wild West town." The early burials at Boothill cemetery were more likely casualties from the rigors of frontier life than the victims of a fast-draw showdown. Clinton Dills and Milton Summer were murdered during the Nez Percé raid of 1877; they had been buried on Joseph Cochran's ranch and were not moved to Boothill cemetery until March 1882. The most likely first interment at the cemetery was David Currier, who died at the hand of John Alderson in 1879. The settlers who died after Currier, like Harry Reed and Fowler Allen in 1880 and Ellen Alderson and Henry Kinse in 1881, were victims of natural causes or accidents. Kinse, for instance, died after being kicked in the head by a horse. Billy Needham was another unfortunate accident victim. A mail carrier for the Lavina-to-Coulson stage, Needham was removing his coat in McAdow's store when his pistol fell, hit the floor, and discharged, fatally wounding him. Young Needham held on to life for a month before dying. A doctor from Fort Custer was summoned, but he arrived too late to be of any assistance.[20]

Needham's plight underscores another harsh reality of early life in the Clark's Fork Bottom: no doctors were available. Doctors were at the Crow agency and Fort Custer, but their primary responsibility lay elsewhere, with soldiers, employees, and the Crow Indians. Rarely could they come to help a sick patient in the Bottom. So the settlers learned to take care of their own. The Erwin brothers at Canyon Creek once nursed back to health a man who stayed in a back room of their store. Alice Reed Shock recalled taking care of several Coulson residents during an outbreak of smallpox. Women often assumed the responsibility of being the community's doctors. They served expectant mothers as midwives and commonly preferred the care of a fellow woman over any services offered by male physicians.[21]

Life was precious on the northern plains—and settlers would risk their own to save the lives of others. In the spring of 1880, a group of settlers from Coulson and Canyon Creek left for the Musselshell country looking for a trader named Snow who had been missing for twenty-three days. During a terrible blizzard in the winter of 1881, Sarah Thompson searched for the missing stage driver, Frank Sanderson. She found Sanderson "all covered with snow and ice." She added, "I took hold of his foot and boot and his leg was like a rock." Thompson dragged Sanderson into her house and nursed him back to health. The best-known rescue involved William A. Allen of Canyon Creek and Pretty Eagle, a Crow chief. During an 1879 blizzard, Allen claimed to have left the safety of his cabin to help Pretty Eagle and the chief's wife and child, in the process establishing a lifelong friendship with this important Crow leader.[22]

The rigors of frontier life were often frightening. A popular escape for both settlers and Native Americans was gambling. For the Crows, gambling served both a social and an economic function, and they loved the sport, especially when it involved horse racing. At some events, the Crows bet thousands of dollars in hides, furs, and horses. More common were simple skill challenges like horse races in Coulson, sometimes between Valentine Wickersham, the army telegraph operator, and Plenty Coups of the Crows.[23]

In addition, the settlers liked card games of all sorts. Calamity Jane, who lived near Coulson in 1880, often played poker at the local saloons. Other active participants in the rough side of life included two of the Bottom's most legendary figures, "Liver Eating" Johnson and "Uncle Billy" Hamilton. These three characters often dominated Coulson histories written in the early twentieth century, yet the contemporary records mention little about them. The three certainly could leave quite an impression: Jane, dressed in men's clothes and swearing, gambling, and drinking with the best of them; "Liver Eating," with his tall tales of Indian fights; and "Uncle Billy," dressed solely in his breechcloth and tanned almost as dark as any Crow Indian. But actually they played no significant role in the early history of the region except to serve the rapidly maturing community as a reminder of the raw frontier past. Perhaps this marginal role helps to explain their prevalence in later historical accounts of Coulson published in Billings newspapers. For even in 1900, when Billings had achieved almost every attribute of a proper Victorian community, it was only a generation removed from

the day when nothing but a sawmill and a tavern had defined its prede-
cessor, the "town" of Coulson.[24]

Although from 1877 to 1881 the Clark's Fork Bottom had its share of
excitement and colorful moments—all-or-nothing horse races and an
Indian raid in which the raiders wore tall stovepipe hats—more typical
were the deadly dull routines of everyday life on the frontier, broken
occasionally by family parties and community dances. If the truth be
told, Coulson was not a "Wild West" town of gunfights, whores, and
drunks: at least not until that agent of progress and civilization from
the East called the Northern Pacific Railroad headed Coulson's way in
the winter of 1882.

CHAPTER 6

Coulson's Boom and Bust, 1882

◻

The majority of people living in the far west have no idea of abiding there until the gray-bearded reaper makes his appearance. In short, we are all Chinamen. We are here to make our pile, then we shall return and enjoy our wealth in a land of congeniality.—A. K. YERKES, MAY 20, 1882

During the first five months of 1882, the Northern Pacific Railroad headed for the heart of the Clark's Fork Bottom, supplanting the bonds of economic and social exchange of the previous five years with the frantic, hurried world of the speculators and quick-buck artists who invariably accompanied the tracklayers of the West. The railroad's impact was multiplied by a heavily capitalized land company, controlled in St. Paul and New York City, which used its railroad connections to purchase the best land in the Bottom and establish a totally new townsite for a city of twenty thousand. Because of these events, Coulson experienced a boom and sudden bust that left this once prominent Yellowstone trade center on the verge of disappearing altogether; in its economic place stood the booming new town of Billings. Life would never be the same in the Yellowstone Valley.[1]

In December 1881, the entrepreneur Perry W. "Bud" McAdow held all the cards to the future of the Clark's Fork Bottom—or so it seemed to the Bottom residents. The topography of the valley, the earlier Northern Pacific surveys, and the railroad's need for a division headquarters and rail yards after crossing well over one hundred miles of the Crow reservation apparently dictated that the tracks would cross the Yellowstone River at the spot where McAdow's ferry and the town of Coulson were located. Rumors of Bud's impending fortune were heard everywhere. One story had the railroad offering McAdow thirty-thousand dollars for his Coulson land. Two weeks later, the future sounded even better as news stories confirmed rumors that the Northern Pacific would build "extensive machine shops" at Coulson.[2]

These stories were so juicy that they caught the attention of Paul McCormick, the Junction City businessman who served as McAdow's chief competitor in the commerce of the Yellowstone Valley west of Miles City. Ever since the Northern Pacific had negotiated its right-of-way along the river's southern bank in the Crow reservation, McCormick had known that the railroad would bypass his town, which was located on the opposite riverbank. But he still hankered for a bit of the prosperity the railroad promised. If he couldn't find it at Junction City, perhaps Coulson was the place. In late 1881, McCormick wrote to Thomas C. Power, the economic power broker of eastern Montana, about the future of Coulson. "There will be a chance to make money in this county next year," predicted McCormick. "When you go east come this way and we can fix Some Thing up. Write me if you know anything about prospects of Coulson."[3]

A week later, McCormick spelled out what "Some Thing" he wanted to "fix up" with Power. Once the railroad got to Coulson, the Junction City entrepreneur suggested, a shipping and warehouse business should be established. "Next year is going to be a good time for you to operate in the Yellowstone Valley," he told Power, adding, "I would like to make some money while this RR is being built." To cinch his argument, McCormick reported a conversation he had just had with Heman Clark, the general contractor for the railroad construction. Clark had advised McCormick to give up his Junction City operations, move to Coulson, and locate a new store and forwarding business there. As an inducement, Clark had guaranteed McCormick twelve hundred boxcar-loads of business annually, plus a railroad rebate large "enough to make it an object." McCormick wanted Power's assistance in this new Coulson venture.[4]

Unfortunately, no evidence exists about Power's response to this information. Neither man made a move until the railroad actually arrived at the Bottom in the summer of 1882, and then Power moved first, establishing a store at Billings. McCormick did not relocate his primary business enterprises from Junction City to Billings until the 1890s. Their decision to stay out of Coulson in the winter of 1881–82 left its future solely in the hands of Bud McAdow and his partner, John J. Alderson.

At the beginning of 1882, Bud's optimism, reported the Bozeman *Avant Courier*, was "consoling" and "rejuvenizing" to everyone interested in the future of Coulson. In mid-January, McAdow tasted his first riches from the approaching Northern Pacific by selling his entire crop of oats—ten thousand bushels—to Heman Clark, the railroad contractor. With this tidy sum in his back pocket, McAdow was ready to escape the rigors of a Montana winter, and in late January he left for California to "luxuriate for a few weeks among the tropical fruits and flowers."[5]

By the time Bud left for his West Coast vacation, Coulson had acquired all of the basic institutions—post office, hotel, and newspaper—to be a fully functional western town. McAdow had established the post office in December 1877, and Alderson had built the hotel, which served new arrivals and symbolized the community's economic prospects, in 1879. The coming of the railroad in the winter of 1881–82 was enough incentive for A. K. Yerkes to establish the third institution: a newspaper called the Coulson *Post*, which first appeared on the town's dusty streets on February 4, 1882. Born in Bordentown, New Jersey, Yerkes was a twenty-three-year-old editor and publisher who hoped to make his start in the Yellowstone Valley. George W. Alderson, a twenty-year-old native of Chicago, was the *Post*'s first foreman. Yerkes and Alderson printed an unabashedly booster press, full of unrealistic predictions of the future greatness of Coulson, along with stories touting the joys of living in the Yellowstone Valley. The booster press, despite its excesses, was an accepted way of life in the American

West, proof to settlers and interested businessmen alike that here, at this tiny spot in the middle of nowhere, a "real" town existed, with cheap land and unlimited economic opportunity.[6]

In February and March 1882, it appeared that Coulson could conceivably match the extravagant claims of unlimited opportunity and unchecked success noted every week in the pages of the *Post*. Coulson had thirteen new businesses by early February. To provide necessary services for the vast number of horses and other draft animals used by the railroad construction crews, Charles Racek and his brother opened a harness and saddlery store, Harry Sanderson established a new blacksmith shop, and H. Sweeney operated a large livery stable.

Another group of businesses served food, booze, and entertainment, mostly of the immoral variety, to the hordes of construction workers, camp followers, and settlers flooding into Coulson. Cross and Brown owned Coulson Restaurant; Robert Peters and T. S. Ash established City Market; Lane and Terrell ran the billiard hall; E. E. Keeley operated a "Vienna Bakery"; and Benjamin Benson opened the first of what would become a seemingly endless number of saloon and gambling halls. Even now Benson had ten other competitors, who stopped at nothing to make a sale. Whiskey sales to Crow Indians reached proportions that disgusted early settlers: John J. Alderson offered a reward of one hundred dollars to curb the practice. The new tavern keepers, however, ignored his plea to stop.

Although local settlers wished the many taverns would disappear, they welcomed the new businesses offering more durable goods. The new stores abruptly ended McAdow's mercantile monopoly, providing a wider selection of goods and services. Silas Blake marketed clothing, boots, and shoes at his shop, E. H. Lee sold dry goods and notions, and Charles W. and Cyrus M. Thompson opened a general merchandise store. Coulson also had its first resident professionals in the guise of Ashton and Lyons, self-described "Tonsorial Artists," and William Owens, a dentist. Two weeks later, these three would be joined by the medical doctors A. J. Hogg and D. M. Parker.[7]

The winter boom at Coulson nevertheless enriched the pocketbooks of both Perry W. McAdow and John J. Alderson as they cashed in their early businesses for large profits. McAdow sold an interest in his

Coulson wholesale and retail store to Jules Breuchaud and Fred Foster while Alderson sold his hotel to C. H. Dewey and E. H. Brown. Alderson's transaction had the more immediate impact on the local economy. Dewey and Brown acquired the property in mid-February and renamed it the National Hotel before furnishing it with the latest in fashion from Chicago and adding a sixty-by-twenty-foot wing to the rear of the hotel. Featured in the new addition was a forty-by-twenty-foot dining room. The largest commercial structure in the upper Yellowstone region, the National Hotel bragged of its large dining facilities and its twenty sleeping rooms, ideal for traveling drummers and newcomers looking for homesteads.[8]

Alderson looked after the management of McAdow's store until mid-March when the new partners, Breuchaud and Foster, arrived with a wagonload of new supplies, a refrigerator, a safe, and a heater bought in St. Paul. Jules's wife, Irene G. Breuchaud, recalled, "The store had been running for many years with an old, inadequate equipment that included few necessities and comforts to help a thriving business to progress adequately." What she thought of the store probably reflects what newly arriving entrepreneurs thought of the Clark's Fork Bottom in general. McAdow's store had been among the best the Yellowstone frontier could offer, but by the spring of 1882 it seemed hopelessly out-of-date for two young men experienced in the latest marketing techniques of St. Paul.[9]

At the same time that Jules Breuchaud was renovating the store, he was also directing the construction of his dwelling. By the end of the month, the Coulson *Post* reported that Breuchaud had almost completed a "fine" residence, but that description hardly fits Irene Breuchaud's recollection. Located on a Coulson lot near the Yellowstone, the house "was tall enough for a two-story building, but there was no upper floor and no stairway." Irene added: "It was just a shell, made of green lumber placed vertically—the drying of which on the sunny side was leaving open cracks, in some places an inch wide. There was no floor, and the small room forming a little ell which was to be used as a kitchen had no sink and no stove. My heart sank! How could such a dearth of every necessary convenience be made a home!"[10]

Irene Breuchaud's response, of course, is predictable for a newcomer fresh from the twin cities of Minneapolis and St. Paul, but it also underscores an interesting difference between the building practices of the early settlers of the Clark's Fork Bottom and those of the settlers during the Coulson boom. The early settlers had assembled their homes with logs, in true vernacular fashion, but they had built solidly, with an eye toward a long-term residence in the valley. Their homes might have been simple and unadorned, but the dwellings were well built. The same was true of major commercial structures such as McAdow's store and Alderson's hotel, both constructed with seasoned logs. But the vast majority of newcomers in the winter and spring of 1882 threw up whatever they could for shelter and for business. One reason was the lack of lumber as the number of new residents quickly outstripped the already meager resources. By February, if lumber could be acquired—the Coulson *Post* of February 11 complained of the severe shortage of building materials—it was typically the green, fresh-cut lumber that proved so useless for the Breuchaud residence. Rather than waste their money on that, most residents built shacks, erected tents, or used other temporary structures. Moreover, veterans of earlier railroad boomtowns knew that it was unwise, and costly, to invest in permanent buildings before the railroad actually arrived. Although the signs suggested otherwise, Coulson could always become another boom-bust town, merely a short-term place to make money before the Northern Pacific tracks moved westward toward new land and new boomtowns.

The number of new businesses and professions listed in the Coulson *Post* of March 18, 1882, thus document the persistent vitality of the railroad boom more than the establishment of a permanent western town. The new enterprises, compared with the limited offerings available in Coulson before the coming of the Northern Pacific, certainly added variety to the business community. The town had two attorneys, Samuel Wilde and Abel Farwell, a jeweler named William Nelson, its first designated builder, John McKay, and the painters McCarty and Sherman, along with a new hardware store, livery stable, and sawmill. But the fastest-growing segment of the local economy catered to the lonely, hungry, and thirsty railroad workers. H. J. Schmiell and Company operated the Le Bon Ton restaurant and "chop house," Harriman and Jones owned St. James Restaurant, and Stull and Lane opened a dance hall in a big tent on Main Street. In addition, the earlier Coulson Restaurant was expanding "with a rush and a roar." The *Post* reported, " A bar has been placed therein and sleeping apartments are soon to be added."[11]

Two weeks later the jerry-rigged, impermanent character of the local commercial district became apparent when a strong chinook wind blew into town, destroying at least two-thirds of Coulson and scattering remnants across the prairie. The only commercial buildings spared extensive damage were McAdow's store, the National Hotel once owned by Alderson, and Jack Skillin's Headquarters saloon. Most businessmen merely resurrected their buildings and tents and went about their business.[12]

It was an ill wind that had blown into Coulson—and a sign of things to come. Throughout the winter, the speculators, businessmen, and workers who eagerly sought out the Clark's Fork Bottom in hopes of making a few quick bucks had looked toward the better-situated entrepreneurs like McAdow and Alderson for hints about the town's economic destiny. In Bud's absence, talk in the saloons, dance halls, homes, and businesses of Coulson centered on several pressing questions. When would McAdow and Alderson sell their land to the Northern Pacific? Were they being too greedy—would they scare away the railroad by making excessive demands for their land? If a deal could be made, what would they do with the money?

These questions were directed at the wrong people—what McAdow and Alderson planned really didn't matter. McAdow and Alderson miscalculated Coulson's future because they ignored the Northern Pacific's preference to bypass existing small towns. In the Yellowstone Valley east of Coulson, the railroad had already bypassed the original settlements at Glendive and the town of Junction City. As the geographer John Hudson found later in neighboring North Dakota, the interest of the northern plains railroads "in a potential townsite was inversely proportional to the amount of investment others had already made, and they characteristically avoided anything that would narrow their options." This is what Coulson experienced in 1882.[13]

A group of St. Paul and New York City capitalists, far richer and more powerful than any eastern Montana entrepreneur, would decide the fate of the Clark's Fork Bottom. On April 1, 1882, the people of Coulson discovered that a huge land company named the Minnesota and Montana Land and Improvement Company had already purchased most of the Clark's Fork Bottom from the Northern Pacific and that this company, not Alderson or McAdow, held the fate of the Clark's Fork Bottom in its hands.

The events that led to the massive land purchase of the Minnesota and Montana Land and Improvement Company began at least two years earlier. On March 27, 1880, Roswell H. Mason, the U. S. surveyor general for Montana Territory, sent Frederick Billings, then the president of the Northern Pacific Railroad, an advance copy of the land office report for the 1878–79 fiscal year. This communication, at first glance, appears routine, but Mason had other things on his mind. He would be leaving office in November and wanted to become the Northern Pacific's land sales officer for Montana. He had already told the railroad's vice-president George Starke, "[If] I could serve the Co. in any way not incompatible with my official duties, it would afford me pleasure to do so." In this letter, Mason took care of official business, then repeated his desire for the land sales position. To demonstrate his loyalty to the Northern Pacific, he gave Billings an advance draft map containing valuable information about the survey delineations along the Yellowstone Valley.[14]

For someone interested in establishing his own Yellowstone townsite, as was Frederick Billings, this map was riveting. Billings and other Northern Pacific officials had selected the Yellowstone for their western route because the territory's population was concentrated in the southwest and because the Yellowstone land was considered to be more valuable than the Musselshell or Missouri river valleys to the north. Land was the company's best asset. As an inducement to construct a transcontinental line, the federal government had given the Northern Pacific the alternating townships for forty miles to either side of the tracks. Northern Pacific officials assumed that the valley possessed vast agricultural potential, and they hoped that settlers would flock to the new lands as soon as the railroad was completed, enriching the company not only by their travel but also by their land purchases.

In addition, Billings and his friends wanted to take full personal advantage of the railroad route through the Yellowstone to create their own city. Throughout his western career, Billings had made judicious investments in potential new townsites, from San Francisco and Port Townsend, Washington Territory, in the 1850s to Tacoma, Washington Territory, and Superior, Wisconsin, on either ends of the Northern Pacific mainline, during his term as company president. The Yellowstone townsite, in time, would prove to be his most personal involvement. But where would be the best place? After reviewing Mason's draft map, Billings and his allies chose a site just north of Coulson because of a fluke in the initial survey. The map showed that the east-west base survey line for Montana cut through the Clark's Fork Bottom near Coulson in such a way that two odd-numbered townships totaling 1,280 acres, both of which by law belonged to the Northern Pacific, "lay side by side across the line, instead of cornering together as they [did] elsewhere." As a railroad engineer, H. W. Rowley, recalled, Billings and the others said, "We will put the town where this line crosses the railroad tract, and get two adjoining sections."[15]

When deciding where to place the new towns and cities of the Yellowstone region, the eastern capitalists sitting at their desks in St. Paul and New York City saw only the abstract lines of the survey map and the terms of the railroad's land grant. In their minds, the dot on the map was reality—not the current land boom in Coulson. Their perfect place for a Clark's Fork Bottom townsite stood on a flat, barren, and largely waterless alkali flat, about two miles to the north of the region's initial settlement.

Frederick Billings resigned the presidency of the Northern Pacific in June 1881 after losing a power struggle with the German financial wizard Henry Villard, but he did not forget about his Yellowstone townsite. As a large company stockholder who still had several close friends among the Northern Pacific's hierarchy, he remained in touch with the railroad's western expansion. As the rails left Miles City and headed for the Coulson ferry, Billings and his allies began to put their plans into action. On March 24, 1882, Billings, Heman Clark, and Thomas F. Oakes, a Northern Pacific vice-president, together with their minor partners John B. Westbrook and Thomas C. Kurtz, filed papers at the

Minnesota state capitol in St. Paul incorporating the "Minnesota and Montana Land and Improvement Company," capitalized at $200,000. The company was empowered to establish a new townsite called Billings and to develop the adjacent Clark's Fork Bottom by purchasing the alternating townships deeded to the railroad. A week later the land improvement company signed a provisional contract for the purchase of 42,791.73 acres (in the final contract reduced to 29,394.22 acres) at and surrounding the Billings townsite for $113,558.86. Ignoring the already thriving frontier town of Coulson, the eastern capitalists had suddenly created *the* city of the Clark's Fork Bottom—and to add insult to injury, they named the town in honor of the one man, Frederick Billings, who had done the most to wreck the hopes of McAdow, Alderson, and the others at Coulson.[16]

On April 1, Heman Clark appeared on the streets of Coulson to announce the creation of Billings—called the "Second Denver" of the west—and detail the plans and prospects of the Minnesota and Montana Land and Improvement Company. He pledged that the company would build eight or nine sawmills, construct a sixteen-mile-long irrigation system (ending the community dependence on McAdow's earlier, poorly constructed ditch), and establish the Bottom's first bank. These steps marked only the beginning of a massive development program. In time, the company would establish a shipping point for the burgeoning eastern Montana cattle industry, build railroads to the mines to the north and south, start a stock-raising company, and do everything possible to assist the rapid settlement of the Clark's Fork Bottom. The Northern Pacific would do its part as well by locating its machine shops at the new town on property donated by the land company. The Billings town plan embodied the "structure" model of town settlement. To control development at this railroad town, the land company chose the site, designed the plat, designated the building lots, and even planned industrial developments before any actual business activity took place.[17]

Clark's promise to inject a massive dose of capital into the development of the region lit the fuse of a crazed land boom. Envisioning that Billings would immediately become a major regional trade center, the land company had planned accordingly, designing a town for twenty thousand inhabitants, complete with broad avenues and city parks. "It was at Billings," the geographer John Hudson has observed, "that railroad design and townsite entrepreneurship were combined in what might be termed 'classic' Northern Pacific fashion." The Billings design largely copied those of Bismarck and Jamestown in Dakota Territory, where "the railroad was the centerpiece, flanked by two streets with business lots facing the tracks, which in turn were backed by an extensive gridiron of business and residential blocks on both sides of the tracks." This "symmetric" plan was a favorite of the Northern Pacific, but rarely did the two sides of the track develop equally.[18]

But that meant nothing on that crazy April day. A city of the size that Clark announced meant that there was plenty of real estate to sell, and Clark had barely finished his speech before eager buyers besieged him. Clark found himself serving as a land agent, selling four hundred lots at whatever price he set in the first week alone. In general, commercial lots brought an average of one hundred dollars apiece, with choice locations going for as much as five hundred dollars, and house lots sold for twenty-five dollars.[19]

Residents in the Bottom soon realized that outsiders—who had inside information about the creation of Billings—had already grabbed much of the prime real estate. Miles City businessmen owned some choice individual lots, and capitalists residing in St. Paul, Chicago, and New York City had bought entire blocks of the new town for speculative purposes. The specter of absentee landlords did not sit well with local residents; the *Post* recorded "very serious discouragement and indignation against the management in the sale of large blocks to people in St. Paul and other Eastern points." These complaints were more than jealous outbursts. The single surviving record of town-lot sales in Billings during these early months indicates that of the first two hundred recorded contracts, two-thirds were signed by residents of either St. Paul or Minneapolis, whereas a mere one-fifth went to Billings residents.[20]

Although unappreciated by local landowners, these outside speculators, most of whom were directly or indirectly affiliated with the Northern Pacific Railroad, had the economic clout to boost the new town's fortunes in a way impossible for local residents. On March 31, for example, Thomas F. Oakes asked a fellow Northern Pacific executive, J. M. Hannaford, to give the future Billings newspaper favorable rates on a "carload of presses." Smaller investors were involved as well, and a few promptly moved to Billings to manage their property. From Dubuque, Iowa, for instance, came C. W. Horr, who opened a real estate office to sell his twenty-eight lots.[21]

During the second week of April, the Billings boom gathered steam with the arrival of George B. Hulme, the land company's official agent. "The rush for lots on Thursday, when the agent arrived," reported *Post* Editor A. K. Yerkes, "was so great that to a stranger, Coulson appeared depopulated. Aside from the 'coon' and ye editor no one was visible on the streets." Yerkes may have remained at his Coulson office that day, but his heart, and good business sense, lay with the new town to the north: the newspaper that announced Hulme's arrival unveiled a new masthead—the Billings and Coulson *Post*.[22]

Perry W. McAdow also appeared on the scene in mid-April. No one recorded his immediate reaction, but Bud must have been shocked to find his Yellowstone world turned upside down, virtually overnight. Nor do we know the reactions of other local residents like the Newmans, the Clarkes, and the Danfords. We do know that the coming of the railroad and the organization of the Minnesota and Montana Land and Improvement Company brought several immediate benefits. The boom gave early settlers a chance to sell their produce to more merchants—at exorbitant prices. Four bags of potatoes fetched as much as thirty dollars. McAdow's store at Coulson and Erwin's store at Canyon Creek suddenly lost their captive market. The settlers could trade with the many merchants who crowded along the river at Coulson.[23]

But trade-offs existed as well. The new economic system was more impersonal, cold and distant. McAdow had lived among the settlers for about six months each year. He offered charity, gave grubstakes for promising newcomers, and sponsored some community social events. Now, wherever they turned, the settlers of the Bottom encountered employees representing faceless land speculators who sometimes lived hundreds of miles away.

Billings, in this sense, would prove to be no different from later northern plains railroad towns. In general, three types of entrepreneurs thrived in these newly established places. First, clerks at businesses from towns created earlier would move to the new city and establish their own ventures. A good example for Billings would be Edgar B. Camp, who first worked in a Miles City hardware store before relocating to the Clark's Fork Bottom and starting his own hardware business. Next, there were the railroad construction entreprenuers who followed the tracks from townsite to townsite, staying only as long as enough construction workers remained to keep their prices high and services in demand. It would not be long, for instance, before the traveling professionals and the owners of the many saloons, taverns, and hotels of early Billings moved their businesses to the next large town on the road, Clark City, the precursor to present-day Livingston. Finally, well-to-do merchants or wholesalers from nearby trade centers would establish branch businesses in the new railroad towns. T. C. Power, of Fort Benton, was the most prominent Montana merchant to open a branch store in early Billings.[24]

More than the business environment had changed in the Clark's Fork Bottom. With the land company owning every odd-numbered section in the region, the days of freely cutting hay, hunting animals, and in general exploiting the local resources were to be greatly circumscribed, if not forbidden altogether. Development of the valley was under way—and for the early settlers that meant a certain loss of the economic freedom and opportunity available only in a frontier setting.

Another part of the dark side of rapid economic development was the sudden destabilization of the settlers' original social world. Visiting, barn dances, and school programs had largely defined the social whirl of the Clark's Fork Bottom. Similar diversions, including a February horse race in Coulson and parties at the ranches of James Westbrook and Orson N. Newman, had marked the beginning of 1882. The town of Coulson opened its first school in the spring, and the teacher, Mrs. Skillin, celebrated by hosting a dance, with the Coulson String Band providing the music and the National Hotel serving the food. But when the children attended school each day they had to pass by a long line of floozies and drunks standing outside saloons and dance halls. As early as mid-February, Coulson had taken on the appearance of a "Wild West" town—and things only got worse. The bars, gambling houses, and dance halls were open twenty-four hours a day. As gambling diversions, gruesome prizefights, like a February bout between two Irishmen named Ryan and Sullivan, replaced the earlier horse races between the Crow Indians and the settlers. Brawls spilled out of the Coulson saloons into the streets. After one nasty fight, John J. Alderson led a fund-raising drive to pay for the medical bills of Ed McHale, who had been beaten almost to death by the gambler Tom Newcomb.[25]

A level of violence totally out of character with the Bottom's early history made Coulson a dangerous place to live. Arthur S. Shannon, a local druggist, recalled watching two drunks riding down Main Street, brandishing their shooting irons. As one neared Shannon, he fired, "kicking up the dust" about halfway between him and the druggist. Shannon was lucky compared with others. Frank Redman walked into a Coulson saloon just after a drunk and irked gambler named Dutch Charley boasted that he would shoot the first man he met. Charley was true to his word and gunned down the eighteen-year-old boy. After a heated argument, Dan Lehey killed Billy Preston, a Coulson saloon owner. A man named Quinn shot Ben Walker without bothering to remove the pistol's ramrod, which passed completely through the victim's body. In a desperate attempt to curb the murders, "Liver Eating" Johnson was appointed a deputy sheriff. His methods of law enforcement, however, were unorthodox. As he explained to the county sheriff, Thomas Irvine, "There ain't no jail here, so when I finds anyone that ain't behavin' I just gives them a good whopping and that's an end of it."[26]

Senseless violence also touched the new town of Billings. A fight in a billiard hall led to the first murder, that of James Russell by George MacArthur. Local citizens buried Russell at Boothill cemetery in Coulson. Then they "race[d] madly back to town on horseback for a fast drink to end the sorrow." As they returned home, however, a cowboy fell off his horse and was trampled to death. The most documented murder involved Muggins Taylor, the popular Coulson resident who in May had become the deputy sheriff for Billings and Coulson. Taylor had gone to the home of Henry Lumpp, who, according to Alice Reed Shock, "spent his time in the saloons while his wife supported him by taking in washing." Taylor wanted to arrest Lumpp for a drunken escapade at a local bar where Lumpp had forced the bartender to dance by

firing repeatedly at his feet. Lumpp resisted arrest, and while strug-
gling for a pistol, he fatally wounded Taylor. Almost the entire town
turned out for Taylor's funeral. In addition to murders, there was even a
suicide. Mrs. Louisa "Lulu" Carter, who worked the dance halls, drowned
by walking into the Yellowstone River after declaring "here goes nothing."[27]

Not everything—or everyone—delivered by the Northern Pacific
Railroad was welcome in the Clark's Fork Bottom. The Coulson *Post*
reported cases of smallpox in early February and again in May. In the
latter outbreak, the community ordered a young man with smallpox to
leave town until all symptoms had disappeared. Other newcomers exploded the earlier racial, ethnic, and occupational homogeneity of the
community. Editor Yerkes demonstrated his bigotry in a slur on a black
man who chose not to participate in the April land rush at Billings.
Keeping watch on the minorities, Yerkes had reported on March 18 that
four Chinese and seven black males resided in Coulson. The appearance of blacks and Chinese on the town's streets undoubtedly upset
the narrow-minded sort. But not all newcomers received such a cold
shoulder. The old bachelors of the Bottom were especially glad to see
the increased number of women. Two of the Salisbury brothers, Win-
field Scott and Van Jackson, married the sisters Kate and Mary Lind-
berg, who had worked their way west cooking for the hungry construction crews of the Northern Pacific Railroad.[28]

The murders and mayhem of the spring and summer of 1882 have
garnered most of the historians' attention, but those events, it should
be remembered, were confined at the time to the Billings-Coulson
area. In other settlements of the Bottom, social life continued much
the same. To ease the boredom of winter, Canyon Creek residents enjoyed innocent diversions such as a "candy pull" in February and a St.
Patrick's Day party in March. The Young's Point community reported
the opening of its first school, with Eva Ash as the instructor, in the
spring. Yet the serenity of these hamlets ended as the Northern Pacific
rail workers moved past Coulson and headed up the valley. On June 25,
1882, Otto Maerdin, a new settler in eastern Montana, described the
Clark's Fork Bottom as "the greatest place for saloons and restaurants
ever seen. We passed one place called Young's Point. There were four

houses in the place and three of them were saloons and the other a restaurant."[29]

Shifting the social and economic patterns of life in the Clark's Fork Bottom, the new engines of development represented by the Northern Pacific and the Minnesota and Montana Land and Improvement Company also gobbled up those foolish enough to offer resistance. The land company, wanting additional room for expansion, made John J. Alderson several offers for his Coulson property. Alderson, however, demanded so much money that the company finally dropped the offer. Greed cost this Englishman his last chance of salvaging something out of his Coulson property. Bud McAdow, on the other hand, did not let his last opportunity slip through his fingers. Within two weeks of his return from California, McAdow had sold 160 acres of his property as an "addition" to the Billings townsite. Far from defeated by his sudden reversals in the Yellowstone, he optimistically reported to T. C. Power on May 6: "A party of engineers are surveying a line from here to [Fort] Benton through the Judith. I think we will be in RR connection with your town in a few years. Everything here is booming." The Billings rush even embraced McAdow's old Coulson store, since he and his partners had moved in May to a new location on the main business street of Billings.[30]

May 1882 was indeed a promising time in the Clark's Fork Bottom. The arrival of the first seventy-five settlers of the "Northwestern Colony Association" from Ripon, Wisconsin, marked the beginning of a Northern Pacific initiative to sell its Yellowstone lands. Each member of the colony would receive two lots, one for a business and one for a residence. The Ripon colony first camped outside McAdow's Coulson ranch before moving to its permanent home at the western end of the Bottom, where the settlers platted the town of Park City. This first Northern Pacific–supported colony, however, was also the last located in the Yellowstone Valley. Many colonists found the land prices of the Minnesota and Montana Land and Improvement Company so expensive that they passed on their options to buy land and returned home to Wisconsin later that summer.

Yet in May 1882, the colony's future looked bright, and its appearance heightened optimism about the future of Billings. If the new town could attract an even larger rush of immigrants, the potential for economic expansion in the region was virtually unlimited. All signs pointed to continued vitality. The firm of Stebbins, Post, and Mund opened its new Billings bank on May 15. The Northern Pacific already had finished its "Headquarters Hotel," a combination office building and bunkhouse for company employees. At Montana Avenue and 28th Street, the Headquarters was the focal point of the new town. The new railroad complex was soon followed by the land company's offices, on the corner of Minnesota Avenue and 29th Street. The land company also filed its corporate charter with the territorial government in Helena.[31]

And to add a bit of the fear of God to the new town, Benjamin F. Shuart of the American Home Missionary Society was busily establishing the First Congregational United Church of Christ. Shuart found Billings in a rough, unfinished state, and he considered himself lucky that a railroad engineer offered the minister a place to stay. As Shuart later recorded in his memoirs during the 1930s, "The only furniture which this shack contained, besides the bed, was one inverted empty nail keg." He added, "I wrote more than one sermon with this keg for my revolving armchair and my knees for a desk." The minister found plenty to do:

> At this early stage in the growth of Billings the gambler, the dispensers of strong drink and women of the "red light" were numerously represented in Billings and plied their several occupations, brazenly and without [shame?]. And at times they rendered the nights hideous, to unaccustomed ears, by the revelries and drunken brawls in progress in the tents. This state of things however did not last long . . . . But a sufficient numer of each sex remained behind safely to insure Billings against being cartooned as a "Saints Rest."[32]

H. B. Wiley's recollections complement Shuart's description of the Billings-Coulson area in early May 1882. Wiley and several friends came to Billings carrying only a large chest in which they had packed "a tent, some cots, bedding and a supply of canned goods." They found Coulson to be just "a small town with a hotel, a few stores and saloons." Wiley and his comrades waited at the National Hotel until their trunk could be delivered. "The first night we had little sleep," remembered Wiley. "Next door to the hotel was a dance house in a large tent, and they made so much noise that there was no sleeping." When they rode into Billings, they found only "one frame building in Billings—the N. P. Ry. Co. Engineers headquarters and some two hundred tents." Even the town's first post office, established in early July by the postmaster Lucius Whitney, who managed a general store owned by T. C. Power, was a decidedly crude affair. According to Wiley, Lucius Whitney "had no fixtures so [he] got a lot of empty beer cases, knocked the bottoms, turned them on edge, and put in glass panes where the bottoms had been, and thus formed letter boxes."[33]

E. V. Smalley, a Northern Pacific Railroad publicist who visited Billings in May, also emphasized the rough, frontier appearance of the new town. Billings "consisted of perhaps 50 cheap structures scattered over a square mile of bottomland." Most residents lived in tiny A-shaped tents or in canvas-covered wagons, the only shelter available until more lumber arrived. Smalley noted the "frightfully dear" prices in the settlement. An order of green lumber sold for $60; potatoes were 8¢ a pound; and flour brought $6 a bag. But to earlier settlers, perhaps these prices were not so shocking; as late as 1880, Orson Newman had paid $6.50 for a sack of flour at Coulson. "The migrating impulse," concluded Smalley, "is the only way to account for the movement of merchants, mechanics, farmers, speculators, gamblers, liquor sellers, preachers and doctors to a point nearly 150 miles from anything that can be called a town."[34]

In her memoirs, Irene G. Breuchaud noted that the tent town of Billings lasted only a few weeks. "As spring developed, stores of a more permanent character were built, and one of them was a two-story house in which hardware was sold." Edgar B. Camp, for years a leading Billings merchant, managed this hardware store. Breuchaud recalled that since "its stock contained everything in the line of building, it prospered as soon as its doors were open for business." Another influential improvement was the construction, on the north side of Minnesota Avenue, of Lucius Whitney's combination post office and general store, which "induced much building on its right and left. Then came the [Stebbins,

Post, and Mund] bank, which occupied a corner on the south side. This proved to be the assurance for steady growth on both sides [of the railroad tracks]. The building of tent stores continued for a time but, gradually, as spring developed, business houses built of rough lumber lined the south side of the broad central street."[35]

Although there were all sorts of rough edges, Billings by the end of May 1882 had two primary business streets: Montana Avenue, on the north side of the tracks, and the busier Minnesota Avenue, on the south side of the tracks, closer to the river and to what was left of the town of Coulson. Billings certainly was a town with a future. The same could not be said for Coulson. The railroad and land company had virtually sucked the town of its economic life. E. V. Smalley dismissed the entire settlement as a place bypassed by progress. Smalley observed, "[Although Coulson] has made some money buying buffalo robes of the Crow Indians across the river, and selling shirting, groceries and whisky to a few herdsmen whose cattle graze in the Musselshell ranges, now it must abandon its score of 'shacks' and shanties or move them up to Billings." To hasten that move, Billings businessmen offered Coulson residents several inducements to do their shopping at the commercial wonders of the new town. Frank L. Mann began building the Billings Street Railway, a horse-drawn wagon on rails, which left from in front of McAdow's store on Minnesota Avenue, passed down the dominant southside business strip to 18th Street, turned south to 5th Avenue South, and followed this street east until reaching Coulson, two miles distant. Once completed, the street railway would lessen the dependence of Coulson residents on the dwindling number of local stores; instead, they could ride the rail to the "city" and select from a wider assortment of goods and services.[36]

This shift in consumer loyalty toward Billings undermined the position of Coulson in the regional market. Once-loyal customers from the outlying Bottom ranches, like the cobbler and blacksmith John Summers, quickly switched to Billings. His diary mentions the new town for the first time on May 22, 1882, when he carried a load of logs to sell at Billings; from that moment on, his diary never mentions Coulson again. Indeed by October 12, 1883, Summers had rented his own shop in Billings from the real estate entrepreneur Clara Tomlinson. Defections like those of John Summers certainly hurt local Coulson businesses but paled in comparison with the loss of Perry W. McAdow's patronage and support. When Bud moved his general merchandise store to Billings, it was a sure sign of Coulson's demise. A similar fate befell the village of Canyon Creek when Sidney Erwin moved his store to Billings that summer. The Billings and Coulson *Post* suspended publication in Coulson on May 20, 1882. The final death blow for Coulson came on June 13, when the town lost its post office designation. Of the three institutional foundations—the post office, the hotel, and the newspaper—only the hotel remained, and competition from Billings so drastically diminished its number of customers that its days as a profitable business were numbered. The hotel even gave its address as "East Billings, Formerly Coulson."[37]

Coulson lost more than its position as the leading trade center of the Bottom; the town was not even a dot on the map of Montana Territory anymore. In one of his last columns for the Billings and Coulson *Post*, Editor Yerkes summed up well the speculative mentality underlying Coulson's brief winter boom and its more rapid bust that summer. "The majority of people living in the far west have no idea of abiding there until the gray-bearded reaper makes his appearance," admitted Yerkes. Their motives were more practical and much more short-term. "In short, we are all Chinamen," he explained. "We are here to make our pile, then we shall return and enjoy our wealth in a land of congeniality."[38]

Coulson did not disappear overnight; some residents stubbornly stayed on for several years. They had paid a dear price for their property, and they could not afford to abandon it. These residents kept some community institutions alive. The Coulson baseball team, for example, had quite a rivalry with the boys from Billings. In the fall, the brewery still pumped out liquid refreshment, and three stores operated along with the hotel. On election day 1882, Coulson males cast sixty ballots—compared with almost seven hundred at Billings. In May 1883, when the street railway finally reached Coulson, local businessmen made a last-gasp effort to drum up new customers by offering a free schooner of beer from T. S. Ash and William Booth's Coulson brewery to any passenger taking the round trip from Billings to Coulson.[39]

Not even that enticement worked. The railway failed within two years and sold for a paltry one thousand dollars. Coulson soon became a ghost town, its buildings demolished or scattered throughout the prairie. Some buildings ended up at Winnett, the county seat of Petroleum County, some one hundred miles to the north, where they lasted through one more boom—the discovery of oil in the early twentieth century. Today the Coulson townsite has no buildings, or remnants of buildings, and serves as a Billings city park.[40]

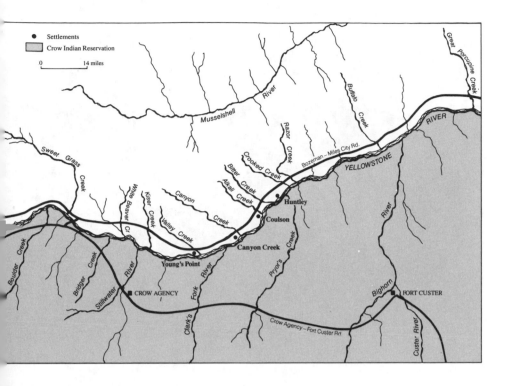

Great Porcupine Creek

Musselshell River

Buffalo Creek

Razor Creek

Crooked Creek

Bozeman – Miles City Rd.

YELLOWSTONE RIVER

Sweet Grass Creek

Bitter Creek

Alkali Creek

Canyon Creek

White Beaver Cr.

Kiser Creek

Valley Creek

River

Huntley

Coulson

Canyon Creek

Boulder Creek

Bridger Creek

Stillwater River

Young's Point

Clark's Fork River

Pryor's Creek

CROW AGENCY

Bighorn

FORT CUSTER

Crow Agency – Fort Custer Rd.

Custer River

Early settlements along the Clark's Fork Bottom of the Yellowstone River, c. 1880. Courtesy of the author.

Treaty Com.
1879 A.M.Quivey Two Belly A.R.Keller Tom Stewart HUFFMAN MILESTOWN

Old Crow Medicine Crow Long Elk Plenticus Pretty Eagle

1. Members of the Crow delegation to Washington, D.C., 1880. C. M. Bell, photographer, for L. A. Huffman photographers, Milestown. Courtesy of Western Heritage Center.

2. Town plat of Coulson, 1881. As initially planned, Coulson featured a linear town plan that focused on the Yellowstone River. Courtesy of Western Heritage Center.

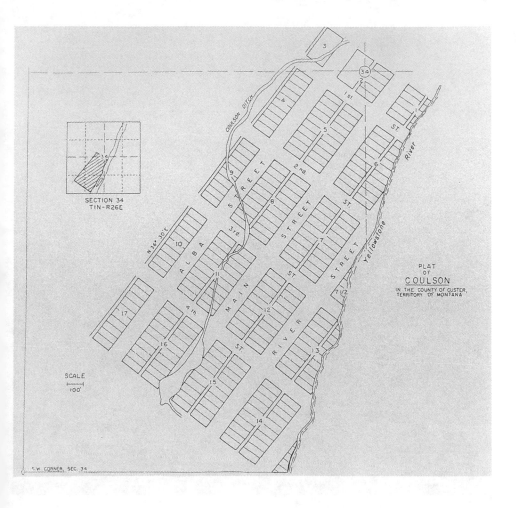

SECTION 34
TIN-R26E

SCALE
100'

S.W. CORNER, SEC. 34

PLAT
OF
COULSON
IN THE COUNTY OF CUSTER,
TERRITORY OF MONTANA

3. Main Street of Coulson, spring 1882. The expected arrival of the Northern Pacific Railroad boomed business activity along Main Street. Courtesy of Parmly Billings Library.

4. Headquarters Hotel of the Northern Pacific Railroad at Billings, June 1882. The arrival of the Northern Pacific on August 22, 1882, put the Clark's Fork Bottom in touch with the national railroad transportation network. Courtesy of Western Heritage Center.

5. Billings, May 1882. The rapid boom of Billings in May and June 1882 earned it the nickname of "Magic City." L. A. Huffman, photographer. Courtesy of Western Heritage Center.

6. Billings *Herald* office, June 1882. The booster press played an important role in the early development of Billings. Courtesy of Western Heritage Center.

7. This detailed map of Township 1S, Range 26E, from the 1889 Yellowstone County Real Estate Tax Records documents Frederick Billings's extensive landholdings in the Billings vicinity. Courtesy of Western Heritage Center.

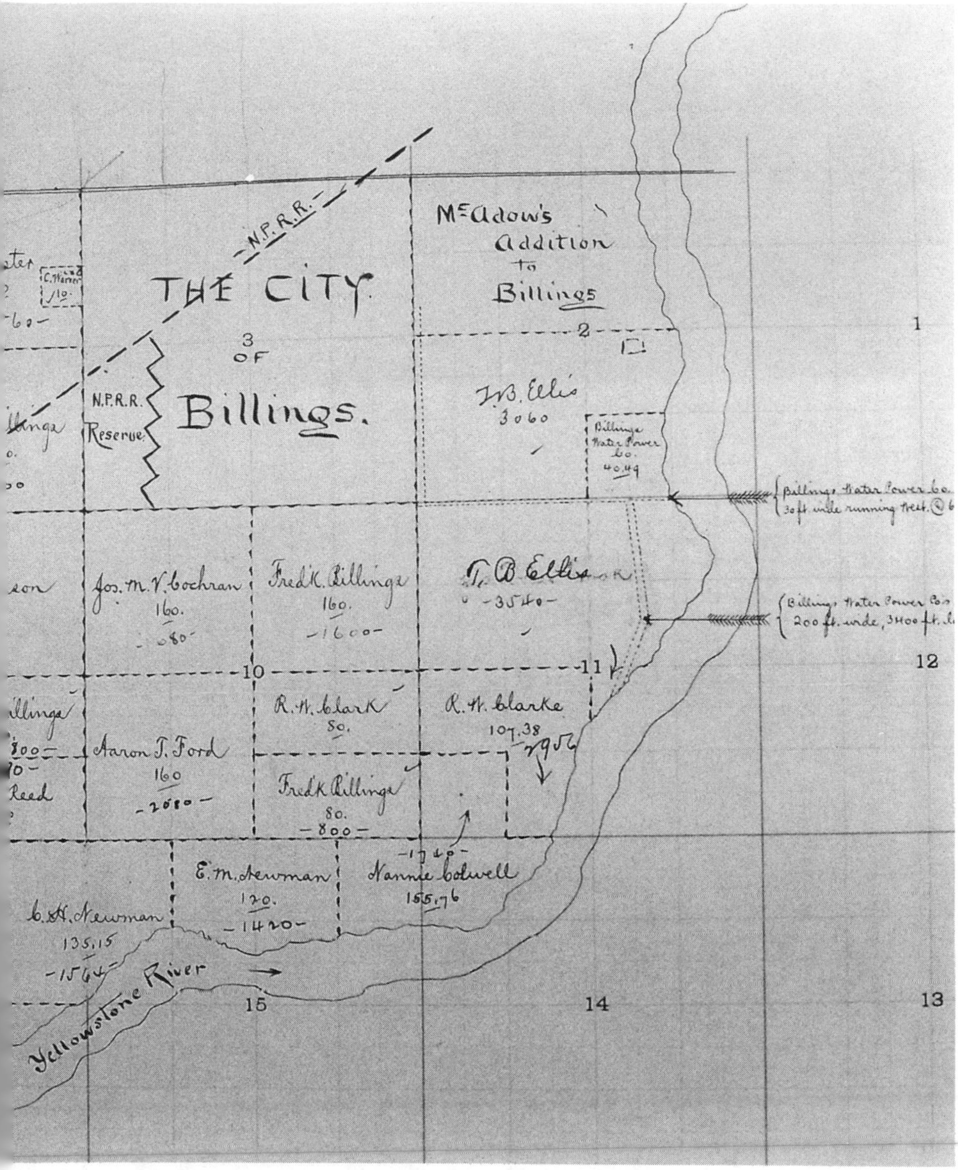

THE CITY
3
OF
Billings.

N.P.R.R.

N.P.R.R.
Reserve

McAdow's
Addition
to
Billings

1

2

F.B. Ellis
3060

Billings
Water Power
Co.
40.49

Billings Water Power Co.
30 ft. wide running West. @ 6

C.Miner

Jos. M. V. Cochran
160.
-080-

Fred K. Billings
160.
-1600-

T. B. Ellis
-3540-

Billings Water Power Co's
200 ft. wide, 3400 ft. l.

10

11

12

R. W. Clark
80.

R. W. Clarke
107.38

Aaron T. Ford
160
-2080-

Fred K. Billings
80.
-800-

E. M. Newman
120.
-1420-

Nannie Colwell
155.76

C. H. Newman
135.15
-1564-

Yellowstone River

15

14

13

8. Bailey and Billings Bank, Billings, c. 1886. Standing at left center is Parmly Billings, resting a hat on his knee. Courtesy of Parmly Billings Library.

9. For entertaining his new Billings neighbors, Paul McCormick used a log cabin, shown in this c. 1893 photograph, as a physical memento of days past in the Yellowstone Valley. Courtesy of Parmly Billings Library.

10. By 1895, as this photograph of Peter Yegen's mercantile business suggests, the depression was over and business was booming in Billings. Courtesy of Western Heritage Center.

11. This detail from a 1904 bird's-eye view of Billings shows the commercial activity concentrated between the tracks of the Northern Pacific (top of the map) and the Burlington (bottom of map) railroads. Courtesy of Western Heritage Center.

12. From left to right, Orson Newman, Paul McCormick, and Joseph Cochran marvel at the modern Billings landscape, c. 1900. Courtesy of Western Heritage Center.

13. Parmly Billings Library, Billings, c. 1900. The new memorial library symbolized the significance of the Frederick Billings family to the settlement and development of the Clark's Fork Bottom. Courtesy of Western Heritage Center.

14. Moss Mansion, Billings, 1988. Preston Moss's dazzling new mansion, built in 1901–3, represented the aspirations of a new class of business leaders who would guide Billings and Yellowstone County into the twentieth century. Photograph by the author.

Searching for Stability,
1882–1883

☐

Today houses are erected on twenty different streets, and new ones are going up on every side, wagon trains laden with merchandise are arriving daily, and the thoroughfares of Billings present a scene of business activity such as is not witnessed in any other town of Montana. The change seems almost as wonderful as some of those related in the old time tales of Eastern magic.
—BILLINGS *HERALD*, JUNE 1, 1882

In the summer of 1882, entrepreneurs, rail workers, settlers, merchants, prostitutes, and speculators came by the hundreds to a new city apparently blessed with some sort of magic. What other place had such enormous potential, fueled by not just one but two engines of capitalism—the Northern Pacific Railroad and the Minnesota and Montana Land and Improvement Company? But as the summer turned to the fall and then to the winter of a new year, those who dreamed of striking it rich at an unparalleled western land boom discovered that neither the railroad nor the land company had the resources to keep the magic alive. The boom faded, and in its place came months of uncertainty as Billings struggled for economic stability and searched for a way to fulfill its self-proclaimed destiny as the "Second Denver" of the West.

The newcomers who walked the streets of Billings in June 1882 could note the many changes the town had experienced in the two months since Heman Clark had first announced the ambitious plans of the Minnesota and Montana Land and Improvement Company. The new city of Billings already was larger than Coulson had ever been— and the railroad would not arrive until late August. An unofficial census on June 1, 1882, estimated the town population at five hundred and counted over two thousand people who owned lots in Billings. Most of these property owners, however, were absentee landlords; three out of every four did not live on the hot, dry, and treeless flat.[1]

Billings had residents and investors galore, but almost no one had a decent place to live or set up shop. On June 1, a mere fifty houses and forty-seven tents lined the streets, and most of these structures were refugees from rapidly disappearing Coulson. New settlers and opportunists must have wondered if this ragged assortment of dwellings and businesses was really a place where "old time tales of Eastern magic" came true. But then they promptly pitched in to turn the promise into reality. By mid-June, eighty-one houses were completed, seventy-five more were under construction, and the number of tents had almost doubled to a total of seventy-nine. Indeed, temporary quarters mushroomed everywhere, forcing Heman Clark to order the removal of "all shacks and tents located in the thoroughfares," an order that forced workers and squatters either to purchase a town lot like everyone else or leave town.[2]

The order to clean up the streets also reflected the desire of the land company to present a proper Victorian townscape to new immigrants and potential investors. How could newcomers be attracted to the company's vast holdings if the town looked like a ragged mining camp? Undistinguished shacks, army tents, false-front saloons, and log cabins, with lawns devoid of trees or any other sort of landscaping, may have occupied the streets of Billings, but at least the streets were neat and were organized into well-defined real estate lots.

This early concern about the city's image extended beyond mere appearances. Local business and civic leaders wanted the town to possess all the proper institutions of "civilized" society, and they borrowed liberally from their collective eastern experience to establish these new institutions. The efforts of the Congregational minister Benjamin F. Shuart, a native of Ohio who had recently moved from Minneapolis, to establish the first church in Billings met with strong encouragement. Another buttress of eastern culture was the community library, and Heman Clark donated several magazine subscriptions to the fledgling Billings Library Association.

Chartered on May 25, 1882, the association listed officers whose names read like an initial Who's Who of Billings businessmen and community leaders. C. W. Horr, the real estate dealer from Iowa, was the president. Minister Benjamin F. Shuart was a vice-president, as was Edgar B. Camp, a merchant who had arrived just two weeks earlier. Camp had been a young businessman in Chicago until one day in 1881 when he read of the rich opportunities of the Yellowstone Valley. He followed the tracks of the Northern Pacific to Glendive, where his first job was loading buffalo hides into waiting boxcars. His next stop was Miles City, where he worked at a hardware business, sleeping in the store to provide nighttime security. Camp's Billings enterprise marked the end of his wanderlust. Over the next thirty years, few businessmen matched his prominence in the town's social, economic, and political affairs as Camp served as everything from a trustee of the Billings Polytechnic Institute to a Republican state legislator. Another newcomer from Miles City was the corresponding secretary, Thomson P. McElrath, who had first chronicled the Clark's Fork Bottom in his 1880 booklet *The Yellowstone Valley* and had served as the influential editor of the Miles City *Yellowstone Journal*. George B. Hulme, the treasurer, controlled the purse strings of the association just as his land company controlled the purse strings of the community in general. Rounding out the officers were three directors: C. P. Saxton, E. A. Bromley of the Billings *Herald*, and Lucius Whitney, the future town postmaster and the unofficial agent for T. C. Power.[3]

Giving Billings a good image was, of course, just part of the land company's strategy to develop its massive landholdings. The next step was to address the town's water shortage, a problem that Billings shared not only with many western towns but with American towns everywhere during the nineteenth century. The water problems of Billings, however, were particularly acute because of the land company's initial decision to locate the townsite where alternating sections could be claimed rather than purchasing the Coulson townsite along the Yellowstone River. The dust produced by the city's new construction projects and the long, hot, dry summer days was a constant aggravation. Other than the Yellowstone, Billings had no water source except for the rather inaccessible and unsuitable waters of nearby Alkali Creek. As the *Herald*'s editor admitted on June 29, "The question of most serious importance that now agitates the people of Billings is that which concerns the water supply." Fifty cents could buy a barrel of water hauled daily from the Yellowstone, but this high price discouraged water use for any purpose except consumption. The lack of an inexpensive water supply threatened to stunt economic expansion before the boom had played itself out.[4]

Northern Pacific officials understood the situation well and hoped to profit by it. In early June, a railroad construction engineer wrote Wilbur Fisk Sanders, a leading Montana Republican and strong Northern Pacific supporter, about a plan to dig artesian wells, which could tap deep underground reservoirs of water. "Everything points toward a future for the new town of Billings," the engineer told Sanders, "but there is lack of good water which will be felt more and more, as the town increases its growth." The Northern Pacific officials wanted Sanders to provide some of the necessary capital to "control the water supply" of Billings. Sanders turned down the opportunity, and the idea of artesian wells was deferred for the time being.[5]

Rather than the quick, but expensive, short-term fix of deep underground wells, the land company offered a long-term solution—build a major irrigation system to open all of the Clark's Fork Bottom for fruitful cultivation. Plans for the "Big Ditch" were first announced in early April, but not until mid-July did the company hire a civil engineer, Henry W. Rowley, to design the project. Rowley planned to tap the Yellowstone River at the western end of the Bottom to build enough constant flow to enable the water to reach Billings with considerable force. Construction was well under way by the fall of 1882. Irene Breauchaud recalled how monitoring the progress of the ditch construction became a popular weekend diversion. Local residents would ride out to the head-gate area, where the engineers would assure them that the construction was on schedule and would predict the completion by next spring. The engineers knew better, but their deception calmed the worries of many residents. "With this great accomodation in view for next summer," Mrs. Breauchaud remembered, "we were disposed to overlook what seemed essential for the winter, and to continue to haul water out [of the Yellowstone] in two barrels."[6]

The problem of scarce and expensive water wasn't enough to stop the economic boom of Billings. A circular released by the banking firm of Stebbins, Post, and Mund on July 5, 1882, captures the aspirations of the business community. Billings was portrayed as the center of all eastern Montana trade, a gateway to Yellowstone National Park, and the home to the "finest agricultural land in the Yellowstone valley." According to the bankers, the town was full of "business men awake to all the possibilities and with ample capital to back their efforts." Could there be any doubts that the town would "grow to be one of the most important centers of the great territory of Montana"? As new businesses multiplied, the population of the town continued to soar, topping eight hundred in early July.[7]

By August 1882, the Stebbins bank circular carried the postmark of the new Billings post office, managed by Lucius Whitney. The formal creation of a local post office came just in time, since no booming town could survive without one. Whitney first operated out of his Billings home, then moved into temporary quarters in a false-front, frame building on Minnesota Avenue. Almost immediately, the post office had a positive impact on local trade as businessmen used the necessity of mail delivery to persuade T. C. Power to establish a stage line between Fort Benton and Billings, serving all of the small settlements in between. This inland transportation link helped to establish the new town as a regional trade center, especially for the scattered cattle operations of the Musselshell Valley and the Judith Basin. The post office also had a social function, soon becoming a gathering point and social center for bull sessions of all types. H. B. Wiley, an office assistant, remembered well a visit by Calamity Jane. She had no mail that day, but she was impressed that Wiley had even bothered to check. "Young fellow, you are all right," Jane remarked. "I came in yesterday and that old feller, without getting up, told me there was no mail for me. I told him to get up off his lazy stern and look."[8]

In August, the land company joined local efforts to boost the fortunes of Billings. Agent George B. Hulme sent pamphlets, circulars, and whatever he could find about the town's prospects to Henry J. Winser, who had been commissioned to write an official guide to the towns along the the line of the Northern Pacific Railroad. Winser was pleased to have such comprehensive information and expressed surprise that the population of Billings had gotten "into four figures so soon."[9]

But such was the case. By August, the number of buildings in Billings had increased by 50 percent since July, and many housed new businesses. Two new ventures, the Heffner quarry and the Montana Realty and Loan Company, had important long-term consequences. William Heffner, who had first come to the Clark's Fork Bottom in 1878 to build mackinaw boats for P. W. McAdow, established a sandstone quarry north of Billings at the foot of the rimrocks. Rock from the Heffner quarry would be used in the construction of many Billings buildings. Chris and Peter Yegen, two Swiss immigrants, were involved in several early Billings enterprises, and their Montana Realty and Loan Company, founded in 1882, contributed to real estate development, especially on the south side of the railroad tracks. Chris served as president, Joseph M. V. Cochran, the Bottom's first official homesteader in 1877, was the vice-president, and H. S. Williston was the secretary and treasurer.[10]

A wider variety of social events mirrored the boom in the local economy during the summer of 1882. The Clark's Fork Bottom experienced its grandest Fourth of July celebration yet, with horse races and fireworks along the graded Northern Pacific right-of-way leading into Billings. A Harvard-educated Texas attorney, Sam Wilde, gave the oration, and a grand ball took place in the evening. As many as one thousand people attended the day-long festivities, which were unfortunately marred by a horse race accident that killed one man.

July also witnessed the new city's first official wedding, between Joseph Lawler and Susie Sheen, with Reverend Benjamin F. Shuart officiating. Later that month, Shuart married Dewitt C. Dye and Mamie Williams at his new Congregational church. This simple, unadorned board-and-batten chapel had been financed by Lucius Whitney, Edgar Camp, and A. Frazer. The local justice of the peace, Charles Racek, married two other couples as well before the end of summer. But the most exciting event of the season belonged to the Boston Comic Opera Company, which presented a "musical extravaganza," called "Magic Doll," in early August.[11]

Musicals and parties aside, the biggest jubilee of the summer was reserved for Tuesday, August 22, 1882, the day when the first Northern Pacific train pulled into Billings. Everyone in Billings toasted the railroad's success. The days of isolation in the Clark's Fork Bottom were over; the region was now connected by rail to all of the eastern markets. After the last hurrahs were shouted, recalled H. B. Wiley, local businessmen took full advantage of the new rail link, setting off still another boom. "Billings grew like a mushroom. Saloons, dance halls, and theaters galore. Stores, offices lined the Main street." Over the next ten weeks, local residents enjoyed another period of unchecked economic growth.[12]

The regional stock-raising industry immediately cashed in on the benefits of a rail connection to midwestern packing plants. By September 15, the railroad was fully operational from Billings to St. Paul, and the very next day, according to the Billings *Post*, the town's first cattle shipments headed east, with Dan Floweree of Floweree and Lowry Cattle Company sending out seven hundred head of cattle. Within three weeks, the Northern Pacific had loaded 354 carloads of cattle at Billings, and by the end of November, 566 carloads had been sent East. The railroad also encouraged T. C. Power to join with the Northern Pacific to provide teamster service from Billings to Fort Benton, linking trade along the Missouri and Yellowstone rivers. This service did not come cheap. According to a Northern Pacific rate circular of October 10, 1882, it cost $13.50 to ship one hundred pounds of goods on the Northern Pacific from St. Paul to Bozeman; Power's "Billings and Fort Benton Stage Company" charged only fifty cents less to ship that same one hundred pounds from Billings to Fort Benton. Despite the expense of shipping goods cross-country, the new stageline contributed to the economic expansion by tying the new city with the largest trade center in northeastern Montana and with the head of navigation on the Missouri River.[13]

The Northern Pacific's presence also forced the Minnesota and Montana Land and Improvement Company to live up to its promise to build a grandiose and striking passenger depot, worth at least sixty thousand dollars. Throughout the summer, Heman Clark delayed construction of the depot as he negotiated with the Northern Pacific to provide unnamed advantages to the land company. The negotiations went nowhere, and by late September, Clark's company finally began to grade a site for the depot, which appeared to be much smaller than originally promised. The delays infuriated railroad officials and local residents alike: what kind of town would Billings be without an impressive gateway? The railroad, according to a report by C. W. Horr, refused to "be bound up with conditions" and took action to utilize its own headquarters building as a temporary depot while its workers finished the adjoining railroad shops and roundhouse.[14]

The developments of the past six months—both the triumphs and the failures—were witnessed firsthand by the town's father figure, Frederick Billings, when he first visited the Clark's Fork Bottom on October 25, 1882. He wrote in his diary, "First impression very favorable—pleased with the prospects for the town." And the town residents were delighted with his words of encouragement, especially his prophecy of "a rapid and substantial growth for the town and surrounding country."[15]

The town had achieved impressive gains during its first six months of existence. The two houses of late April had mushroomed into 250 dwellings by the first week of October. Fifteen "business houses" were open, with ten more under construction. And these new establishments were much more substantial than the rickety fly-by-night enterprises that had first followed the construction crews of the Northern Pacific. When bricks and stone became available in October, C. W. Horr and Lucius Whitney promptly abandoned their poorly assembled frame buildings to erect new brick stores. These were permanent structures, designed to serve the consumers of the Clark's Fork Bottom for many years. No longer could a strong chinook wind blow down the business district, as it had in Coulson the previous April.[16]

Yet as the seasons changed, a degree of uncertainty about the town's future infected the businessmen and entrepreneurs of the Clark's Fork Bottom. In part, their anxiety focused on the failure of the land company to build the promised grand depot, seven or eight sawmills, bank, and other institutions necessary for Billings to become the "Second Denver" of the West. This lack of capital investment scared away new investors and settlers. By October, for instance, many of the original Ripon colonists had abandoned their Park City lands at the western end of the Bottom. In addition, local leaders sensed a change in attitude from the Northern Pacific. Because major railroad stockholders like Frederick Billings and key Northern Pacific officers like Vice-President Thomas F. Oakes were major investors in the land company, local residents had assumed that the land company and the railroad would work together. But antagonism between the railroad and the land company grew, first evident in the controversy surrounding the Ripon colony and then in the depot spat. It became even more apparent when a letter from Thomas F. Oakes to General James S. Brisbin, a booster who coined the phrase "Billings, the Magic City," became public knowledge. Oakes had commented:

> I trust your predictions in regard to the settlement of the Yellowstone Valley may be fulfilled. I confess—to some skepticisms on the subject. I think we are going a little too fast. . . . The reports that reach us from people who have visted the Yellowstone Valley . . . are not as favorable as we could wish. We have plenty of territory that commends itself to intending settlers without forcing the country upon the attention of emigrants against their own convictions.[17]

Until the railroad and land company could settle their differences, the boom in Billings appeared to be on hold. The Billings *Post* of November 25 encouraged the city's businessmen to seize the initiative. The paper suggested creating a "reception committee," composed of "influential and representative citizens" who could provide "some mode of obtaining united action in relation to matters affecting the well being" of Billings. A committee was immediately formed, and it made plans to build good roads to outlying areas, especially to the Musselshell Valley where several thriving cattle ranches operated along with the gold and silver mines of the Judith Mountains. The construction of the cattle road began in early December. As a further inducement to stock raisers, the committee also worked to interest outside investors in a glue and tanning factory.

The committee frankly addressed two basic problems facing Billings in late 1882: the lack of water and the rampant crime of the city. It raised five thousand dollars to build five artesian wells as a short-term solution to the water problem, and it hoped that nine hundred dollars for a new jail would deter criminal activity. Billings businessmen realized that the town's reputation for wild fights and crime detracted from its image as the "Magic City." As a *Post* editorial explained: "It is about time that the Devil took a dip net and scooped in some of the thieves and pimps who make their headquarters in this town. . . . The respectable people do not propose to have the good name of the town smirched by the evil deeds of a few scoundrels."[18]

Local businessmen might not have turned so quickly to their own resources if they had known that another engine of outside capital— Frederick Billings—was planning to invest more of his personal fortune in the Clark's Fork Bottom. The favorable impression gained during his October 1882 visit persuaded the Vermont capitalist to invest more. No one in Montana, however, knew of his personal interest because Frederick Billings refused to confide in anyone, including his partner Heman Clark and his own land company agent, George B. Hulme. To guarantee his anonymity, Billings accepted an offer from the Congregational minister, Benjamin F. Shuart, to do his bidding.

The two unlikely partners already knew each other. During his October visit, local businessmen had asked Frederick for a donation so that a proper Congregational church could be built. His wife, Julia Billings, had immediately donated five thousand dollars, and the land company had provided a lot. After Frederick had inspected and approved the construction plans, he offered to pay the full cost of the church, which proved to be another eight thousand dollars. These donations initiated a fascinating economic partnership between the Billings family and Shuart, the minister and ever hopeful entrepreneur.[19]

The correspondence that winter between Shuart and Billings began innocently enough. Shuart kept Billings well informed about the progress of the new church and its various activities. "We have competent builders, under carefully drawn contracts & heavy bonds," he told Billings at the end of November. The next week he reported, "The building is already exciting much admiration for itself, to say nothing of the giver." But from the very first letter, Shuart offered more than flattery, telling Frederick Billings about promising, and cheap, sections of land available for purchase. "I shall esteem it a privilege to furnish you from time to time with any confidential information you may desire," Shuart promised. Although none of Frederick's responses to Shuart have survived, the content and the tone of later correspondence indicate that Billings accepted Shuart's offer. The minister would be Frederick's agent, and no one initially would know that Shuart was purchasing property for the Vermont capitalist.[20]

The early months of 1883 were a key period in the economic development of Billings as local business leaders aggressively pursued new opportunities and as outsiders like Frederick Billings and T. C. Power extended their investments in the region. The new year began with good news from Helena when the territorial legislature established Yellowstone County on January 23, 1883. The new county became a fully operational legal entity a month later, ending the time-consuming and expensive necessity of traveling to Miles City to conduct routine legal affairs. A late January public meeting at the Billings Opera House named John Gerish, Fred Foster, and Paul McCormick interim county commissioners and selected Billings as the county seat of government, an additional boost to future economic growth.[21]

Business reports also spoke well of the community's future. By January, the silver mines in the Judith Mountains, along with the mineral strikes north of White Sulpher Springs, had shipped almost 100,000 pounds of silver bullion to Billings. That summer, Billings received an additional 203,000 pounds of bullion from the mines around Cooke City. The stagecoaches from Fort Benton arrived three times a week, and in April, the Billings *Herald* had enough subscriptions and advertising revenue to become a daily paper. That same month, the Crow Indians began to cross the Yellowstone once again to trade with Perry McAdow and other local merchants, who "reaped a good harvest" of furs from the Crows. This year, however, the profits from the Crow trade were a pleasant bonus, not the economic necessity they had been in the past.[22]

The cattle industry of central Montana continued to expand its shipping operations at Billings, where twelve outfits had established offices. "It is simply astonishing to see the beef which is on sale here in Billings," observed Benjamin Shuart, especially since the steers "have been exposed through all this cold winter." The year proved profitable for stock raisers as cattle and then sheep fattened themselves on the thick natural grasses of the Yellowstone Valley and rich rangeland to the north. Indeed, Billings emerged in 1883 as a major wool shipping point. When the stock-raising efforts of the year were tallied, over 600,000 pounds of wool and 20,000 head of cattle had been shipped out on the Northern Pacific Railroad.[23]

The cowboys who accompanied the cattle to the Billings stockyards brought welcome business to the hotels, brothels, saloons, and restaurants of the town. They also took advantage of the goods available at local stores to stock up for the next season. But aggressive merchants like Heman Clark, who had established his own mercantile operation called H. Clark and Company, did not wait for the cowboys to come to Billings. Clark and other local businessmen loaded wagons with merchandise worth over thirty thousand dollars and carried these goods directly to the ranches and mining camps of central Montana and south to Cooke City, re-creating, in one sense, the old rendezvous of the fur trade era. But this time, rather than accepting beaver furs and buffalo robes, the merchants took only gold and silver in exchange for their food, whiskey, clothes, and equipment. And although the business community welcomed the cowboys and the hard money they exchanged at the stores, new settlers were often terrified by the ways of the range. Mrs. T. W. Wilkinson Polly, a Missouri native who moved to Billings with twenty-five friends and relatives in the spring of 1883, recalled:

When we arrived here, I guess all the cowboys in the neighborhood decided they should welcome the pilgrims, and show them
what the west was like. A bunch of them rode up and down the
street shoot[ing] revolvers, and one of them rode his horse right in
the door of a saloon.

We were a terror-stricken lot of women and girls, and I remember my mother leaning out of the conveyance which had stopped
before the Magnolia hotel, and calling to father, who was out on
the street, in an agonized voice: "Andrew, come here. You will be
killed." That only served to increase the evident glee of the cowboys at our consternation.

It was a tearful set of women and children that evening. There
was not a tree, and hardly a blade of grass —only sagebrush and
dusty streets and untidy surroundings, making it seem as if we
had come to very last place on earth.[24]

Billings might look like the last place on earth, but mere appearances
did not discourage the city's "smart-looking real estate brokers" from
besieging the Missouri immigrants with land deals. Few newcomers
failed to be swayed by the persistent arguments of the brokers. One of
the most persuasive, and most controversial, was Clara Tomlinson, a
fifty-year-old woman from Detroit, Michigan. Clara had arrived in Billings with her husband, C. E. Tomlinson, a physician aiming for a new
start in the Yellowstone Valley. When her husband suddenly died,
Clara had the choice of remarrying or striking out on her own. She took
the latter option, working as a clerk at the Northern Pacific offices in
Billings. Clara soon gave up this dead-end job to take on the male-dom-
inated world of real estate. By the spring of 1883, she had established
her own business, with "a nice three-room office on the main road, and
as she lived there, she was ready for business at any time." Confident in
her ability to sell property, Clara soon became a "quite popular" broker.
As Irene Breauchaud remembered, "She was a very free and easy talker,
and amused the boys much by the description of the way in which she
managed her business." Although both men and women in Billings
made fun of Tomlinson's "very high idea of her business ability," Clara
enjoyed the last laugh. In 1884, she married Perry W. McAdow, and by

using his mining know-how and her capital, she developed the famous Spotted Horse mine at Maiden. Clara made her fortune and later retired to Jackson, Michigan, a suburb of Detroit, to live in elegance in a grand Victorian mansion.[25]

Another broker stalking the streets of Billings was much more secretive about his work. Benjamin F. Shuart, the respected minister of the Congregational church, toiled throughout the winter months to locate valuable land for his patron, Frederick Billings. Shuart especially preyed on the many early homesteaders of the Clark's Fork Bottom; as he explained to Frederick, "[They] are poor & have neither means to prove up nor to improve after proof & who are therefore ready to sell in some instances very cheaply."[26]

Among Shuart's targets were ranches belonging to such early pioneers as the Newman, Clarke, and Walk families. Their land lay along the well-watered bottoms of the valley, between the town limits of Billings and the Yellowstone River. In early March 1883, Shuart urged Frederick Billings to buy the properties before new immigration drove up land prices and the early settlers realized how much their land and improvements were worth. Billings agreed, and before the month was out, he had bought eighty acres from Newman and given his approval for negotiations with John Walk for his entire ranch. Shuart wanted some of the Walk property for himself. Only $1,000 to $1,500, he told Billings, would turn the homestead into a dairy farm, which Shuart would gladly rent, splitting the profits with his patron. The reverend had worked on dairy farms before and knew everything about the business. As he calculated, "Butter & milk are both very high here and must continue to be so for the present summer." At from fifty to seventy-five cents per pound for butter, a dairy of twenty-five cows would pay for itself in the first year.[27]

Shuart's dealings with the early settlers did not always go smoothly. Some held on to their property, no matter the price. "[Richard Clarke] will not set a price at all—says he does not want to sell," complained the minister. Similar encounters with other stubborn ranchers left Shuart frustrated with his inability to buy the land Frederick Billings wanted. The minister ended his secrecy to consult with George Hulme of the land company. That was a mistake. Miffed that Frederick Billings had bypassed his office, Hulme soon let the identity of Shuart's patron become public knowledge. Buyers now demanded even more money. John Walk, who initially had agreed to sell, changed his mind and left for Oregon to purchase milk cows for his own dairy. In desperation, Shuart urged Billings to order Hulme to intimidate Walk into selling his land and improvements—a two-story log cabin and stable—for between $500 and $600. Eventually Walk did sell, but for $1,000. County records detailing the amount of land owned by Frederick Billings in the immediate Billings townsite area do not exist for these early years. The land-ownership records for 1888, however, reveal that the majority of land in sections 10 and 11, which lay south of Billings between the town and the Yellowstone River, belonged to the old-time settlers James Westbrook, Henry Colwell, Aaron Ford, and Richard Clarke. But Frederick Billings also owned 240 acres of this prime property.[28]

As Frederick Billings used the dealings of Benjamin Shuart to extend his personal involvement in the Clark's Fork Bottom, so too did T. C. Power of Fort Benton become more directly involved in the local economy. Power used the railhead at Billings as the debarkation point for freighting his beef and grain contracts to the Crow agency. In May 1883, the Billings banking company of Stebbins, Post, and Mund, which also served Frederick Billings, invited Power to invest and become a director in their new national bank. "We think it will be a paying investment," asserted Herman H. Mund.[29]

The local business community of Billings also took steps to solidify the economic gains of the first year. The historian Waldo Kliewer characterized the local entrepreneurs Heman Clark, Edgar Camp, Perry McAdow, and Albert L. Babcock as "more of a 'farseeing, enterprising, and thrifty class' than usually fell to the lot of towns along the railroad." In the spring of 1883, concluded Kliewer, "speculators, transients, and the like became scarce," and the entrepreneurs took control of the local economy, concentrating in retail trade and entertainment and working with the railroad.[30]

In mid-March 1883, the town's businessmen formally established a Billings Board of Trade. Its constitution, drafted by the banker Herman H. Mund, pledged "to facilitate and promote the business interests and general welfare of the town of Billings; to create harmony and good will among its business men and to form a body devoted to the advancement of any enterprises for the common good." The establishment of the Billings Board of Trade began a local tradition of "civic capitalism" that shaped the town's economic growth for the following generation. As the historian John Cumbler demonstrated in Trenton, New Jersey, late-nineteenth-century American cities relied on entrepreneurial capitalists to spur local economic development. "Each of these men," Cumbler argued, "sought his own profit, but each understood that his welfare was bound up with the welfare of others of his kind and the city that nourished them." Billings would prove to be a good example of this phenomenon in a much smaller, and more frontier, context. The Billings Board of Trade was the town's first serious attempt to harness the energy of its disparate business interests for the common good. The most immediate concern was to extend trade connections throughout eastern Montana by encouraging the construction of new railroad spur lines, wagon roads, and mail lines to Fort Benton and the mining camps of Cooke City, Barker, and Maiden. Later in the summer, the board provided the capital to improve the road between Billings and the cattle ranches along Flat Willow Creek in central Montana.[31]

Like any chamber of commerce, the Billings Board of Trade also produced colorful propaganda about the future prospects of the town. The board's first circular in April 1883 bragged about the town's population of fifteen hundred, its four hundred buildings ("many of the buildings would be no discredit to an Eastern city"), and its active community and social life. The circular also documented the resources of the Clark's Fork Bottom, giving first billing to the "finest" climate in the Northwest before boosting the area's cattle industry, excellent farmland, and coal deposits. "The prospects of the town are unexcelled by any other in the Northwest," the circular concluded, "and those selecting a new home and desirous of bettering their prospects cannot do better than to carefully examine the inducements offered by Billings and the adjacent country."[32]

In addition to class and economic solidarity, the entrepreneurial capitalists of early Billings needed a board of trade for another reason. They needed an institution to counteract the power of bureaucratic corporatism—the emerging national economy dominated by bureaucratically managed corporations represented here so well by the Northern Pacific Railroad—on the local economy. The creation of the board was both a statement of independence and a reaction against the railroad's failure to do more to assist the development of Billings. Indeed, some residents believed that the railroad was determined to ruin the town. An early agent who drank and gambled to excess had been particularly disliked. In addition, local businessmen believed that the Northern Pacific had deliberately deceived prospective immigrants headed for the Clark's Fork Bottom. Benjamin Shuart told Frederick Billings about travelers who "very frequently" spoke of the "apparently bitter prejudice against Billings & C. F. Bottom which they encounter[ed] among the N.P.R.R. men in St. Paul." He recounted a recent conversation with a Brooklyn immigrant who claimed that St. Paul officials had described Billings as "a humbug" and "that God-forsaken hole." In these railroad employees' unsolicited opinion, the "worthless" Clark's Fork Bottom had "nothing worth stopping for . . . short of Livingston." Shuart, along with everyone else in Billings, was outraged. They all knew that railroad officials were heavily involved in Livingston real estate, but they were shocked to hear that company officials were defaming Billings in order to lure settlers to the Livingston area.[33]

Allegations of such brazen conflict of interest upset Frederick Billings as well, and he demanded immediate explanations from Thomas F. Oakes and Leonard K. Kidder of the Northern Pacific. Frederick's old friends at the corporate offices in New York City promptly responded by ordering the St. Paul office to cease "misrepresentations" about the Clark's Fork Bottom. Both the St. Paul land commissioner, Charles Lamborn, and the ticket agent, G. K. Barnes, pleaded innocent to the charges. And, perhaps to abate the anger of Billings businessmen, the railroad announced in mid-April 1883 a cut in its wool freight rate, as the board of trade had suggested. But misleading stories persisted at the St. Paul office. In late April, Shuart reported another case, this time involving two settlers from Grinnell, Iowa, who were told in St. Paul that no land was for sale at Billings. The prospective farmers heard nothing of the vast holdings of the Minnesota and Montana Land and Improvement Company.[34]

The hard feelings between local businessmen and railroad officials turned more bitter when the two groups clashed over the development of coal mines discovered in the Bull Mountains north of Billings. Northern Pacific officials insisted that the mines lay within the forty-mile right-of-way through the Yellowstone country granted the railroad when it built through the valley. But some Billings businessmen believed that the land was free for the taking. Benjamin Shuart, as early as December 1882, advised Frederick Billings to ignore the advice of the railroad and invest as soon as possible in the coal mines. "It is my conviction that the mine is one of immense value," argued Shuart on April 14, 1883.[35]

What really worried the minister, as he explained in another letter two days later, was that Northern Pacific executives, including Herman Haupt, the general manager, and Charles Lamborn, of the St. Paul land office, would develop the mines in ways antagonistic to the interests of the town of Billings. The Northern Pacific men wanted to connect the mines to the railroad's main line with a branch running from Junction City or Pompey's Pillar, and not from Billings. The new branch line was of crucial importance to the future growth of Billings—the town had to have it. If the line went elsewhere, Billings might wither away and be replaced by Junction City. Convinced that the railroad deliberately planned to injure the town's future, Shuart begged Frederick Billings to use his influence at the railroad's corporate office to have the Bull Mountain branch line based in the Clark's Fork Bottom.[36]

Shuart had his own interests in mind as well as those of his patron and the town of Billings. On May 3, 1883, he purchased for Frederick Billings the most significant claim in the Bull Mountains for thirty-five hundred dollars, without obtaining the prior approval of his patron. He lamely explained his rash action as an emergency—if Billings had not bought the property, it would have fallen into the hands of Haupt and Lamborn, and the future course of the branch line would have been set. But Shuart also had his eye on some coal property, and after he bought the mine for Frederick Billings, he claimed 160 adjacent acres as his own.[37]

The antagonism between the railroad and the local business community during the spring of 1883 merely added to the worries faced by those who had gambled on the future of Billings. A few months earlier, rumors had claimed that the Northern Pacific would be initiating another boom by constructing a new northern line from Billings to Fort Benton. Some residents had even been ready to pay for the survey themselves to prove that the road could be constructed. Now those rumors seemed to be without foundation, and the future looked bleak. "We do need the road very much," despaired Benjamin Shuart, "as business is becoming much depressed."[38]

As Billings reached its first birthday, the town faced additional problems. Throughout the winter, no one paid much attention to the increasing amounts of garbarge and waste as successive snowstorms and cold temperatures kept the mess frozen. But as the winter snows melted, an almost unbearable stench rose across the Clark's Fork Bottom, and newcomers smelled Billings before they actually saw the town. An editorial in the *Post* complained, "The condition of the town is filthy in the extreme, [a] virtual mass of corruption that in itself is enough to sicken a turkey buzzard off its nest." Abel K. Yerkes, the former Coulson *Post* editor who now worked at the Bozeman *Chronicle*, liked almost everything he saw at Billings during a June 1883 visit except "the filth" that was "allowed to accumulate in the alleys and backyards." He added, "The expense of cleaning up would be small and the beauty and health of the town greatly enhanced."[39]

Garbage disposal was an urban problem that Billings shared with many other nineteenth-century American cities.[40] But in this case, most citizens placed the blame for the town's disgusting appearance and lack of economic growth squarely on the shoulders of the Minnesota and Montana Land and Improvement Company. Complaints against the land company fell into two general categories: the indifferent, if not fraudulent, administration of Heman Clark and George Hulme; and the failure of the company to finish the irrigation ditch as promised.

Benjamin Shuart's doubts about the land company's management had already flared into outright hostility. The minister flatly predicted to Frederick Billings in mid-May 1883 that "great prosperity" would come to Frederick, the town, and the valley if he merely replaced Heman Clark as administrator of the land company. Shuart stressed, "All that is needed to make Billings a flourishing town—independently of branch R[ail]Roads—is an intelligent & liberal policy with respect to public improvements, manufacturers, etc." The dirty streets, filthy alleys, and general economic stagnation proved that Clark was incapable of developing the enormous potential of the valley. "The vice of Mr. Clark's policy, & I speak advisedly, is that he seeks to build upon the capital of others [namely F. Billings] & to pocket the proceeds himself. Where money is needed he is always ready to say 'Go' but never 'Follow' & our business men complain of this bitterly and justly." Billings businessmen, in Shuart's opinion, possessed "a true spirit of self help & of enterprise," but without the necessary capital, they could do little to "take the initiative in public enterprises."[41]

Entrepreneurs in Billings further charged Clark with deception and misrepresentation in selling real estate. Most wanted to locate their businesses in the center of town, ideally across from the passenger depot on either Montana Avenue (the north side of the tracks) or Minnesota Avenue (the south side), but Clark had never been very forthcoming about where the "center" or the depot would be. The town's temporary depot stood in block 110 on 27th Street; later the land company's own map of Billings placed the permanent station, which Clark still had not constructed, in block 112. When the land company failed to build an adequate passenger station by 1883, the Northern Pacific took matters into its own hands, moving the Headquarters Hotel to block 109 for use as a depot. As property values skyrocketed in that block, lot owners in blocks 111 and 112 felt cheated—and blamed Clark for their misfortune.[42]

Perhaps the land company could have survived this controversy if not for its April 1883 demand that all lot owners immediately pay the final installments on their property. This announcement outraged R. J. Anderson, who had built the fancy Windsor Hotel in block 112. He sued the Minnesota and Montana Land and Improvement Company for twenty thousand dollars in damages because the company had failed to build the railroad depot as specified in its own town plan.[43]

Actions by the Northern Pacific Railroad soon added to the legal troubles of the Minnesota and Montana Land and Improvement Company. Benjamin Shuart understood that railroad officials such as Charles Lamborn and Herman Haupt believed that "Mr. Clark did not recognize them in a sufficiently substantial way in founding the town" and were "therefore determined to punish him for it." Upset in general over the railroad's financial straits, caused in part by its failure to attract new immigrants, Northern Pacific President Henry Villard expressed little confidence in the management of Heman Clark. When Villard visited the Clark's Fork Bottom for the first time in May 1883, the earlier disaster of the Ripon colony, as well as the railroad's problems with squatters in the Yellowstone Valley, weighed on his mind. What he saw that day left him unimpressed. The banker Herman H. Mund reported that Villard "revealed a strong feeling" against Heman Clark. Hearing the same story, Shuart concluded that Clark was "a dead weight upon the town & valley." He added, "There is so much antagonism to him in R. R. circles—to say nothing of the citizens here— that prosperity for the town & valley seem impossible under his leadership."[44]

In late July 1883, the Northern Pacific sued Heman Clark and the land company for failing to build the sixty-thousand-dollar passenger depot promised when the land company initially purchased the Billings townsite. Facing the dual suits of Anderson and the railroad, Clark quickly constructed a cheap depot, valued at ten thousand dollars, on block 112 at 25th Street and Montana Avenue. The railroad refused to accept this building and continued to use its own Headquarters Hotel at block 109 at 28th Street and Montana Avenue as the town's official passenger station. Trains arriving in Billings would stop briefly at the Clark depot before pulling into the railroad building. Despite the negative impression this left passengers, the odd arrangement continued for years.[45]

Whereas the real estate and depot scandals particularly soured local speculators and businessmen on the Minnesota and Montana Land and Improvement Company, the company's failure to complete the irrigation ditch by the spring outraged everyone. The "inexcusable tardiness" and the "dilly-dallying" of the land company, insisted Minister Shuart, had "paralyse[d] the faith of the settlers, both actual & prospective." He concluded, "One thing is certain, unless something is done soon to restore confidence & bring in the settler we shall suffer a most serious backset." Delay was one problem; shoddy design and construction were others. When the water was released in May 1883, the ditch broke in several places, and water did not reach Billings until the fall. Local disgust turned to anger when it became known that Henry Rowley, the land company engineer, told County Commissioner Fred Foster that he had never planned to finish the ditch in the spring. Benjamin Shuart reported, "As an inducement for him [Rowley] to remain at Billings, [George Hulme] had promised him that his salary should be continued at $150 per mo. & that the completing of the ditch should be strung along so that his job should last a year longer."[46]

In despair for a good water supply, the town's civic capitalists explored two solutions. In April 1883, a group of Billings entrepreneurs formed the Montana Artesian Well Company. The trustees included George Hulme of the land company, Benjamin F. Shuart, Fred Foster, John R. King, Herman H. Mund, Perry W. McAdow, and Walter Matheson, the editor of the *Post*. Another major shareholder was Frederick Billings, with 150 shares worth fifteen hundred dollars. The investors did not particularly like or trust each other. Shuart told Billings that the men were "of our best citizens," but he added, "They are nevertheless not only virtual strangers to you, but also to me & each other; & are therefore untried men." The mutual goal of good water kept the group together. The first experiments took place near the roundhouse on land belonging to Frederick Billings. Yet even after the well reached nine hundred feet, no water was forthcoming, and the company failed.[47]

Another alternate water supply considered in the summer of 1883 was the small irrigation ditch that Bud McAdow had initially constructed in the late 1870s to meet the requirements of the Desert Land Act. In late July, McAdow, Herman H. Mund, Henry W. Rowley, and Henry Belknap established the Billings Water Power Company. This enterprise planned to supply piped water to downtown businesses, but it was not fully operational until three years later.[48]

As if the land company's difficulties with the irrigation ditch, the railroad, and local real estate were not enough, Heman Clark and George Hulme found themselves embroiled with Frederick Billings on the question of a new school for the town. Billings had agreed to donate four thousand dollars for construction of the school, and the land company, Fred Foster, and J. E. Kurtz had donated a building lot on the north side of the tracks, four blocks from the railroad line at Fourth Avenue between 29th and 30th streets. According to Benjamin Shuart, however, the location was terrible, near the town dump, and Clark wanted the school there merely "for the purpose of enhancing the value of his property" on the relatively undeveloped north side of town. Clark and Hulme even threatened to withdraw the land company's donation of one thousand dollars if the school was not built on Clark's property. This was too crass and self-serving for Frederick Billings, a capitalist noted for his liberality. In August, he remarked that George Hulme was "a first class fraud." Certainly he did not think much better of the land company's administration.[49]

The lawsuits, squabbles, petty differences, and personality clashes of the spring and summer of 1883 were temporarily forgotten in September as the community of Billings prepared itself for Henry Villard's "last spike" excursion. To mark the completion of the Northern Pacific, the railroad president had invited dignitaries, financiers, journalists, and influential politicans, including former President Ulysses S. Grant, from America, England, and Germany, to take a cross-country trip on a specially prepared Northern Pacific train. Eager to see the frontier West, many dignitaries accepted, including Lord Justice Sir Charles Bowen of the Bank of England, Secretary of Interior Henry Teller, the financier August Belmont, the railroad men James J. Hill and George Pullman, and Carl Schurz, the editor of the New York *Evening Post*. Towns along the Northern Pacific line made every effort to impress the newspapermen, prospective investors, politicians, and railroad executives. In Billings, the residents swept the streets and hung colorful bunting from their new brick buildings. The dignitaries would see, so hoped the Billings *Post*, "a thriving town which only 15 months ago had no existence except upon paper, an orderly, intelligent, law abiding population." To make a distinctive impression, local residents built a "summer house" of wheat and oats, topped by two stags' heads and surrounded by piles of melons, squashes, cabbages, turnips, and potatoes. To one side was a huge pile of coal and representative samples of gold, silver, and copper while on the other side hung a large beef carcass.[50]

The Villard party arrived at 9 A.M. on September 6, 1883, and Frederick Billings left his private car, the *Northern Adirondack*, to give a rousing speech to the crowd surrounding the Headquarters Hotel. Billings was a "great town" located in a "great valley," possessing "all the elements for great material prosperity." The Vermont capitalist was proud to be associated with this bustling town; yet, strangely, he denied any close involvement with its destiny:

> I suppose you consider me the father of this town, but a father is supposed to know something of the child before it is born, and I know nothing of this town before its birth. So I can't be its father. Nor am I its Godfather for a Godfather is supposed to be present at the christening and I had nothing to do with the naming of this town; and moreover, far from being its owner, I have unluckily never possessed a lot in the place. Being neither father, godfather, nor owner I suppose I am what the lawyers call an accessory after the fact.

Perhaps this description of his relationship with the town was meant as some kind of inside joke, but it puzzled rather than humored local residents. Frederick Billings had been among the founders of the land company; he had agreed to Heman Clark's request that the town be named in his honor. Then after his October 1882 visit he had donated money for the local church and school, and his investments in local property totaling in the thousands of acres were widely known. Frederick Billings was far more than "an accessory after the fact" in the development of the town of Billings and the Clark's Fork Bottom. Why he characterized himself in this manner remains a mystery.[51]

Before leaving town several hours later, Billings again congratulated local residents for making a good impression on the Villard party. The visitors, Billings remarked, now possessed an "unqualified admiration of the location of Billings, and the preparation which the citizens have made to show what can be raised here." He pledged his lasting friendship to the town. Looking back at the day's events a week later, the Billings *Post* was also very pleased. Local residents had achieved a "great success" and could "assure themselves" that they had "lost nothing"

but would be "amply repaid, for their efforts in future [benefits] accru-
ing from their magnificent display to the Villard party."[52]

On September 14, the day after the *Post* editorial, the first water
from the irrigation ditch reached the streets of Billings, and the combination of the completed water project and the visit of the Villard party
revitalized local spirits. The thirty-nine-mile canal had cost $125,000
and taken sixteen months to complete, but now that the water was
here, past difficulties could be forgotten. "The doubting Thomases,
who long predicted that we should never see water in the ditch near
town, and the suspicious ones, who averred that the ditch was never intended to carry water," asserted the Billings *Herald*, "can now find
their answer in the beautiful stream." The water, the editor predicted,
would solve the city's dust problem and provide much needed irrigation for trees and gardens.[53]

As the fresh water supply helped Billings bloom, business in the valley picked up in the fall. Fred Oberland reopened the old National Hotel at Coulson, where he served lunch daily in his "beer garden." The
Herald reported that businessmen were investing $150,000 in new
brick and stone buildings. Heman Clark expanded his freighting business in the outlying areas of eastern Montana and formed a new partnership with Bud McAdow to dominate the local mercantile trade. In
addition, T. C. Power expanded his freighting activity between Fort
Benton and Billings and encouraged tourists to use his line to visit the
wonders of the Yellowstone Valley and the national park.[54]

The better business climate encouraged town leaders to renew their
calls for a branch line connecting Billings, the Bull Mountain coal
mines, and Fort Benton. Yet Frederick Billings remained unconvinced
that his town needed the line or the mine development. Not even
Shuart's claim that Northern Pacific officials, together with the territorial representative Martin Maginnis, were plotting to throw open the
Crow reservation in order to establish a new Yellowstone competitor
opposite Junction City could budge Billings. When words failed to
move Frederick forward, "thoroughly alarmed" local businessmen
asked Shuart to offer Frederick "large gifts of town lots" if that would
secure his support for the branch line. Perry W. McAdow, Fred Foster,

and John Alderson stood "ready to make large sacrifices" if necessary, Shuart explained.[55]

Frederick Billings still said no, but it appears that the Northern Pacific was willing to consider such large land bribes in exchange for new branch lines. George Hulme told Shuart that the Northern Pacific would "require" one hundred acres of town lots for the "running of the coal road from Billings." Shuart asked Frederick Billings if the demand was true, noting, "If it is the requirement of the road itself, the land will be forthcoming." What the town entrepreneurs did not realize was that the Northern Pacific was broke; completing the transcontinental line had almost bankrupted the company. In addition, a national economic recession in 1883 had damaged the railroad's ability to earn or borrow needed capital. A month after the "last spike" celebration at Gold Creek, Montana, the company directors announced a severe policy of retrenchment to steer the railroad through the hard times. Because of the national economic situation and its own financial vulnerability, the Northern Pacific lacked the resources to build any branch lines, no matter what kind of inducement the civic capitalists of Billings could offer.[56]

Another economic initiative of late 1883—persuading the Marquis de Mores to build a large slaughterhouse at Billings—also would fail. The marquis had already established a large slaughterhouse facility at Medora, on the Northern Pacific main line near the Montana-Dakota territorial border. The Billings Board of Trade hoped to persuade de Mores to build another on 120 acres of free land in the city. In addition, the businessmen offered to construct an icehouse large enough to keep one thousand tons of ice. But the board of trade encountered immediate difficulties with land acquisition. The first 40 acres cost five hundred dollars, but the Northern Pacific wanted eight hundred dollars for the other 80 acres. Shocked by this price, the board asked Thomas F. Oakes, the railroad's vice-president, to intervene. Oakes suggested a compromise. If the railroad donated the land, the community would promise to raise the funds necessary to build a bridge across the Yellowstone River at Billings. The railroad wanted to capture the trade of cattlemen in northern Wyoming, but the cattle companies needed a new bridge to cross the river. The deal was struck, and the contracts were signed, but the slaughterhouse never was built because of the marquis's financial difficulties. Even his operations at Medora, Dakota Territory, would soon fail.[57]

That November, the men of Billings took their first vote on the incorporation of the city, but few business leaders or workers were ready to place the town on a new legal footing. The measure failed by 163 to 17. The people of Billings had looked around at the meager progress of the past eighteen months and chose not to burden themselves with the expense and taxes of local government. They decided that their options were better as an open settlement than as a legally established town.

Despite the disappointments and setbacks of 1883, town dwellers and investors could still brag of significant achievements during the past eighteen months. The city directory of 1883, produced by C. S. Fell and J. E. Hendry, is one way of documenting the progress of settlement and development in the Clark's Fork Bottom. The directory began with a history and description of the area, aimed at prospective immigrants; it even included instructions on how to claim government land. Full of enthusiastic booster rhetoric, the directory claimed: "It is needless to say that the town has been uniformly prosperous. Our merchants have engaged and still experience a large and constant flow of trade, while mechanics and laborers have found no difficulty in obtaining employment at highly remunerative prices."[58]

The second half of the directory documented the success of the town through a detailed listing of the governmental, social, and economic institutions of Billings. According to the directory, five corporations operated in Billings by the end of 1883. The Minnesota and Montana Land and Improvement Company topped this list; in fact, the land company's George Hulme served as an officer in three of the other four corporations and as president of the Bull Mountain Coal Company. The newcomer W. E. Edwards headed the Montana Lumber Company, whereas old-time residents Perry W. McAdow and John R. "Commodore" King directed the activities of the Billings Street Railway Company (which connected the town to Coulson) and the Artesian Well Company. Then there were the offices, shops, and stockyards of the Northern Pacific Railroad, the town's largest single employer.

In addition to the corporations, the number of business and professional firms had also multiplied since June 1882. Most workers were employed in one of six occupational categories: transportation, merchandising, services and entertainment, trades, professions, or farming and ranching. One-fourth of local workers (25.0 percent) were involved in the transportation industry, be it the lone ferryman at the Yellowstone River or the ninety-four men who toiled for the Northern Pacific as rail laborers, skilled repairmen, clerks, or conductors. The railroad, however, was not the only way to move goods and people across the Yellowstone Valley, and twenty men worked either as freighters or for the Billings-Benton stage line.

Almost as many residents (21.9 percent) worked in merchandising. About sixty individuals operated their own businesses, ranging in size from the large houses of Heman Clark, Perry McAdow, and Edgar Camp to the much more modest Champion Bakery of Emil Faust. Two Chinese men had opened laundries, adding an ethnic diversity to Billings that had never existed in the early history of the Clark's Fork Bottom.

The third-largest category of occupations, services and entertainment, included local restaurant, saloon, and hotel owners as well as the maids, cooks, porters, barbers, waitresses, and musicians who worked at those establishments. Almost one in five workers in Billings (19.1 percent) belonged to this category, perhaps the best indication of the lasting economic impact of the construction of the railroad in 1882 because most of these businesses had initially been established to serve the tracklayers of the Northern Pacific.

The categories of transportation, merchandising, and services and entertainment account for 66.0 percent, or two-thirds, of the jobs held by early Billings residents. By late 1883, the town's professional class was still small (8.9 percent), and few independent tradesmen (10 percent) had established shops, although thirty-seven carpenters and builders, together with eight painters, were doing their best to meet the demand for new dwellings and businesses. Stockmen and farmers were few in number (6.6 percent), since most lived outside of town. Of the workers, 8.5 percent were scattered among other occupations. Compared with 1880, when farmers had dominated the occupations given for settlers in the Clark's Fork Bottom, in 1882 the growth of Billings over the past eighteen months had given a decidedly commercial, even industrial, character to the area work force.

New social institutions matched the economic maturation of Billings. In the fall of 1882, a literary society, headed by the hardware merchant Edgar Camp, joined the earlier library association. Billings also had a "Young Man's Social Club," along with lodges for the Masons and Odd Fellows. Local political parties had been established, with vigorous competition existing between the Republican party, led by Fred Foster, Albert Babcock, and Sidney Erwin, and the Democratic party, led by the old stalwarts Perry McAdow and John Alderson. The new brick school donated by Frederick Billings and the land company was under construction, and a Congregational church and an Episcopal church catered to the religious needs of local residents. Although Billings remained an unincorporated town, it had developed the institutions—literary clubs, fraternal lodges, churches, and political parties—associated with the frontier "volunteer community," where mutual interests, more than a legal structure of governmental services and obligations, bound the settlers.[59]

By the end of 1883, through their joint activities at the lodge meetings, the board of trade strategy sessions, and Sunday church services, Billings residents increasingly shared common interests as well as common ground in the Yellowstone Valley. The authors of the city directory concluded:

> "[Billings] has grown and prospered with a rapidity and vigor that is more remarkable than the mushroom growth and ephemeral existence of a mining camp. From nothing but the mere townsite, twelve months have seen the growth of a noble town, well worthy of the name of city. It is an instance of western development more remarkable than anything on record."[60]

CHAPTER 8

The Billings Family Takes Charge, 1884–1889

The first eighteen months of settlement had tested the citizens of Billings. Building a new town on dusty alkali flats involved its share of disappointments and setbacks, but they had survived these demanding times, and recent developments pointed toward a brighter future. With a renewed sense of optimism, the citizens of Billings faced the new year of 1884. Stock raisers dreamed of great wealth, since the Marquis de Mores had just announced plans to build a large slaughterhouse complex. (No one knew in January that the venture would soon fail.) A more secure source of capital was available, it appeared, after the private firm of Stebbins, Post, and Mund received its federal charter as a national bank. In addition, the postal service recognized the growth and stability of the town by designating Billings as a third-class post office. Perhaps just as important, the town's first permanent school, North School, opened in a handsome two-story, gothic brick building.[1]

The promising start of the new year, however, did not eliminate the frontier era's legacy of economic uncertainties. More than a new school, bank, post office, or even modern stockyards was necessary before Billings and the Clark's Fork Bottom could prosper. Town leaders remained convinced of the need for a railroad to the region's rich coal deposits. They were equally certain of the city's need for new branch lines connecting its businesses to the national marketplace. And they still entertained hopes that someone new would take control of the Minnesota and Montana Land and Improvement Company and shake it out of its lethargy.

From 1882 to 1884, Billings suffered from erratic short-term business activity, a pattern it shared with Grand Junction, Colorado, another western town heavily dependent on the whims of a dominant land company and a railroad corporation. But at Grand Junction, the land company served as a major employer in the construction trades— establishing a hotel, brick factory, and irrigation ditch—and maintained good relations with the Denver and Rio Grande Railway. In Billings, the land company appeared to more and more investors and residents to be an impediment to future growth.[2]

Sitting in his study in his gracious Woodstock, Vermont, mansion, Frederick Billings also worried about the future of his Yellowstone investments. His visit during the Villard excursion had reinforced his faith in the region's potential, but at the same time, it had undermined his confidence in the management abilities of his local agent, Benjamin F. Shuart, and of Heman Clark and the others at the land company. The Bull Mountain coal mines, mired in legal entanglements spun by jealous competitors at the Northern Pacific Railroad, were of immediate concern. The Northern Pacific Coal Company and Shuart were now in court, fighting over the title to the mines. Wanting to avoid legal difficulties, Frederick gave serious consideration to selling the property, but Shuart urged him to wait until the court had made its decision. As only a minister can, Shuart assured Billings that he was in the right and that right would win out in this case.

Frederick soon regretted taking this advice. On February 1, 1884, the Congregational minister excitedly informed Billings about a secret visit by Wilbur Fisk Sanders, the Helena capitalist and a key advisor to the railroad in Montana Territory. Sanders had urged Shuart to play it smart—why cause trouble for a company that counted his boss, Frederick Billings, as a stockholder? Sanders had offered Shuart a deal: drop the suit against Northern Pacific Coal Company, and the railroad "would withdraw the contests" against Shuart. The minister had agreed—and immediately wrote Billings to brag of his "victory."[3]

Frederick Billings didn't think much of this "victory." The crafty Sanders had hoodwinked Shuart into believing that Frederick Billings, the coal company stockholder, would approve the deal. But Frederick was not a stockholder—a crucial point that Shuart, in his eagerness to strike the bargain, never checked. Instead he had trusted Sanders and assented to the deal. Very upset, Frederick wanted to know why the minister ever trusted anything Sanders uttered. Besides chastising his agent, he also sent his nephew, Edward Bailey, to the Clark's Fork Bottom to personally survey the situation and reach some type of agreement with Sanders and the rival coal mine interests.[4]

Another problem troubling Frederick Billings centered on the persistent reports of mismanagement and fraud at the Minnesota and Montana Land and Improvement Company. In mid-March, Benjamin Shuart admitted to Samuel Kilner, Frederick's private secretary, that Frederick's farmland would never be cultivated unless the ditch was "better developed this year than it was last." No one trusted the land company. "Some tell me that they are afraid to take the risk of putting in a crop. Everybody is praying that Mr. Billings will buy the thing out. Things will boom if he does for confidence in his integrity & executive ability are so universal."[5]

Frederick Billings and his advisors listened closely to the grievances of Shuart and the others. In 1884, Frederick owned just over 4,545 acres in Yellowstone County, in addition to his stockholdings in the land company. He had too much invested to let Heman Clark ruin his holdings through lazy management. To ensure the development of his own landholdings, as well as to encourage new immigration to the holdings of the Minnesota and Montana Land and Improvement Company, Billings assumed personal control over the land company. By the first of April 1884, the Vermont capitalist had reached a settlement with Heman Clark and the other major investors for an undisclosed amount of money. The *Post* praised Billings's acquisition, adding the hope that he would reverse past policy and sell land "at reasonable prices to the actual settlers [so] the valley [would] soon be filled up." Shuart advised Billings to take two actions immediately: promise to have the ditch operating properly so that every farmer would have adequate water for the season, and break up virgin land for cultivation. If these steps were delayed, Shuart warned, the valley might well suffer from a mass exodus of farmers.[6]

Frederick Billings's takeover of the land company inaugurated a new era of cooperation among the company, the citizens of Billings, and the Northern Pacific Railroad. Relations especially improved between the land company and the railroad, with Northern Pacific officials, in one case, taking care to assure settlers that their land titles purchased from the Minnesota and Montana Land and Improvement Company were free and clear. Billings also took steps to resolve several land controversies involving squatters on his property while settling his old differences with the Northern Pacific Coal Company. The railroad left the Bull Mountains, opting instead to "obtain a footing on Rock Creek, in anticipation of the early opening of the [Crow] Reservation to settlement." Ironically, by sticking to his initial claims and pushing the railroad out of the Bull Mountain mines, Billings forced the railroad to find coal elsewhere; around the mines of Rock and Bear creeks would later develop the town of Red Lodge and by far the richest coal deposits found in the Yellowstone country.[7]

As Frederick Billings extended his personal involvement in the development of the Clark's Fork Bottom, he encountered many who wanted to jump on his bandwagon of capital improvement. One interesting exception was Bud McAdow. After Billings acquired the land company, McAdow contacted several Minneapolis investors for capital to build new flour and woolen mills. Rebuffed there, he asked Shuart to name a price for controlling interest in the land company. Shuart ignored him. With his local political and commercial ties, McAdow might be able to confront Frederick Billings, but he could offer no serious threat to the Vermont capitalist's wealth, power, and railroad connections. Billings was now Frederick's town; perhaps McAdow, as the founder of Coulson, a territorial representative, and later a partner of Heman Clark's, found that hard to accept. Or perhaps he wanted to leave for another frontier community where once again Bud McAdow could call the shots and serve as the leading entrepreneur. Whatever the reason, McAdow sold most of his Billings property, and for the rest of the decade, he and his wife, Clara Tomlinson McAdow, concentrated on developing their mining properties at Maiden and the Judith Mountains.[8]

In June 1884, Frederick Billings dispatched his secretary, Samuel Kilner, to inspect the Yellowstone operations. Kilner got the ditch into working order and reviewed Frederick's various landholdings in the Bottom and in the Bull Mountains. He met as well with Benjamin Shuart to discuss the local economic situation. Judging from the tone and content of later correspondence between Kilner and the minister, the visit left Kilner rather unimpressed. He returned to New York City determined to reorganize the Yellowstone investments.

First, Kilner placed the Shuart-Billings relationship on "a more business basis" and ordered the minister to set a value on his services for the past fifteen months. Shuart, who had already asked Kilner whether Frederick would be interested in purchasing his coal claim, shyly demurred on naming a price at first, but then turned around and said that thirty-five hundred dollars for an enlarged dairy operation and private ranch would do nicely. Refusing to immediately meet Shuart's price, Kilner placed the idea under consideration. Kilner also found out that no one was officially in charge of the land company's office at Billings. Shuart, for his part, maintained only a rather indirect and aloof involvement, whereas the local businessmen Fred Foster and Herman Mund wanted John R. King to be appointed manager of the land company.[9]

Kilner and Billings wanted someone besides Shuart to manage the Yellowstone investments, but they refused to choose another local businessman to take his place. They had in mind someone trustworthy who would keep the family's interests always in mind. But who could that be—who would want to go to Montana? Frederick Billings found his answer at the family dinner table. One night his son Parmly, just returned from a semester at Amherst College, proved "so talkative and self-asserting" that Frederick was put "all out of sorts." This was just the most recent annoyance Parmly had caused his father; this time, Frederick Billings did something about it. As Frederick's biographers have remarked, " 'send him out to a ranch in Montana' has been a popu-

lar prescription for the troubled parents of unruly youths for genera-
tions." Parmly was soon Montana bound.[10]

Late July 1884 was the first time Parmly Billings visited the Clark's
Fork Bottom. He moved to the north, where he and three others—his
cousin Edward Bailey; A. J. Seligman, the son of a prominent New York
banker; and Percy Kennett of Helena—owned and operated the I J
Ranch, near the army post at Fort Maginnis. Parmly did not live in Billings, but he was close enough to keep an eye on affairs there, a situation
that seemed to threaten Benjamin Shuart. In his weekly dispatches to
Vermont, the minister took great pains to emphasize all of his devoted,
unselfish work. He did his best to bolster Frederick's confidence, pre-
dicting to Samuel Kilner, "Unless some unforseen accidents occur,
next year will demonstrate to him the wisdom of his land purchases
here in a most satisfactory manner." Later that summer, Shuart had an
opportunity to plead his case directly with the Vermont capitalist
when the Billings family arrived on August 11 for a brief inspection trip.
Frederick visited the works of the water company, the irrigation ditch,
and his own ranchland before departing for a West Coast vacation.[11]

He also discussed with Shuart new land acquisitions along with the
disposition of the Bull Mountain coal claims, even consenting to buy
Shuart's adjoining claim for whatever price Shuart and Samuel Kilner
decided. The friendly relations of that summer, however, did not renew
Frederick's confidence in Shuart's business ability. After returning
home, he asked Parmly Billings and Edward Bailey to leave their Judith
Basin ranch to investigate matters in the Clark's Fork Bottom. The
minister graciously took the young men on a detailed inspection tour
of Frederick's considerable holdings in the region. At the same time
Joseph Zimmerman, who owned the Boston One Price Clothing House
in Billings, asked Parmly for a loan of two thousand dollars to build a
new brick store on block 110. Parmly ignored this request but forwarded Zimmerman's letter to Vermont in case his father was interested. Shuart's tour and their own contacts with local businessmen
convinced Parmly and Edward of the Bottom's economic potential, but
they shared Kilner's assessment that Benjamin Shuart was not the
right man to tap that potential. Edward Bailey nominated himself and

Parmly, writing to his uncle: "If you should see fit to put the ditch property into our hands I think we would be able to manage it. By another spring the stock [at the ranch] will not require so much attention." He and Parmly would thus be able "to attend to other matters."[12]

That winter Frederick Billings decided to replace Benjamin Shuart with Bailey and Parmly. Evidence indicates that he hated to make the change, but Shuart's inability to solve squatter disputes and to get along with Parmly and Bailey gave Frederick little choice. And the switch allowed Frederick Billings to have direct family management of the land company while, at the same time, he could reward the minister for past loyalty by making Shuart the manager of the family ranch (later known as Hesper Farm), a model demonstration farm complex west of Billings located between the waters of Canyon Creek and the newly completed "Big Ditch" of the land company. At this location, the Billings family owned or controlled over 2,500 acres. Shuart also received his own ranch of 320 acres for payment of past services.

The events that led to Shuart's removal to the countryside had begun in September. The Billings family wanted to clear squatters off its land but, in the interests of fair play, had offered to pay the squatters for any improvements they had made. Some old-time settlers, including Edward Johnson, refused to set a price on their homesteads, and that September, Shuart, Parmly, and Bailey visited Johnson, demanding that he leave the farm. The minister let young Billings lead the negotiations, and Shuart thought that all parties had consented to outside arbitration, with three local residents, Richard R. Crowe, George Lamport, and Orson Newman, setting a price on Johnson's improvements. Shuart closed the deal on that basis.[13]

Frederick Billings promptly repudiated the transaction; he would offer nothing for improvements. This telegraph message shocked Shuart, who professed total ignorance of the change in policy. Shuart reminded Frederick that Parmly had conducted the negotiations and that Shuart had merely carried out Parmly's orders. To reject arbitration now would severely damage the minister's credibility. "I cannot believe Sir that you would intentionally do me a wrong but if you adhere to the determination which you have expressed in this matter, you will inflict upon me a most cruel wrong," Shuart asserted. "I have done nothing to merit such treatment at your hands." Desperate to clear himself, Shuart submitted signed affidavits, from himself and Edward Johnson, that frankly implied that Parmly was a liar.[14]

Frederick Billings had had enough. He asked his son and nephew to submit their own sworn statements about Shuart's unauthorized arbitration. With that, the correspondence between Shuart and Billings abruptly ended. Naturally siding with his son and nephew, Frederick finally removed Shuart as his personal agent and asked the minister to manage, instead, the family ranch along Canyon Creek.

The minister accepted his new assignment with grace, leaving the real estate business with few regrets. With Frederick's encouragement, Shuart took the first steps in developing the property as a model "scientific" operation specializing in alfalfa production. Over the next decade, first under the leadership of Shuart, and then of I. D. O'Donnell, the family ranch became known as Hesper Farm and served as a regional attraction, a mini-bonanza farm in the Yellowstone Valley.

Indeed, the development of Frederick's farmland in the Clark's Fork Bottom during these years is reminiscent of the Northern Pacific's earlier successful experiments in modern, corporate agriculture in North Dakota. In the late 1870s, while he was Northern Pacific president, Billings had encouraged the establishment of the Cass-Cheney demonstration farm, which popularized the "bonanza farm" boom of the late 1870s and swelled land sales. Although a similar boom did not take place in sales of the Minnesota and Montana Land and Improvement Company, the Billings ranch became the region's pacesetter in modern agricultural practices for the rest of the century. Shuart stayed there until May 1892, when he sold his interests to Bailey and O'Donnell.[15]

As the first buds of spring 1885 appeared in the Clark's Fork Bottom, Parmly Billings and Edward Bailey assumed personal control of the Minnesota and Montana Land and Improvement Company. The Billings *Post* of March 12, 1885, reported their arrival, especially noting Parmly's offer to sell or rent "broken" land "on the most favorable terms." The paper noted, "Seed and water furnished if desired." Parmly and Bailey rented five hundred acres for oat production to James Westbrooks, who had previously worked P. W. McAdow's large valley farm. Parmly also made a preemption claim of 160 acres adjoining the family's Hesper Farm, but he failed to build some sort of dwelling in the required thirty days. Frank Church jumped the claim, and Parmly reacted by contracting with a builder to erect a cabin. That night, Parmly and a co-worker from the ranch stayed at the crudely constructed cabin. One night in such rustic surroundings was enough for Parmly. The next morning he proclaimed: "I'm through. I would not put in another night like that for all the land in the Valley. Frank Church can take the land and go straight to ———— with it. He can have the cabin to boot." Parmly promised his friend, "When we get to Billings I will get you a good breakfast."[16]

That friend was Ignatius Donnelly "Bud" O'Donnell. The Billings family made many significant contributions to the early history of the city of Billings, but perhaps the most important was introducing young O'Donnell to the potential of the Clark's Fork Bottom. O'Donnell was born in Ontario, Canada, on September 19, 1860, the second child of second-generation Irish immigrants, Daniel and Margaret McIntosh O'Donnell. His family moved to Saginaw, Michigan, four years later, where his father worked in the timber industry for several years before buying his own farm in Midland County, Michigan. O'Donnell attended the public schools of Saginaw until his early teenage years, when he started work in the local timber business. "Many a day," he later remembered, "have I split rails, cut ties, and guided logs down the river." He continued this labor until the age of twenty-one, when a friend persuaded him to look for work in Chicago.[17]

O'Donnell was only twenty-two when he first arrived in the Yellowstone Valley. Following the tracks of the Northern Pacific, he left the train at Miles City and took a job with the Northern Pacific, cutting ties along the Tongue River. With that grubstake in hand, O'Donnell left for the mines at Maiden. Quick riches, however, slipped through his fingers at Maiden and the other places where he tried his luck. The grubstake now gone, O'Donnell signed up for something completely new—putting up hay for a government contractor—and learned the new skills of building corrals, stables, and fences. This experience set him up for his next job: as a cowboy at the I J Ranch, a stock-raising enterprise owned by a bunch of kids from back East. Here he became fast friends with the new owners, Parmly Billings and Edward Bailey, having nothing in common with the rich kids except a determination to have a grand time on the northern plains. When Parmly and Bailey moved to Billings in the spring of 1885 to administer the family property, they called on O'Donnell to help supervise the family's ranchland in the Clark's Fork Bottom. His charge was similar to the one the family had earlier given Benjamin Shuart—to prove beyond a doubt that the land of the Clark's Fork Bottom was productive, valuable farmland, so that new immigrants would be encouraged to move to the valley. O'Donnell would soon institute some of the region's earliest experiments in scientific farming, dry-land farming, and irrigation.[18]

The Billings family's impact on the area was immediate. Parmly Billings had arrived on the town's dusty streets at a particularly opportune time. This small Yellowstone town had finally taken an important step in its future urban development by exchanging its informal civic arrangements for a legally established government structure. Local residents had recently voted to incorporate, and they had established their first city charter, which allowed every adult taxpayer (including women) the right to vote. Some citizens approached Parmly about running for mayor even though the charter stipulated that the mayor must have lived in Billings for at least one year. Somewhat amazed at the offer, Parmly wrote his sister Mary: "We are going to elect a mayor and three aldermen. And would you believe it, I had some people come to see me and ask your reprobate brother, exiled from home and friends, to let them use his name as a candidate." The town had exciting prospects, but Parmly couldn't resist poking fun at some of the booster rhetoric that surrounded him. "I would rather be mayor of the city of Billings than president of the U.S.A.," he joked. "We intend to annex New York and there is some talk of hitching on Boston."[19]

Parmly Billings was not elected mayor, but the business class of Billings usually treated him like a prince. His mere presence promised to keep the benevolence of Frederick Billings flowing toward the city. In addition, Parmly quickly joined the local civic capitalist network through his enthusiastic support of the determined effort to secure new railroad lines for Billings. Days after his arrival, young Billings joined the businessmen Herman Mund, Walter Matheson, and Fred

Foster to petition the territorial legislature for permission to transfer county tax dollars for the construction of a Bull Mountain branch line. But even the Montana legislature, by this time accustomed to requests from capitalists who wanted to raid the public treasury for their own greedy purposes, found this petition hard to swallow. It died in committee.[20]

Parmly Billings and Edward Bailey also proved to be quite an engine of capitalism in their own right. In 1886, they extended operations throughout the area. Under their management, the land company enjoyed much more success than in the past, selling forty-seven town lots to new immigrants in one week of May alone. That spring, the two easterners also established the bank long promised by the land company, taking their own funds and borrowing more from Frederick Billings and the American Exchange National Bank in New York City to establish the private firm of Bailey and Billings. The young capitalists continued their ranch operations as well. In October 1886, according to the Billings *Gazette,* Parmly traveled to the Missouri River country, making arrangements to drive north a herd of eight thousand cattle to graze on land leased from the Canadian government. Nor were Billings and Bailey ignoring the development of the Bottom's farmland in favor of city improvements. Throughout the winter the land company advertised, "Fine farming lands in the fertile valley of the 'Clark's Fork' bottom for sale on easy terms; favorably situated for the advantages of markets, schools, churches, etc." Buyers had only to contact the local agents, Bailey and Billings, or write Samuel E. Kilner, the land company's secretary and treasurer, on Broadway in New York City.[21]

The big-city boys were in charge of the destiny of the Clark's Fork Bottom, and for many local entrepreneurs, the direct, personal involvement of the Billings family in the fortunes of the town and the surrounding countryside offered many benefits. By competing with Herman Mund's national bank, the Bailey and Billings private bank opened new avenues for loans and capital investment. The orderly management of the land company brought additional advantages as increased sales of town lots and farmland strengthened the local market economy. Because of the better relationship between the Billings family and the Northern Pacific, no longer did ticket agents along the line discourage new immigrants from moving to the Clark's Fork Bottom. In his willingness to assist efforts for new branch lines connecting Billings to other commercial and resource markets in eastern Montana, Parmly Billings had also become part of the local civic capitalist network of economic development.

But other businessmen worried that too many Billingses might be bad for the city of Billings. The Billings family might be doing well, but the city had not developed into the major trade center initially envisioned by many investors and local entrepreneurs. The real estate agent C. W. Horr still expected the land company to build that sixty-thousand-dollar depot in downtown Billings; he wanted to sell his property and leave town "without so great a loss." He griped to T. C. Power, "I improved my lots, and bought them from Co. in good faith, expecting they would live up to what they promised." He added: "If I knew how to reach them, I can assure you I would not be long in taking proper measures. I do not think I will be so easily caught next time, by a lot of unscrupulous fellows, booming a little place, and deceiving people."[22]

Those bitter feelings were shared by Heman Clark as he watched his Yellowstone empire crumble away. Of course, Clark had been among that "lot of unscrupulous fellows," but he too suffered substantial financial reverses in the mid-1880s. Consider Clark's situation. The Minnesota and Montana Land and Improvement Company was a partnership among himself, Frederick Billings, and Thomas F. Oakes and other minor investors. Billings brought capital to the venture, along with good connections to New York financial markets. Oakes brought his own share of money and, hopefully, the goodwill of the Northern Pacific Railroad. Billings and Oakes certainly had made sizable investments, yet these represented only a fraction of the two men's worth. Clark, on the other hand, staked almost everything he had made as a Northern Pacific contractor on the land company venture. And whereas his partners could sit safely tucked away in their grand offices in New York City, Clark maintained a Billings residence, where he alone had to endure the constant whines and complaints of local citizens who expected miracles overnight. Living with the aggravation was one thing when Clark was the only major partner living in Billings, a situation that afforded him a degree of social and economic prominence that no one else approached. But then Parmly Billings and Edward Bailey arrived on the city streets in 1885, effectively undermining Clark's unique position as the only direct representative of the land company in the town.

Adding to that aggravation, the young capitalists arrived at a time when Heman Clark was experiencing problems with his general merchandise and wholesale store in Billings. By the beginning of winter 1885, George Hulme had returned to work at the store, which maintained its business through the following year only by taking in a third partner, Thomas Hanlon. But business did not improve. Then came the legendary winter of 1886–87, which destroyed Clark's once thriving outfitting business with central Montana stock raisers. In March 1887, Lucius Whitney reported to T. C. Power that the partners were "in trouble amongst themselves" and had no choice but to offer the business to Bailey and Billings.[23] Although Whitney thought about buying the firm in order to operate its warehouse and forwarding business, neither Whitney, Power, Bailey, nor Billings came to the rescue. The *Stock Gazette* of April 21, 1887, announced that H. Clark and Company was "closing out their stock as rapidly as possible" and lamented the departure of the store from the local commercial scene.[24]

In 1882 or 1883, the failure of Heman Clark would have sent shock waves throughout the economy of the Clark's Fork Bottom. By the spring of 1887, the news merely rippled through the business community. Perhaps the failure didn't matter, many assumed, because it seemed certain that a new railroad was coming to Billings. Talk of a new railroad boom gripped local residents and excited local businessmen. That was enough to keep the economy prosperous. Two rival projects had been announced. The Billings, Clarke's Fork, and Cooke City Railroad would connect the town to the lucrative gold mines at Cooke City and would establish Billings as a northeast gateway for tourists headed to Yellowstone National Park. It was the favorite project of local residents. The other, the Rocky Fork Railroad, was the favorite of the Northern Pacific. Company officials owned large chunks of the venture, which would connect the main line with the company's coalfields to the south, near present-day Red Lodge.[25]

Politicians in both Helena and Washington also preferred the Rocky Fork line. Samuel T. Hauser, the Democratic territorial governor who owned the largest bank in Montana, had been an advocate and economic ally of the railroad ever since its completion. The relationship had not been without its difficult moments. In the summer of 1885, for instance, Thomas Oakes of the Northern Pacific threatened to make things "hot" for Hauser and promised him, "You will think the Devil is after you." But in general Hauser and the Northern Pacific worked together to develop the territory and pocket large profits for themselves. In 1886 Hauser became interested in a scheme to develop the coalfields of the southern Yellowstone Valley, but to mine the coal he needed three things: a federal charter, federal approval to build a railroad line through the Crow reservation, and the willingness of the Northern Pacific to build a branch line.[26]

Hauser, as a Democratic governor with a Democratic administration in Washington, was in a perfect position to lobby for the necessary federal consent. The Northern Pacific also was ready to support its friend Hauser. In early March 1887, Congress approved the creation of the Rocky Fork Railroad. The decision in favor of the Rocky Fork line rather than the Cooke City branch disappointed several Billings businessmen, but as Walter Matheson, the editor of the Billings *Gazette*, argued, "[the] road will be of incalculable benefit to the city, in furnishing it with cheap fuel, and a vast additional trade." A *Gazette* editorial on January 15, 1887, even promised that the new line would "at once set Billings on the high road to prosperity beyond all former dreams of its inhabitants" and "open up unlimited possibilities to this city."[27]

In fact, railroads were all the talk of eastern Montana in the spring of 1887. James J. Hill, the St. Paul railroad executive, had undertaken the massive construction project of extending his Manitoba railroad to Great Falls, Montana, building to the north of Billings along the Missouri and Milk rivers. The possibility of a new northern connection intrigued many Billings businessmen. But the *Gazette* warned everyone not to fall back into old patterns in which businessmen and community leaders waited for outsiders to make the crucial economic decisions. "We are living in a progressive era," the editorial stressed, "and to accomplish anything [we] must stir ourselves, and work in the present and not follow the example of men who came to this country five years ago, and are still meditating over the best and most advantageous way to turn." The Rocky Fork scheme was a golden opportunity—businessmen should make the most of it. "Undoubtedly" the new line would "have a good deal to do with the prosperity of the city," the *Gazette* observed a week later.[28]

Despite the *Gazette*'s prodding, the expected boom in the local economy developed slowly because businessmen waited for Samuel Hauser and his partners to make the first moves. The railroad received its right-of-way through the Crow reservation in the spring of 1887, but for almost a year no tracks were laid. Before launching the project, Hauser wanted as many Northern Pacific men involved as possible, and getting everyone to agree was not easy. Thomas F. Oakes energetically supported the Rocky Fork scheme, and he promised that his friend Frederick Billings would soon join the venture. With the problems of the Bull Mountain coal mines fresh in his mind, however, Frederick Billings had no interest in the Rocky Fork line unless Hauser was in complete control of the venture, owning at least 52 percent of the railroad stock and at least half of the coal property. To help Hauser gain control, the extended Billings family, represented by Edward Bailey, offered the Helena banker a 106-acre coal claim along Bear Creek.[29]

The speculation about a Rocky Fork line and the news that the Northern Pacific had sent out surveyors to locate a line between Billings and Fort Benton were encouraging developments for Billings businessmen. Perhaps the city would receive the economic incentives it needed. Then, in the second week of May 1888, the city of Billings received the shocking news that Parmly Billings, traveling home to Vermont, had unexpectedly died of uremic poisoning at the age of twenty-five.

What did this sudden turn of events mean for the future of Billings? Surprisingly, although Parmly's death lessened the Billings family's direct, personal involvement in the local economy, the tragedy spurred new family investment in the Clark's Fork Bottom. Proud of Parmly's maturation in Montana, Frederick was determined not to abandon his son's hard work. In July 1888, the Minnesota and Montana Land and Improvement Company announced plans to spend $30,000 expanding and improving the irrigation of the "Big Ditch," under the direction of I. D. O'Donnell, who used this experience to become one of the country's leading irrigation experts. O'Donnell also purchased Parmly's half in the family's agricultural operations. The new partnership of Bailey and O'Donnell, as the latter recalled, owned "a number of bands of sheep, took up various land holdings and kept a quality of range." O'Donnell recalled, "It was through these experiments that I caught a glimpse of a great future for farming in the Yellowstone valley."[30]

The Billings family also decided to join the other Northern Pacific officials and investors in Hauser's Yellowstone coal ventures. Shortly after his son's death in May, Frederick bought ten thousand shares for $125,000 while the Northern Pacific's Henry Villard and C. B. Wright grabbed eight thousand and four thousand shares, respectively, in Hauser's "Helena and Livingston Smelter and Reduction Company," to be powered with coal taken from the Red Lodge and Bear Creek mines. By September 1888, Hauser had acquired control of both the Rocky Fork Railroad and the associated coal mines, and as promised, Frederick Billings joined the Red Lodge syndicate, which now included such notable capitalists as Thomas F. Oakes, Henry Villard, and C. B. Wright of the Northern Pacific, and Marcus Daly, James Haggin, and E. L. Bonner of Montana.[31]

The capitalists used $713,000 to establish "the Rocky Fork Railway & Coal Trust," with Henry Villard as trustee. To build up a capital fund for construction and development, the trust sold part of the company stock to investors at rock-bottom prices, with insiders like Billings, Haggin, and Wright paying only eighteen cents on the dollar. These machinations soon had a direct impact on the Clark's Fork Bottom. On December 18, 1888, Hauser, on behalf of the trust, signed a contract with the Northern Pacific to build a branch line from Laurel, a new railroad town established on land company property located near the abandoned village of Canyon Creek, to a new townsite called Red Lodge near the coal mines. A month later Hauser formally incorporated the Rocky Fork Coal Company. The new year, 1889, appeared to be one of great promise in the Yellowstone Valley.[32]

Northern Pacific officials became closely involved with the development of the railroad line between Laurel in Yellowstone County and the new Red Lodge townsite. On February 18, 1889, Thomas F. Oakes wired Hauser: "Immediate steps should be taken to start town site at Red Lodge. Now is the time just as emigration is commencing to have things in readiness. A great many people could be diverted to that point if matter[s] are put in shape." To boost the town's fortunes, and publicize its connection with the Northern Pacific, the trustees of the Rocky Fork Railroad changed the name of the new town from Red Lodge to "Villard," following the earlier example of the town of "Billings." But Henry Villard, despite owning thirty thousand shares in the Rocky Fork Town Site and Electric Company, registered an immediate objection, and the name change was rescinded. If Villard had said nothing, the two primary communities of what was then Yellowstone County would have shared more than a rail connection; they would have shared the trait of being named for presidents of the Northern Pacific.[33]

Hauser's various development schemes in 1889 reflected the new realities of doing business in the Yellowstone country. During the past decade, the economy of the Clark's Fork Bottom had evolved well beyond its prerailroad reliance on Crow Indian trade, buffalo products, and the exchanges between local farmers and entrepreneurs such as Perry W. McAdow. From 1880 to 1889, the region's economy had changed beyond recognition. Measured by any indicator—the change in population, the amount of trade, the amount of capital available for investment, the number of corporations established, or the quality of available transportation—a new economic world had been created along the Yellowstone Valley.

Traditional patterns of exchange, for instance, no longer bonded the peoples of the Yellowstone. New economic realities defined relationships between the Crows and the white residents of the Clark's Fork Bottom. For decades, the Indians had been at the center of the region's trade; without their involvement, success in the fur trade would have been exceedingly difficult, if not impossible. Then, in the early years of settlement, they had had a close, personal, and often friendly trading relationship with the newcomers to the Bottom. Now, in the age of the schemes of Frederick Billings, Samuel Hauser, and Henry Villard, the

Crows played no role in the local economy, except for controlling the land and the transportation corridors south of the Yellowstone River.

Having lost their central role in the economic structure of the region, the Crows found themselves increasingly abused and ignored by newer Yellowstone residents. Only earlier settlers, such as William A. Allen, maintained friendships with Crow leaders. Plenty Coups summed up well the tribe's frustration: "White men with their spotted-buffalo [cattle] were on the plains about us. Their houses were near the water-holes, and their villages on the rivers. We made up our minds to be friendly with them, in spite of all the changes they were bringing. But we found this difficult, because the white men too often promised to do one thing and then, when they acted at all, did another."[34]

The "Sword Bearer" incident of 1887 only made things worse. That year had witnessed the passage of the Dawes General Allotment Act, which promised to substitute tribal ownership of reservations with individual family allotments of 160 acres, allowing the remaining millions of acres to be opened for white settlement. The Crow Indian Sword Bearer and his followers were very angry about the proposed allotment process because they knew the new law would further impoverish the already desperately poor tribe. That fall, they rebelled against the authority of the Crow reservation agent, Henry E. Williamson, by conducting a horse raid against the Blackfeet. After Williamson threatened to arrest them, Sword Bearer and his followers rode into the agency in full warrior regalia and shot up the place. The agent panicked and asked Fort Custer for protection. When the troops found Sword Bearer and his followers, both sides were ready for action. Cooler heads prevailed, however, and bloodshed was averted.[35]

The Billings *Gazette* translated this incident into a full-scale Indian outbreak that demanded swift and sure retaliation before the Crows attacked every settlement in the valley. "Nothing discourages the Indians more than a judicious display of force," argued the newspaper. The army responded with orders to arrest every defiant Indian, and on November 5, 1887, a brief skirmish between the soldiers and Sword Bearer's supporters resulted in the death of one soldier and eight Crow Indians, including Sword Bearer. Although Billings had never been threatened during the entire incident, local leaders used Sword Bearer's defiance to call for the immediate opening of the reservation to white settlement. The Crows had demonstrated their bloodthirsty nature, according to the *Gazette*, and the newspaper demanded their immediate subjugation. In the local parlance north of the Yellowstone, the only good Indian was now a dead Indian.[36]

Just as the earlier friendly relations between the settlers of the Clark's Fork Bottom and the Crow Indians had disappeared some time ago, so too had the primary resource exploited by the early homesteaders—the buffalo. With the coming of the Northern Pacific Railroad, the vicious, senseless extermination of the buffalo accelerated. By 1884, the animal had been hunted to near extinction in the area, leaving behind a ghastly sight: thousands of tons of bleached buffalo bones littering the prairies. These piles of bones, moreover, were worth something—at least twelve dollars a ton. Settlers and entrepreneurs made small fortunes during the next three years by collecting the bones to be shipped, usually to the Michigan Carbon Works of Detroit where they would be processed for their minerals.[37]

The new economic world also largely eliminated the intimate, personal relationship between entrepreneur and settler, a relationship that had once existed between Perry W. McAdow and the early residents of the Clark's Fork Bottom. The dealings of the land company, the investments by capitalists such as T. C. Power and Frederick Billings, and the power of the Northern Pacific Railroad had eclipsed the significance of this exchange network. But McAdow and most of the early settlers remained involved in the local economy, even though their actions no longer held the same importance. Perry McAdow, for instance, had done well in the new town of Billings during its early years, leading the local Democratic party as a territorial representative, operating a mercantile and wholesale liquor store, and serving on the boards of several local companies, including the water company and the First National Bank. His marriage to Clara Tomlinson had given him a valued and wealthy economic partner, and in 1885 his and Clara's investments in the mines at Maiden began to pay off handsomely. As it became clear that the Billings family would chart the destiny of the "Magic City,"

Bud sold his Billings store to W. V. Jobes and moved to the Judith Basin.[38]

McAdow experienced good times and bad times in his new abode. According to the historian Muriel Wolfe, Bud was paralyzed and bound to a wheelchair by the time he reached Maiden. How this happened is unknown. Despite the handicap, he directed the overall operations of the mines while Clara assumed management. In 1885, her capital bought a ten-stamp mill, which finally allowed the McAdows to process the rich ore of the two mines. Almost immediately they turned to T. C. Power for further investment capital. In August, the McAdows offered Power half-interest in the War Eagle, along with the option of renting the other half and purchasing the stamp mill. Within a month, the negotiations were over, and Power assumed operation of the War Eagle while the McAdows reinvested their profits into improving the Spotted Horse. Within the next two years, this one mine made the McAdows an estimated one million dollars. They then sold the Spotted Horse to a syndicate headed by Samuel T. Hauser and Anton Holter, who failed to make much from the property and allowed it to revert back to the McAdows by the summer of 1890.[39]

The couple's successful economic partnership, however, stirred up old ghosts. Several years earlier, according to the Miles City *Yellowstone Journal*, Imogene Dupont—a "Spanish woman, whom [McAdow] met in one of his trips through the southern country in search of health"—had become McAdow's mistress. When Bud reneged on his promise to marry her, choosing instead Clara Tomlinson, an irate Dupont sued for damages shortly after the marriage in 1884. A Miles City jury that year reviewed 140 letters, which were "decidedly nasty in their tone and created a great sensation when they were read in the court," and found in favor of Dupont. McAdow eventually won the case on appeal in 1886, but his relationsip with Clara did not last much longer. By 1889, Clara was living in a spacious Victorian mansion in her hometown of Jackson, Michigan, while McAdow was in Montana managing the mines.[40]

The diary of John Summers, an early Canyon Creek settler, from 1882 to 1889 provides another perspective on the new economic world of the Clark's Fork Bottom. The formation of the city of Billings brought employment and trade opportunities never available at Coulson or Canyon Creek. Throughout the decade, Summers and his sons were often busy working on the Bottom's irrigation ditches and in the construction of new bridges. Yet, their farming activities remained as important as in the past. Cabbage, corn, squash, lettuce, turnips, rutabagas, and potatoes provided food for the table and for trade. Eventually, however, the lure of the town proved too strong, and from November 1887 to January 1888, Summers relocated his blacksmith and cobbler shop from near Canyon Creek to Billings while continuing to operate the family homestead. Initially, business was slow in Billings, and Summers had to assume all sorts of odd jobs, from smoking and packing meat to cutting and stacking ice, to make ends meet. It was a hard life in the city.[41]

Whereas Summers moved to Billings in the late 1880s and failed to do as well as he hoped, Bud McAdow had abandoned Billings for the brighter horizons of Maiden in 1885. The economic decisions of these two early residents of the Clark's Fork Bottom underscore a reality that was hard for everyone to accept: Billings was no "Magic City." Only three months after its founding, the town's population had topped one thousand, but it took three years to add another five hundred residents, and in the late 1880s, Billings even lost population.

Why did Billings struggle so? The failure of the land company, even with the active involvement of the Billings family, to inject enough capital into public improvements and commercial institutions was one important reason. The promised sawmills, flour mills, and other industrial enterprises never materialized. The lack of support and cooperation from the Northern Pacific Railroad, especially its inability, until late in the decade, to build additional branch lines from Billings, was another. The town still lacked a crucial connection to the Missouri River towns of Fort Benton and Great Falls.[42]

A third reason was a lack of support from the territorial government in Helena. Local political leaders and businessmen blamed territorial politicians such as Joseph K. Toole for the federal government's failure to open new areas of the Crow reservation for settlement. Billings residents were particularly incensed at Toole's refusal to introduce into

Congress an 1885 agreement, supported by the Dawes Commission, by which the Crows would cede five million acres for the paltry sum of one dollar per acre. The *Gazette* charged that Toole merely represented "a few of the millionaire miners and speculators in the west." The newspaper added, "It was and to their interest that the progress of Eastern Montana be paralyzed."[43]

Billings also had its share of bad luck. A disastrous fire in 1884 wiped out the center of the town's business district, costing some forty-five thousand dollars in losses. A year later, fires once again damaged the business district, destroying almost two complete blocks of buildings. These disasters, however, had a silver lining, since local businessmen quickly replaced their old false-front frame buildings with handsome multistoried brick buildings. In October 1885, construction began on the Grand Hotel on the northwest corner of First Avenue and North 27th Street. This three-story brick building with an understated Victorian facade was the best hotel in Billings and was a physical symbol of the town's determination to put bad times behind and look with renewed confidence toward the future. In the new year, the massive beauty of the Grand Hotel was matched by a new ten-thousand-dollar hardware store for Edgar Camp and Brothers.[44]

But the streak of bad luck had yet to run its course. The legendary winter of 1886–87 (Paul McCormick at Junction City reported heavy snows and temperatures down to forty-two degrees below zero) wiped out the region's stock-raising industry. Whereas the Stockgrowers Association had routinely shipped sixteen thousand head of cattle annually from Billings, the killing winter of 1886–87 crippled the stock raisers and the local merchants who depended on their trade. More than a decade would pass before the stock-raising industry would fully recover from this natural disaster. Then, after the spring thaw, another fire in May 1887 destroyed several downtown businesses.[45]

Throughout the 1880s, Billings was a town still in search of its destiny. New economic relationships, market development, and transportation networks had been established in the Clark's Fork Bottom. But the early dreams of Billings as another Minneapolis or Denver were now laughable; reality had set in, and most boosters realized that Billings would do well to evolve into a secondary trade town on the Northern Pacific's route. As in other years, however, 1889 began with plenty of optimism. After all, it was the year of statehood, and perhaps that new political status would bring benefits to Billings. Management of the land company was in sound hands; successful irrigation projects could lure new immigrants; several residents and businessmen enjoyed electricity; the long-desired branch railroad to Red Lodge was nearing completion; the federal government might soon open the Crow reservation for white settlement; and rumor had it that new railroad lines would soon connect Billings to Fort Benton and to the cattle country of Wyoming.

Yet the problems of the past had not disappeared. Billings and Yellowstone County might still have a chance of recapturing a bit of that "old-time eastern magic," but it would take more investment, willing capitalists, aggressive entrepreneurs, continued national prosperity—and a little bit of luck. As a new decade beckoned, the people of Yellowstone County warily awaited their future.

CHAPTER 9

"The Star of the Yellowstone Is in the Ascendant": Billings Rebounds, 1890–1900

When the census takers traversed Yellowstone County and Billings in 1890, they found a community of 2,065 people, a number that represented a considerable population gain since the roughly 200 residents of 1880. But numbers can sometimes be deceiving. Local residents realized that Billings in 1890 was a declining, rather than growing, community. According to their estimates, Billings had lost as much as half of its population in the last five years.[1]

People left largely out of frustration: Billings and Yellowstone County had never experienced the economic miracle their boosters promised. New businesses dotted the landscape, but the commercial district of Billings had never really recovered from the disastrous fires and lack of investment of the 1880s. The cattle market was busted. Nor did the future of the Northern Pacific Railroad, the county's major employer, look very promising. Due to its financial instability, the corporation had never been the engine of capital expansion and improvement that town leaders had expected. After the recent failure of the London bankers Baring Brothers, the railroad was too concerned about saving its own neck to risk any further investment in the Yellowstone Valley. The land company had enjoyed better management by the Billings family, but many of its promises were still unfulfilled. Then, on September 30, 1890, Frederick Billings died at his Vermont home, prompting new questions about the future of the land company. With his death, the Billings family soon abandoned most of its personal involvement in the Yellowstone, leaving only Edward Bailey active in local real estate. The city of Billings had lost the one capitalist who had devoted his time, money, and family to cultivating the Clark's Fork Bottom.[2]

With Frederick Billings's death, the railroad's poor health, and the town's decreasing population, one might expect that over the next generation Billings would develop into nothing more than a railroad town of a few thousand residents along the Yellowstone Valley. It had enough energetic local capitalists—Fred Foster, Henry Rowley, Paul McCormick, Albert Babcock, and Herman Mund—to ensure that much. But Billings did much better than that in the 1890s and the decades to come; in 1910, its 10,000 residents made Billings the biggest city in the Yellowstone Valley. By reviewing the major economic changes of the 1890s, this final chapter explores the forces that reshaped the destiny of the town of Billings in this crucial decade.

The elimination of the Billings family from direct involvement in the affairs of the Clark's Fork Bottom was the first turning point of the 1890s. As rich, powerful eastern capitalists personally active in Yellowstone County in the 1880s, the family had served as a bridge between the highly personal nature of the market relationships of the frontier era and the highly impersonal, distant corporate relationships of the late 1890s. From 1890 on, Samuel Kilner directed the land company from his New York City office, with Edward Bailey making periodic visits to the Yellowstone properties. The land company too became a cold, distant corporate player in the development of the region.

The second turning point came on August 1, 1890, when the forty-four-mile railroad line from Laurel to Red Lodge opened for operation.[3] The branch established Laurel as an important transportation link on the Northern Pacific's main line while it extended the economic dependence of Billings on the railroad, the outside market, and the financial developments that served to buttress or weaken the well-being of the Northern Pacific.

Next came the opening of the western end of the Crow Reservation in 1892 and new local business initiatives that boosted the local economy. Because of the town's strong ties to the Northern Pacific, the depression of 1893 abruptly ended this period of expansion. The depression led to the bankruptcy of the Northern Pacific and introduced Billings to the specter of bitter labor strife.

Out of this same depression, however, emerged new forces to shape the economic future of Yellowstone County. The arrival of the Chicago, Burlington, and Quincy Railroad in the fall of 1894 opened new avenues of commerce. As the railroad built through the north side of town, a new commercial center emerged between the tracks of the two competing lines. At the same time, corporate America began to reorganize the nation's railroad system with a series of decisions that imposed a different economic order on the Yellowstone Valley.

Herein lies the final, and perhaps most important, key to the economic resurgence of Billings during the decade. Negotiations among several men—James J. Hill, the president of the Great Northern Railway; J. P. Morgan, the international private banker; George Stephen, the British capitalist; and representatives of the Deutsche Bank of Berlin—consolidated the once rival Northern Pacific and Great Northern railroads into one northern plains transportation network. This chapter reviews their dealings in detail because the Morgan-Hill corporate alliance soon led to James J. Hill's control of all of the railroads in eastern Montana, and, more important, to his selection of Yellowstone County as the hub of his railroad empire. That decision would establish the crucial transportation foundation for the economic expansion later experienced by Billings and Yellowstone County, the boom that in the twentieth century finally justified the city's self-proclaimed nickname of "Billings, the Magic City."[4]

In March 1891, the Billings *Gazette* announced, "Two million acres of land, mountain and hill, meadow and plain, valley and highland, grassland, mineral, timber, farm and grazing land, is soon to be thrown open to settlement, and as we have several times exultantly remarked, and remark again, it is all within the confines of Yellowstone county and a part of our inheritance."[5]

The politicians, businessmen, and farmers who had moved into the

Yellowstone Valley during the 1880s greedily awaited the day when the federal government would open the Crow Indian reservation for full settlement and exploitation. For years, white residents had complained bitterly about the Crows' ownership of so much land south of the Yellowstone River. Why did those Indians need it? If Montana businessmen and speculators controlled the land, prosperous towns would grow along the Northern Pacific main line between Miles City and Billings, settlement in Yellowstone County east of Billings would be stimulated, and the cattle industry would thrive in the rich grasslands to the south.·

The hard times of recent years amplified the settlers' cries for more land, especially cheap Indian land. In February 1890, Paul McCormick of Junction City bluntly informed the new U. S. senator from Montana, Thomas C. Power: "We want to see the Reservation opened & want it done soon. To have so much good land kept idle is an outrage." As McCormick reminded his sometime business partner, "Yellowstone county people are good friends of yours & opening the Reservation will please them better than any other measure you can get through at present." Deferring to the cry for more land, Power and the other senator from Montana, Thomas Carter, urged the Indian Bureau to implement the allotment procedure as quickly as possible. That summer, federal commissioners arrived on the Crow Reservation to assign permanent allotments and negotiate a new land-cession treaty.[6]

But Paul McCormick's worries were not over. Would the Interior Department agents act soon enough, and would they properly "supervise" the Indians in selecting allotments? It would be a shame if the Crows took all the good land. McCormick complained to Senator Power that the Crows were "selecting all the hay lands, all the bottoms easily irrigated, in fact all the lands worth anything to settlers whenever the Reservation should be thrown open." The opposite should be the case, he argued. His attitude reflected a common assumption among most white settlers. The Crows, they reasoned, should be assigned the marginal farmland, whereas valuable property should be reserved for ranchers who knew how to exploit the land to best advantage.[7]

The Crows, however, persisted in their right to claim good reservation land as their allotments; they refused to be limited to boundaries that eliminated valuable resources from their control. In the 1890 round of negotiations over the western section of the reservation, roughly from Boulder Creek to the western side of the Bighorn River, the Indians frankly distrusted the commissioners and chastised the agents for the government's failure to enforce the treaties of the early 1880s. Initially, Chief Plenty Coups refused to sell the land under any terms, but later he and other Crow leaders relented, if the federal government promised to build new day schools and extensive irrigation systems while supplying tribal members with more cattle and direct cash payments. "The country we are selling," Plenty Coups asserted, "is worth lots of money. . . . Promise me that the Great Father will not trouble us about our land any more." The chief's goodwill was abused; the deal struck by the federal agents slighted the Crows in favor of the government. In exchange for about 1.8 million acres, much of it potentially valuable mining property, the tribe received $946,000, or about 50 ¢ an acre. The Crows retained previously granted allotments in the ceded area, but they were encouraged to sell this property back to the government and take new allotments in the reduced reservation.[8]

On December 8, 1890, Paul McCormick wired T. C. Power that the federal commissioners had secured the "consent of Indians ceding west end of reservation." McCormick had hoped the cession would extend beyond the Bighorn River and would open land for development south of his major base of operations at Junction City. Despite the development of Billings to the west and Miles City to the east, McCormick had remained at the mouth of the Bighorn River, convinced that one day his Junction City would have all the land necessary to become a major trade center. The failure of the 1890 treaty to include land east of the Bighorn finally forced him to abandon Junction City and search for greener pastures. The place on the Yellowstone River that for decades had nurtured American entrepreneurs, from the fur trader Manuel Lisa to the merchant Paul McCormick, became a ghost town by the early twentieth century. During the next spring, McCormick moved permanently to Billings, residing in an eclectic Victorian-style dwelling on the corner of Fourth Avenue North and 31st Street. He soon became a fixture in the social, political, and economic affairs of the town, hosting many gatherings at his old log cabin, which he had moved behind his new house.[9]

The Crow negotiations of 1890–91 also disappointed others, for vastly different reasons. The Chicago commission merchant P. B. Weare, another business acquaintance of T. C. Power's, told the senator, "I am also disgusted with the price that the Crows were bamboozled into accepting for the West end of the Reservation, but suppose that 'Discretion is the better part' and that we had better keep our mouths shut, and let the thing go." Weare believed that the Crows should have received one dollar an acre, or double the actual purchase price. "I am in favor of the Indians selling it," he admitted, "but I think the price that the Government paid them is outrageous, and for an enlightened, civilized people to take advantage of their wants in this way is beneath the dignity of a great nation like ours."[10]

Needless to say, few in the Clark's Fork Bottom agreed with the Chicago merchant. They had wanted this land for eight years—and if it now came at a bargain price, so much the better. Some squatters crossed the river to make their claims as soon as news of the treaty became public. In early 1891, T. C. Power introduced the treaty to Congress and pushed for its immediate approval. But the rush of new settlers to the cession, squatting before the Indians had relinquished formal title to the land, combined with deficiencies in the government survey of the reservation to delay congressional ratification. Not until the fall of 1892 did Senator Power receive official notification of ratification and the presidential proclamation opening the western section of the Crow reservation.[11]

The new Crow treaty, formally ratified or not, spurred the Clark's Fork Bottom economy from 1890 to 1892 because local businessmen, anticipating a new land boom, improved their stores and expanded their stock for the expected new settlers. T. C. Power's activity in the fall of 1890 is a good example of how the promise of new, cheap federal land stimulated investment. Assuming that the treaty would attract thousands of new settlers to the area, Power tried to position his store as the leading mercantile firm in Billings. He pressured the Northern Pacific for the right to erect a new store directly on the railroad right-of-way so that newcomers could step off the train, walk into his store, and buy all the things they needed to start life anew in Yellowstone County. But the Northern Pacific rejected Power's proposal. J. M. Hannaford ruled, "Our management does not approve of our right of way being devoted to general merchandise stores for retail purposes, fearing that it would create complications, which would lead us into endless trouble." The senator would receive no special favors in Billings.[12]

Despite the lack of railroad cooperation, business activity accelerated during the spring of 1891. The key development happened in April when Albert L. Babcock reorganized the former Bailey and Billings private bank as the Yellowstone National Bank. In 1882 Babcock had left his Illinois grocery business to try his luck in Billings. He proved successful in several different ventures, from a hardware store to real estate. His business acumen led to political prominence, and Babcock served as the chairman of the board of county commissioners from 1885 to 1889 and had recently been elected the county's first state senator. Now forty years old, Babcock grasped the local leadership mantle in the economic development of the community. His bank funded his own ventures while providing a new source of investment capital for other entrepreneurs. On August 18, 1891, to further encourage new enterprises, Babcock and other local businessmen established the Billings Club, an association of like-minded boosters and the direct forerunner of the Commercial Club and the Billings Chamber of Commerce. Like the earlier board of trade of 1883–84, the new Billings Club served to bind the town's disparate entrepreneurial capitalists into one powerful lobby for economic development.[13]

As the institutional fabric of Billings changed in 1891, so too did the everyday rhythm of work. The Northern Pacific adopted "standard time" in late March 1891, forcing local businessmen, citizens, and railroad workers—who wanted to be on time with the railroad—to change the way they counted the hours in a day. First established in 1883 by the General Time Convention, standard time divided the country into the zones of eastern, central, mountain, and western time that we use today. Previously, different towns along the railroad line had set their own time, often baffling train travelers. In announcing the new policy, the Billings *Gazette* remarked that the railroad would "require each engineer and conductor to have his watch examined once every six months." But the impact of standard time extended well beyond regular watch examinations for railroad employees. In a town heavily dependent on the railroad, the new time changed the daily rhythms of life, adding a new degree of standardization to the workday. The adoption of standard time also continued the integration of Billings into the mainstream of the national economic system.[14]

In 1891 the physical fabric of Billings experienced fundamental change as well. In late July, a fire destroyed what had long been the symbolic heart of the business district—the Northern Pacific's Headquarters Hotel, which had served as the original depot and telegraph office and had been the first building erected by the railroad in the spring and summer of 1882. The Maverick Hose Company, the city fire fighters established just two years earlier, did little to stop the blaze because most residents were glad to see the building go. "This unsightly pile had long been an eyesore," observed the Billings *Gazette*. Town leaders announced plans to raze the site so that 28th Street could be extended south of the tracks and become a major commercial artery, renamed "Broadway." The fire also forced the railroad to build a more suitable depot, a one-story brick building of Victorian design, which opened in the following March.[15]

During the early 1890s, local businessmen and county leaders also aggressively sought to expand their agricultural markets. In late 1891, the rancher Charles Bair staked his future in Yellowstone County, leasing thirty-three hundred acres of T. C. Power's land near Lavina for his sheep herds. Bair would soon become the region's dominant stock raiser, especially renowned for his outstanding wool production. On the benches north of Billings, Bair joined other ranchers such as Joe and Frank Zimmerman, who moved their twenty-two hundred head of sheep every summer via the Zimmerman Trail, a rugged, winding road built by Frank in 1890. In 1892, I. D. O'Donnell and Edward Bailey took full control of the Hesper Farm. Further modernizing the property, O'Donnell extensively irrigated the ranch and planted alfalfa and sugar beets. Within a year, the Billings *Gazette* reported that O'Donnell and Bailey's operations in the Clark's Fork Bottom embraced five thousand acres of prime ranchland where the two men practiced "mixed farming on a big scale, for in addition to large crops of grain, hay, and vegetables, they run 7,000 or 8,000 head of sheep, and are extensive cattle and horse growers." The Bottom's "bonanza farm" continued to grow in prosperity and reputation.[16]

Also in 1892, O'Donnell founded the county's principal agriculture promotional vehicle, the Yellowstone Fair Association. O'Donnell conceived the fair not only as a way of improving local agricultural yields through new crops, farming techniques, and irrigation but also as a way of attracting new settlers to the still considerable landholdings of the Minnesota and Montana Land and Improvement Company, which he served as manager. As the association president, O'Donnell raised twenty thousand dollars by private subscription to place the fair on a sound financial footing. Over the next ten years his annual fair boosted the agricultural reputation of the county as had no other promotion in Billings.[17]

For the residents of Yellowstone County, the opening of the western end of the Crow reservation and the success of several local entrepreneurial initiatives in 1891–92 set the stage for a period of economic expansion and growth. The town also had benefited from the construction of Eastern Montana Prison at the base of the rimrocks. Population certainly had been on the upswing, with Billings reaching an estimated sixteen hundred residents by the end of 1892, approximately a 60 percent increase in just two years. Reflecting both the recent population growth and a new confidence in the future was the January 1893 vote to reincorporate the town as a "second class city" under the laws of the state of Montana. An 1892 proposal to update the city's legal standing had failed badly, but the 1893 referendum passed with only four dissenting votes. The official Northern Pacific guide for that year described Billings as a trade center of great potential, complete with "six hotels, three churches [actually four], two banks, two public halls, two brick yards, a brick and stone court-house, two daily and weekly newspapers, a flouring mill [operated by Albert Babcock], and numerous stores of all branches of trade."[18]

Another factor besides local initiatives, productive farms, and cheap land was fueling the expansion of early 1893—a rumor that the Chicago, Burlington, and Quincy Railroad, a powerful midwestern carrier, was planning to expand into the Yellowstone country. In 1888–89, the railroad had sought the approval of the Montana territorial legislature for a branch line, called the Big Horn Southern Railroad Company, to stretch from Wyoming to Billings. The legislature had incorporated the company in December 1888, with federal approval to build across the Crow reservation coming in February 1889. That year the Burlington had entered the northeast corner of Wyoming, apparently headed for Yellowstone County, but in December 1889, the railroad had unexpectedly stopped at Cambria, Wyoming, still hundreds of miles from the Clark's Fork Bottom.[19]

For the next three years, local businessmen kept a close eye on Burlington activities for any sign of movement northward. In February 1892, the Burlington announced plans to float a multimillion-dollar bond issue for new construction. "This looks as if they intend to do something this season," Paul McCormick told T. C. Power. "Do you know anything about their plans?" McCormick's instincts were right on the mark—the railroad had decided to extend its track into the rich cattle land of Wyoming. By November 26, 1892, its Grand Island and Northern Wyoming Railroad Company had reached Sheridan, Wyoming, just south of the Montana border and the Crow Indian reservation.[20]

As the Burlington moved toward Montana, Paul McCormick and T. C. Power debated its probable route. Newspaper and other contemporary accounts called the proposed road the Burlington and Missouri, although corporate records indicate that the branch line was always officially known as the Big Horn Southern Railroad. From reading the newspapers, McCormick decided that the railroad was headed toward central Montana. In December, he predicted to Power that the new line would follow the Little Bighorn to Fort Custer, where it would cross the Bighorn River and then head north, "following down Fly Creek to within a few miles of Pompey Pillar leaving that stream and crossing the Northern Pacific track between Clearmont station and Huntly [sic]." At that point, the railroad would head westward toward Billings before veering off into the Judith Basin and ending at Great Falls.

Power fully agreed with this assessment. He ordered McCormick to look for good land to buy along the north bank of the Yellowstone between Huntley and Billings. McCormick, however, hesitated to act without better intelligence. On February 5, 1893, he gave Power three reasons why they should "get on the inside on this Railroad deal." First, if the railroad crossed at Fort Custer, supplies for the fort could be shipped via rail, saving Power the expense of freighters. Next, the two businessmen could make money on "the furnishing of ties, piling and lumber." Most important, McCormick added: "If they will give us the exact location of their line into Billings and the location of th[e]ir work shops we can make money on lands here. But the matter can not be delayed too long." What could McCormick offer in exchange for this valuable insider information? He noted, "[The] rail road people should understand that one man is all that should know what is wanted from the Indians." McCormick asserted that he was that one man.[21]

The Burlington welcomed the offers from Power and McCormick, but its construction plans were not so grandiose. The railroad planned to resurrect the charter of the Big Horn Southern Railroad, extending its line from Sheridan to Huntley. (Today, Interstate Highway 90 generally follows the Burlington Route from Sheridan to Billings.) From there the company would build along the Yellowstone River into Billings, locating its depot and its yards on the north side of town, approximately five blocks north of the Northern Pacific's depot and yards.

In February and March 1893, the Burlington sought the necessary legal permission from the Montana state legislature, where the company expected—and found—plenty of support. One representative informed T. C. Power, "If I can be of service to the Burlington people at any time, of course, they can command my services, and if they will reciprocate it will probably only be fair." His support came cheap. "I shall probably want to make one or two trips East this year, and if you can put in a word for me it will be appreciated." The Burlington also received numerous local offers of assistance. O. F. Goddard, an influential Republican attorney and the Billings state senator, wanted to become the railroad's state attorney. He asked T. C. Power for assistance. "You may rest assured that such confidence will not be betrayed," Goddard promised, "and such information will be duly appreciated, and it may be I can profit thereby." Goddard got what he wanted: as a corporate lawyer for the Burlington, he established the basis for a successful career as an attorney and judge, later topped by his appointment as chief justice of the Montana Supreme Court in 1938.[22]

With supporters easily outnumbering detractors, the railroad proposal sailed through the legislature, and the Burlington immediately began to survey its new line between Huntley and Billings. Its approach thrilled Paul McCormick, for the railroad construction was a sure "opportunity to make some money."[23]

The news of the Burlington extension boomed the economy of Billings in May 1893. "Billings is going to the front this season more rapidly than has ever been known in the history of the town," the *Gazette* exclaimed. "Every house has a tenant and store and office rooms are at a premium. The assurance of the advent of the Burlington & Missouri this season was all that was needed to keep the hammers going and pushing the city forward." Although the sudden "stringency of the money market in eastern financial centers" somewhat tempered the editor's optimism, he was confident that Billings could withstand any delays. The town could even afford to await another year for the Burlington to arrive.[24]

What appeared to be a minor financial panic in May became a disastrous depression during the summer of 1893, leading to the failure of 573 banks and 8,105 major businesses across the country. By early June, the oncoming depression had reached Chicago. The grain merchant P. B. Weare observed to T. C. Power:

> I want to say to you in confidence, that nothing has ever been known like the experience of this week. The run on our banks here was as vicious and ugly as it was possible to conceive, and you can understand that things were in pretty bad shape when Armour, Field, Higginbottom, Leiter, and John B. Drake [major Chicago capitalists] were spending their time walking up and down the lines of depositors, giving them good advice and tell[ing] them there was no danger, but confidentially I tell you there was plenty of danger, and lots of property was sacrificed here in the way of stocks and grain at fearful loss, in order to strengthen people engaged in finances.

You can be sure of one thing T. C. and that is that here [*sic*] is going to be a general liquidation from this on.[25]

Weare's "general liquidation" soon counted the Northern Pacific Railroad among its victims, rocking the economy of Billings and the Clark's Fork Bottom, where so many Northern Pacific workers resided and where local businessmen still depended on the stability of this transportation system. On August 15, 1893, the railroad filed for bankruptcy in the U.S. Circuit Court for the Eastern District of Wisconsin at Milwaukee, and the court appointed Henry C. Payne, Thomas C. Oakes, and Henry C. Rouse as receivers. Interestingly, both Oakes and Rouse had intimate knowledge of the Yellowstone Valley. Oakes, who had traveled in the valley several times, had been an original investor in the Minnesota and Montana Land and Improvement Company. Rouse's acquaintance with the valley dated to an 1878 trip, when settlement in the Yellowstone region had just gotten under way and when the area that was now Billings had been known as McAdow's Mill.[26]

That fall, two parties interested in the fate of the Northern Pacific investigated the bankruptcy. A secret report prepared for the company's German investors emphasized that disastrous Wall Street management had undermined the railroad. The other, more official investigation, conducted by the receiver Henry Rouse, placed emphasis on the company's failure to attract new settlers to its enormous landholdings. Rouse observed, "I was very familiar with the region some years ago, and I was surprised to see how little progress in settlement had been made in many parts of it." He urged, "An active policy of inducing settlement should be immediately inaugurated." Despite these differences in emphasis, the two investigations agreed on the Northern Pacific's considerable liabilities: its excessive debt, unprofitable branch lines, and poor management. Rouse even mentioned the threat posed by the Chicago, Burlington, and Quincy's extension into Billings.[27]

Yet the Burlington threat worried few of the railroad's executives and major creditors. They addressed the more pressing issues of reorganization: what would happen to the Northern Pacific, and who would emerge in control of the line? The debts were a serious problem, but the line possessed valuable assets—the land grant through the western

states alone was worth millions—which attracted all types of speculators, corporate executives, and financiers. Throughout the winter and
spring, different factions among the company's directors, creditors,
and executives battled to control the reorganization of the Northern
Pacific. One group of company directors—headed by August Belmont,
who had visited Billings as part of the Villard excursion in 1883—demanded that the Wisconsin federal court remove the receivers and
charged Oakes with malfeasance and fraud. And as the battle waged
on, little was done to keep the railroad in full operation; men were laid
off, and wages were slashed. Cities like Billings, which depended on
the Northern Pacific for their commercial lifeblood, suffered accordingly.[28]

Temporarily compounding the troubles of the 1893 depression in
the Clark's Fork Bottom was the Burlington's decision to halt its Yellowstone extension. The company reported that "owing to the money
troubles and bad outlook for business generally," construction would
cease until financial stability returned to the markets. The delay
proved to be short. By the spring of 1894, the Burlington had recovered
enough to resume the project. With the unemployment caused by the
Northern Pacific's bankruptcy, the tight and expensive credit, and the
sluggish commercial markets, this news gave the business community of Billings something to cheer. The *Gazette* of April 21, 1894,
boasted: "Billings will double its population within the year and an era
of prosperity hitherto unknown will dawn upon us, for everything is
now coming our way. The star of the Yellowstone is in the ascendant."[29]

The workers of Billings, especially those who toiled for the bankrupt Northern Pacific, did not share the editor's optimism as bitter labor disputes racked the working-class community that spring. Only a
week after the Burlington resumed construction of the Yellowstone
branch, railroad laborers from Billings assisted the three-hundred-plus
army of William Hogan, who had commandeered a Northern Pacific
train in Butte and was headed eastward to join the "Coxey's Army"
march on Washington to demand unemployment relief. Hogan's followers left Butte on April 24, 1894, and Northern Pacific officials ur-
gently wired the Yellowstone County sheriff's office to stop the train. A

deputy either thought the wire was a practical joke or decided to treat it like one, replying: "County attorney and sheriff out in Bull Mountains laying out additions to Billings. All of ablebodied men are busy selling real estate. Stop Coxey's army at Livingston." When the stolen train stopped in Billings on April 25, Hogan and his men received a hero's welcome, and one hundred additional recruits offered their assistance. They also encountered Federal Marshal William McDermott and his sixty-five deputies, who moved to arrest Hogan and his followers. A brief gunfight broke out, wounding both deputies and protesters and killing one Billings resident. The train hurriedly left Billings and moved down the valley until it ran into the U.S. Army, which had blocked the tracks near Forsyth with a cannon. Hogan and his men surrendered to the authorities.[30]

The Hogan affair was a mere precursor to a much more bitter labor conflict during the summer of 1894. Two weeks after Hogan's surrender at Forsyth, the American Railway Union, headed by Eugene V. Debs, announced a strike against the Pullman works outside of Chicago. The Pullman strike inflamed railroad workers throughout America; the union refused to handle any Pullman cars, to show sympathy to striking brothers and sisters in Chicago. Because most railroad workers in Billings belonged to the union, the town soon found itself embroiled in a labor dispute that it had not started and had no direct control over.

In late June 1894, the Northern Pacific fired several employees in St. Paul for assisting the boycott. In retaliation, local union leaders at Livingston threatened to close the entire division between Livingston and Billings. Mail trains would continue to operate (in order to keep the federal government from entering the dispute), but the union vowed not to run any other Northern Pacific trains. When railroad executives refused to consider union demands, a strike was announced for June 27, 1894.[31]

Rail traffic came to a complete halt in Billings, with over three hundred Northern Pacific employees on strike. The impact of the strike on the local economy split the business community. Some merchants sided with the railroad on ideological grounds—strikes and labor unions must be opposed at all costs. Other merchants favored the railroad workers because of the business the laborers and their families brought to the stores. Stock raisers were especially antistrike, whereas the small farmers in the Bottom generally supported the union. In a sermon on the first Sunday of the strike, the local Methodist minister and union supporter J. W. Jennings compared the Pullman boycott to the Boston Tea Party of the American Revolution. Jennings chastised both the state and the national Democratic party for abandoning "the faith of the Jacksonian fathers." Rather than defending "the rights of the people against aggression and oppressive corporations," party leaders were "the pliant tools of the codfish monied aristocracy who seek to dominate this country."[32]

The heated rhetoric heard on the streets of Billings during those hot summer days, as the historian Olivier Zunz reminds us, was also heard in other western railroad towns grappling with the corporate power of the nation's railroads. Zunz's study of the Chicago, Burlington, and Quincy during the 1880s found that labor protests included "many an independent entrepreneur who felt the pinch of corporate growth and power." Zunz discovered that these entrepreneurial capitalists "even lent occasional support to workers striking the railroad lines, for their vision of a nation founded on independence, social justice, and fairness was at issue in these disputes."[33]

Yet although the strikers enjoyed support from segments of the business community, the strike soon lost momentum after the federal government entered the scene. In July, those "pliant tools" detested by Jennings sent federal troops to open the Northern Pacific. On July 9, soldiers under the command of Captain B. C. Lockwood reached Billings, where they received a chilly reception but no violence. The next day, Lockwood's command arrived in Livingston, the heart of the strike in the Yellowstone Valley. Overreacting to the hundreds of union supporters who surrounded the troop train, Lockwood nearly precipitated a riot by striking several citizens. Calmer heads prevailed, however, and the train left a small detachment and headed down the line. By July 23, 1894, the federal occupation of the Northern Pacific was complete, and the Pullman strike in Montana was over. Once the railroad returned to operation, company officials weeded out workers who had supported the union; over the next five years, blacklisting and economic restructuring reduced the Northern Pacific's labor force in Billings by approximately 40 percent.[34]

The fires of the summer labor unrest must have smoldered for some time afterward, but by reading the local newspapers in the late summer and fall of 1894, one would think that the depression had hardly affected Billings. The booster press continued its theme—"everything is now coming our way"—while the business community focused on the pending arrival of the Burlington. Businessmen looked to the new branch as an economic stimulus on a par with the runaway boom brought about by the arrival of the Northern Pacific in 1882. When the first train pulled into Billings on October 4, 1894, it was greeted as the town's savior. The Burlington line, so claimed the *Gazette,* would make the town "the supply and distributing point for all that southern country for 300 miles." Certainly the new branch opened the southern half of the valley to local merchants and entrepreneurs. But by concentrating on the immediate region, the *Gazette*'s editor missed the bigger picture. As the Burlington 1894 annual report stressed, the Billings connection formed "a shorter route than any other between Omaha, Kansas City and St. Louis, on the south, and Montana and the region west of there, on the north." The new railroad link placed Billings at the center of the western railroad network and ended the Northern Pacific's monopolistic stranglehold on local transportation.[35]

A description of Billings published in the September 1894 edition of *Northwest Magazine* emphasized the obvious. "[The Burlington extension] will bring considerable new trade to the town, especially from Fort Custer, which it touches, and its shop men and train men will add a new element to the population. As the only town in the valley with competing railroads to the East, Billings will once again feel new life." A new commercial core, located in the blocks between the Burlington and the Northern Pacific tracks on the north side of town, began to redefine the urban landscape of Billings. By the early twentieth century, all of the major religious, political, commercial, and educational institutions of the town would be located on the lots between the two sets of tracks.[36]

A new development in western land legislation further contributed to the economic recovery and expansion of Billings and Yellowstone

County in late 1894. The U.S. Congress approved the Carey Act, to encourage the reclamation of the arid plains through irrigation. The act gave six states, including Montana, federal land on the condition that the states sell the property, at the lowest possible cost, to private irrigation companies. I. D. O'Donnell, the president of the Montana Irrigation Society, had lobbied hard for the new legislation, and the Carey Act was a godsend for his operations in the Clark's Fork Bottom. It revived interest in western land sales, which helped to attract new buyers to the holdings of the Minnesota and Montana Land and Improvement Company, and it created opportunities for new irrigation schemes. O'Donnell later used the provisions of the Carey Act to establish the High Line Ditch Company in 1899 and, with Preston Moss and Henry W. Rowley, to create the Suburban Homes Company, which provided irrigated farms for the thousands of new residents who flocked to Billings and Yellowstone County in the first decade of the twentieth century.[37]

The immediate future of Billings and the Clark's Fork Bottom looked brighter indeed, but room for improvement still existed. Just think, the Billings *Weekly Times* remarked in November 1894, if the government in Helena had been more supportive of eastern Montana in general and Billings in particular, the city would be enjoying an unparalleled boom. Instead the Helena capitalists who controlled the government had always been "strongly antagonistic to development here." For instance, the Eastern Montana Prison, now built, had never been funded and stood empty. Because of the recent railroad developments, however, the negative effects of the state government's indifference no longer meant so much.[38]

The most important events of late 1894, however, centered on what the "codfish monied aristocracy" planned as the fate of the Northern Pacific Railroad. The manipulations of these corporate capitalists in St. Paul, New York City, London, and Berlin over the next three years imposed a solution to the railroad's chronic financial and managerial instability, a solution that, in turn and largely inadvertently, profoundly influenced the economic future of Billings and the Clark's Fork Bottom. The resurgence and economic expansion of Billings at the turn of the century cannot be understood without an examination of the corporate alliances and resulting railroad networks established during the reorganization of the Northern Pacific.

The powerful private banking firm of J. P. Morgan and Company dominated the railroad's first reorganization committee, headed by Edward D. Adams, a former Henry Villard employee trusted by the company's German investors. Morgan had already tasted success as the financial wizard behind several eastern railroad reorganizations. But even with his assistance, the committee resolved nothing due to bitter infighting between directors and investors in the Northern Pacific.[39]

In the fall of 1894, the railroad's frustrated German investors, represented by the Deutsche Bank of Berlin, turned to James J. Hill and George Stephen, of the Great Northern Railway for assistance. Tough as nails, shrewd, and ruthless, Hill was generally recognized as the best railroad manager in the Northwest, perhaps in the country. Together he and Stephen, the former Montreal banker and Canadian Pacific president who had recently retired to his estate outside London as Lord Mount Stephen, had made the Great Northern Railway a highly efficient and profitable corporate machine. Both capitalists, but particularly Hill, had earlier considered acquiring the Northern Pacific, so they eagerly awaited the German offer.[40]

In October 1894, Dr. Georg Siemens, of the Deutsche Bank, visited Stephen at his English estate and presented a plan, as Stephen excitedly revealed to Hill, "by which Northern Pacific would practically disappear and be absorbed by Great Northern, which would then . . . control whole business from St. Paul and Duluth to Pacific Ocean." The offer made sense to Hill, who thought that the Northern Pacific's primary problem was poor management. Always confident in his own abilities, Hill believed that if he could run the Northern Pacific, "it could be made [a] great property." Hill observed, "Its capacity to earn money is good, but it has not been run as a railway for years, but as a device for creating bonds to be sold." Indeed, Hill reported back to Stephen about another offer from the "old 'Billings' crowd" urging him to take control of the Northern Pacific reorganization. The more he considered the offers, the more Hill became convinced that grabbing the railroad was the right move. He predicted to Stephen that the Northern Pacific would soon realize "how much more" they could do with the property "than any other organization without exception." As the Great Northern president commented to the New York banker Jacob Schiff, the acquisition of the Northern Pacific was "beyond doubt a very desirable thing to do," but at the same time it called for "the greatest caution and wise forethought."[41]

Unfortunately Hill forgot his own warning. In his eagerness to take control of the Northern Pacific, Hill almost threw caution to the wind during the winter and spring of 1895 as he worked with Edward Adams to prepare a reorganization plan. He did not keep a close enough eye on Adams's behind-the-scene maneuvers in favor of the Northern Pacific and J. P. Morgan. The reorganization chairman developed an elaborate scheme that combined the Northern Pacific and the Great Northern into a giant transportation company, a deal favorable to Morgan and the Northern Pacific and not so favorable to Hill and his allies. Hill immediately rejected the plan and scrambled to assure his friends that he was not willing to dismantle the Great Northern to have control of the Northern Pacific. His friends were not listening. George Stephen called the Adams plan "the invention of [a] professional reorganizer and not worth discussing." Gaspard Farrar, a London financier, sarcastically described the reorganization as "a work of art" and wondered why its title had been ommitted—"A scheme to scale and reorganize Great Northern in the interest of the Northern Pacific." Farrar wrote Hill, "[This plan] sweeps away in an hour the work which for seventeen years you and your friends have been toiling to build up."[42]

As experienced international capitalists, Stephen and Farrar lost confidence in Hill's ability to negotiate a reasonable agreement. In late April, Stephen began meeting with Dr. Siemens and J. P. Morgan to hammer out a compromise plan. When the bankers had decided on the outlines of a reorganization, Stephen summoned Hill to London. After a few tense days of negotiations among the financiers, Hill, and Adams, the parties signed a memorandum of agreement, known as the "London agreement," on May 10, 1895.[43]

The London agreement of 1895 called for the Great Northern to guarantee payment on the principal and interest of a newly reorganized Northern Pacific; in return, Hill's railroad would receive half of the new company's capital stock, joint use of certain selected tracks and depots, and in general, friendly relations in all traffic questions. News of the agreement met with swift and favorable reactions among American capitalists. Marcus Daly, the copper king of the Anaconda mine at Butte, and Charles Pillsbury, the flour king of Minneapolis, believed Hill had struck a wonderful bargain. John G. Moore, of the New York City banking firm Moore and Schley, reported, "Thoughtful men of this town, who know the railroad situation, approve thoroughly of your having the Northern Pacific property."[44]

But support for the agreement was not unanimous among northern plains residents, who feared a Hill railroad monopoly. The "Empire Builder" returned from London to a storm of popular protest. Nor did Northern Pacific executives and members of the reorganization committee all approve of the plan, and by early June their opposition led J. P. Morgan to reconsider his initial support. Serious questions had been raised about the legality of the transaction. Minnesota state law might not allow the Great Northern to acquire the Northern Pacific because the latter was a competitor with largely parallel trackage through the state. If the agreement precipitated a lawsuit, Morgan worried, the case could discredit everyone involved, especially the bankers. The criticism did not deter Hill, however, and he remained committed to the London agreement, although he was willing to carry out "reasonable and necessary changes" to end the wrangling.[45]

Questions about the legality of the agreement persisted throughout the summer of 1895, and to quiet his critics, Hill arranged for a test case of the London agreement in the federal circuit court at St. Paul. Hill won the case, but the mere fact that he was willing to use litigation persuaded J. P. Morgan and the Deutsche Bank to join forces against the London agreement. Weakened by this defection, the London agreement of 1895 was dealt a mortal blow by a Minnesota state court that ruled, in a suit brought by the attorney general, that the London agreement violated state antitrust laws. That fall Jacob Schiff advised Hill to allow Edward Adams and the Morgan interests to proceed with an independent reorganization in which individuals, and not companies like the Great Northern, would take control of the railroad. In urging

Hill to give up the London agreement, Schiff argued that the Great Northern would still be able to "secure a sympathetic management" and achieve most, if not all, of its original goals.[46]

The failure of the London agreement of 1895 embittered James J. Hill. "Next year the parties who are now shouting huzzas for independent reorganization will have another song to sing," Hill predicted to Stephen. "At any rate there will be a more solemn note in their music long before they reach a reorganization on any basis." Morgan, the Deutsche Bank, and the reorganization committee spent the winter of 1895–96 preparing a new plan. Wanting Hill's cooperation, Morgan asked to meet with the Great Northern president in New York City, but Hill declined. Instead he worked on his own reorganization, which stressed reducing the per-mile capitalization of the Northern Pacific, but his plan was never seriously considered. On February 25, 1896, Hill received the Morgan plan, which possessed the basic characteristics of all "Morganized" railroads: (1) financial reorganization through increased capitalization, (2) adoption of the community-of-interest principle, in which corporations would work together for common interests rather than engage in ruinous competition, and (3) the voting trust, dominated by Morgan himself, empowered to direct company policy for five years.[47]

Hill was wary of all three ideas. Increased capitalization would mean high debt payments, making it much more difficult to turn the railroad into a profit maker. Inherent in the community-of-interest principle was shared power and decision-making; Hill liked neither. And he certainly cared little for leaving ultimate control to Morgan and the bankers for the railroad's first five years.

The Morgan plan was released to the public on March 16, 1896, and two weeks later, James J. Hill again sailed for London to reach a compromise with Morgan, the Northern Pacific, and the Deutsche Bank over the control of his railroad rival. On April 2, Morgan, Hill, Stephen, and Arthur Gwinner, a director of the Deutsche Bank, signed the London "memorandum." This document stipulated that Hill and Stephen would "do all in their power to further" the independent reorganization of the Northern Pacific, and in return, the Great Northern and the Northern Pacific would "form a permanent alliance, defensive, and in case of need offensive, with a view of avoiding competition and aggressive policy and of generally protecting the common interests of both Companies." The memorandum meant that the two major railroad companies of eastern Montana were to work together to achieve their mutual goals.[48]

During the next several months, Hill and Morgan clashed over the interpretation of the 1896 agreement. For example, the New York financier enraged Hill by selecting, without consultation, Edwin P. Winter as the new president of the Northern Pacific. Then in June, Hill outraged Morgan, Winter, and their corporate allies by announcing plans to build new branch lines into the valuable Red River valley territory of the Northern Pacific. His rivals realized that the "Empire Builder" had decided to follow his own course and to hell with the wishes of Morgan and the Northern Pacific. At the end of August 1896, J. W. Kendrick, the general manager of the Northern Pacific, complained that James J. Hill had "never hesitated for an instant to make such extensions as would, in his opinion, best serve the interests of his road," and now Hill threatened to disrupt railroad traffic in the Yellowstone Valley by using steamboats to move freight in the summer months. The corporate capitalists continued to wrangle over the nature of the Great Northern–Northern Pacific alliance into the new century, when Morgan dissolved the voting trust, Hill took control of the Northern Pacific, and Morgan financed Hill's purchase of controlling interest in the Chicago, Burlington, and Quincy.[49]

The Morgan-Hill alliance had both immediate and long-term benefits for Billings and Yellowstone County. The alliance allowed the Northern Pacific Railroad to emerge from bankruptcy court in February 1897 as a stronger corporation, with new capital reserves to improve its physical plant and expand its markets. One railroad historian, Louis Renz, has concluded that "vigorous rejuvenation was the best way to describe the Northern Pacific" from 1896 to 1900. Once again acting as an engine of capitalism in the Yellowstone Valley, the railroad spent millions in improving its Yellowstone operations. In the Billings area, it built a much desired spur line off the Rocky Fork branch between Rockvale and Bridger in 1898. Three years later, upriver at Livingston, the Northern Pacific injected millions of dollars into the Yellowstone economy by greatly expanding its machine shops and rail-road yards. By 1909, Livingston was home to 1,178 railroad employees and the largest Northern Pacific machine shop complex between the Pacific and Brainerd, Minnesota.[50]

Increased corporate spending was not the only immediate impact. The railroad, after years of uncertainty about both its operations and the towns it served, now represented stability and future expansion, which in turn encouraged all sorts of local economic initiatives. From 1895 to 1899, Billings recovered from the depths of the depression. Confidence in the Northern Pacific's future stability attracted new investors, as well as encouraged the town's entrepreneurial capitalists to develop new ventures. Three entrepreneurs in particular—Albert Babcock, Preston B. Moss, and I. D. O'Donnell—asserted a leadership role in charting the future of Billings and the Clark's Fork Bottom.

From 1895 to 1897, Albert L. Babcock, now the minority leader of the Republican party in the state senate, solidified his key economic and civic position within the community. He established the Yellowstone Valley Flouring Mills and the eight-hundred-seat Billings Opera House, served as a partner in the Automatic Telephone Exchange Company, and became the "Exalted Leader" of the town's B.P.O.E. Elks Club, first chartered in December 1897.[51]

A second important capitalist, Preston B. Moss, was a relative newcomer. A native of Missouri, Moss had moved to Billings in late 1892 and became the vice-president of the First National Bank, once headed by Herman Mund. In January 1896, Moss was elected president of the institution, and he soon inaugurated a period of rapid expansion for the bank. Moss worked closely with the county stock raisers, especially Charles Bair, and actively encouraged new farming ventures throughout the Bottom.

By the middle years of the decade, I. D. O'Donnell had emerged as a third important entrepreneurial leader. Now the general manager of the Minnesota and Montana Land and Improvement Company, O'Donnell not only was involved with the agricultural development of the county, such as the new High Line Ditch Company established with Carey Act support in 1899, but also further interlocked the interests of his company with new commercial ventures throughout the community. In 1899, for instance, he joined with Preston Moss and Henry Rowley to create the Suburban Homes Company out of the remaining Billings-area landholdings of the Minnesota and Montana Land and Improvement Company. Two years later, with Albert L. Babcock and other important local businessmen, he served on the board of trustees for the new city library. The common enterprises and interests of O'Donnell, Moss, and Babcock significantly influenced the development of the city over the next decade.[52]

Local business activity from 1895 to 1900 introduced Billings to a new urban landscape. Across from the Northern Pacific depot stood a handsome, three-story, Romanesque-style brewery. Montana Avenue had shed itself of the cheap, false-front stores that had once littered the city; property owners poured over $205,000 into improvements in 1899 alone. Permanent brick buildings of some architectural pretension now greeted residents. On the north end of town stood another impressive Romanesque-style building, St. Vincent Hospital, built by the Sisters of Charity of Leavenworth, Kansas, in 1898. In a special issue on October 6, 1899, the *Gazette* marveled at the recent advancements. "This is not a boom town, although it has doubled its population within the last five years," bragged the editor. Billings was a "commercial town" that did "not depend upon a single industry for support."[53]

Considering the railroad's importance to the local economy, this last claim rings hollow. Yet the number of railroad employees had significantly decreased since 1894. In that year, the Northern Pacific had employed 300 workers; five years later it worked only 180 men while the Burlington had 47 workers. This decrease of approximately 20 to 25 percent in the number of railroad employees living in Billings combined with the considerable population increase among the town's commercial and industrial sector from 1895 to 1899 to produce an economy far less dependent on railroad jobs than in the past, although the railroads remained vitally important to the future of the community.[54]

Billings and Yellowstone County lost more than railroad jobs during these five years. Political decisions in Helena shrank the size of Yellowstone County. In 1895, the legislature created Carbon County (Red Lodge) and Sweet Grass County (Columbus), which effectively took away much of the land that Yellowstone County had gained from the 1891 Crow cession. This loss of land and population makes the gains recorded in the 1900 census even more impressive. The census takers of 1900 counted 3,221 residents in Billings, about a 100 percent increase in five years.[55]

By 1900, developments on the regional and local levels, the arrival of the Burlington, and the reorganization of the Northern Pacific had spurred Billings and the Clark's Fork Bottom to new heights of growth and prosperity. Appropriately, a local photographer placed Orson Newman, Paul McCormick, and Joseph Cochran near the town's busiest corner to graphically represent the progress achieved since the frontier days. Perhaps these three early settlers would have agreed with the later assessment of the historian John Reps: "The foundation of Billings may have been based largely on promises and promotional exaggeration, but in the competition for urban survival on the western railroad frontier, Billings succeeded in living up to the expectations of its planners." Certainly those expectations were met during the next decade as Billings enjoyed a new boom that quadrupled its population. Here is where the long-term effects of the Hill-Morgan corporate alliance had their full impact on the economic development of the region.[56]

By the early 1900s, assisted immeasurably by his alliance with the banker J. P. Morgan, Hill controlled the three railroads that carried the freight of eastern Montana: the Northern Pacific, the Great Northern, and the Burlington. Already the Northern Pacific and the Burlington were linked in the Clark's Fork Bottom. In the fall of 1900, Billings residents received news that Hill planned to build the "Great Falls and Billings Railway," which not only would connect his Great Northern Railroad and the Northern Pacific but also would tie both lines to the Burlington at Billings. Finally, the city would have that northern rail connection businessmen had wanted since 1882–83. The editors at the Billings *Gazette* correctly predicted that the railway "would soon make Billings the trade center of eastern and central Montana." During that winter as well, the Burlington announced plans to build a new 128-mile branch line from Toluca, through the Crow reservation, to Cody,

Wyoming, extending the wholesale trade of Billings into northern Wyoming.[57]

The announcement of new branch railroads closed a period, 1890 to 1900, of remarkable change in the Clark's Fork Bottom. The new lines quickly strengthened the position of Billings as the leading commercial town of eastern Montana as it became an important hub of Hill's northwestern railroad empire. The city also enjoyed the benefits of booming population growth at rates not experienced since the initial railroad boom of 1882, progressive agricultural leadership, and a renewed spirit of civic capitalism. Billings at the turn of the century stood at a crossroads between its legacy as a developing frontier town and its promising future as an urban transportation center for the northern plains.

Leading the way would be a new generation of civic capitalists, and two events in 1900 and 1901 perfectly symbolized the changing of the guard. In October 1900, the farmers served by the irrigation ditches of the Minnesota and Montana Land and Improvement Company took over the project and incorporated themselves as the Big Ditch Company. The mighty land company, first envisioned as the town's savior and then blamed for almost every misfortune the town suffered, was no more.

A year later, local citizens recognized the symbolic end of the Billings family's influence in the Clark's Fork Bottom, turning out en masse for the dedication of the Parmly Billings Memorial Library. Designed by the town's best architect, Charles S. Haire, the library was donated by Frederick Billings, Jr., in honor of his brother. The Billings family had a strong preference for the massive masonry arches favored in Richardsonian Romanesque style. In the mid-1880s, Frederick had donated a library to the University of Vermont, selecting Henry Hobson Richardson himself to design the building. The family returned to that style for the new library in Billings. The building symbolized that earlier era when the Billings family had meant so much to the town; now the torch had been passed to a new generation of civic leaders.[58]

And that torch shone brightly at the grand mansion of Preston B. Moss at 914 Division Street. Arguably the most important financial leader in Billings, Moss had staked his claim to the new century by hiring the noted New York City architect R. J. Hardenbergh (who designed both the Waldorf-Astoria and the Park Hotel) to design a city estate of monumental proportions and architectural daring. Hardenbergh gave Moss exactly what he wanted: a huge three-story home of striking reddish-brown Lake Superior sandstone, with a magnificent Moorish-influenced interior designed by W. P. Nelson and Company of Chicago. When initially constructed, the mansion stood alone on the western boundaries of Billings, where it became a symbol of the town's new confidence in its future.[59]

Soon other prominent Billings businessmen, including Moss's partners I. D. O'Donnell and Henry Rowley, built new homes here as well, creating a neighborhood that physically represented the power and prestige of this new class of civic capitalists in Billings. After Moss, O'Donnell, and Rowley established the Billings Sugar Factory in 1905—a million-dollar industry that would dominate the county's economy for decades—there could be little doubt that the heart of the business community lay within this little group of homes on the newly platted west side of town.

Moss, O'Donnell, and Rowley may have lived outside of the city center created by the parallel tracks of the Burlington and the Northern Pacific, but they could not escape the power exercised by the corporate railroad network of James J. Hill on the future of Billings and the Clark's Fork Bottom. The impact of the Morgan-Hill alliance spread into the county proper in 1906–7, when Hill located, at nearby Laurel, the joint division point for the Great Northern, the Northern Pacific, and the Burlington railroads. By this time, explains the geographer John Hudson, Hill "had so consolidated his control over the Northern Pacific and Burlington that he needed a site for a large yard where the companies could interchange traffic." Billings had grown so large that it no longer had enough room for the rail yards, but Laurel, the little railroad town that had eclipsed the early hamlet of Canyon Creek, had plenty of room.[60]

The creation of the Laurel hub initiated a decade-long boom in Yellowstone County. In the spring of 1907 alone, Billings residents witnessed the construction of a $25,000 electric light plant, a $100,000

YMCA building, an $85,000 Masonic Temple, a $60,000 opera house, and a $40,000 addition to the Northern Hotel. Although the town shared traffic and operations with the new Laurel yards, Billings enjoyed a phenomenal increase in its number of rail passengers and permanent settlers. Billings became the largest and most prosperous city in the Yellowstone region, with its population reaching 10,031, a 211 percent increase in just ten years. "The growth of Billings has been the wonder of the state," admitted a regional history in 1907. "From the little struggling village it had always been, since the boom it has grown to be one of the principal cities of the state of Montana. It is again properly designated the 'Magic City.'"[61]

The growth altered the built environment of the town. A bold neoclassical-style county courthouse dominated the central city district between the tracks of the Burlington and the Northern Pacific. Many new small businesses had been established, including stores: five meat, three cigar, three grocery, three liquor, two hardware, and two candy. From 1905 to 1907, over a million dollars was spent in constructing new buildings. As a contemporary account emphasized: "All sorts of new enterprises have started in Billings. It has become a manufacturing center because of cheap water power; it has a large wholesale trade because of its location as a railroad center; [and] its always large agricultural shipments are increasing."[62]

The economic changes in the Yellowstone Valley over the thirty years from 1877 to 1907 had totally transformed the landscape. Where once there had been cottonwood log cabins, tents, and Indian tipis now stood two- and three-story brick and masonry buildings and fine Victorian-style residences. Shiny bands of steel crisscrossed the valley in place of the old rutted wagon roads and Indian trails. As the traces of the old frontier landscape disappeared, so too did the sense of economic independence. Distant corporate capitalists, who saw Billings as nothing more than a promising spot on the map, and new local capitalists, who made Billings their outpost for wealth and prominence, now worked together to effectively determine the course of the city's development. The "star of the Yellowstone" was, finally, "in the ascendant," and a new chapter in the history of Billings had been inaugurated.

Notes

◻

Commonly used abbreviations in footnote citations:

BCMSU: Merrill G. Burlingame Collections, Montana State University Library, Bozeman

MNHS: Minnesota Historical Society, St. Paul

MHS: Montana Historical Society, Helena

NA: National Archives, Washington, D.C.

NPR: Northern Pacific Railway Company Records, Minnesota Historical Society, St. Paul

PBL: Parmly Billings Library, Billings, Montana

WHC: Western Heritage Center, Billings, Montana

INTRODUCTION

1. Among the more accessible studies are George C. Frison, *Prehistoric Hunters of the High Plains* (New York: Academic Press, 1978); Lawrence Loendorf, "Prehistoric Settlement Patterns in the Pryor Mountains" (Ph.D diss., University of Missouri, 1973); William Mulloy, *The Hagen Site: A Prehistoric Village on the Lower Yellowstone* (Missoula: University of Montana, 1942); idem, "An Indian Village near Pompey's Pillar Creek, Montana," *Plains Anthropologist* 14, no.4, (1969): 95–102; and William B. Vincent, "The Late Prehistoric and Historic Periods in Northern Yellowstone County: A Comparison of Archaeological and Historical Evidence"

(Master's thesis, Washington State University, 1976). For short, insightful summaries, see C. Adrian Heidenreich, "The Native Americans' Yellowstone," *Montana: The Magazine of Western History* [hereinafter cited as *Montana*] 35 (Autumn 1985): 2–17, and Stuart Conner's dated but still useful "Prehistoric Man in the Yellowstone Valley," ibid. 14 (Spring 1964): 14–21.

2. The most important work on the Crows is that of Robert Lowie. See his *The Crow Indians* (New York: Farrar and Rinehart, 1935) and *Indians of the Plains* (Garden City, N.Y.: Natural History Press, 1963 [1954]). Other useful studies of the Crow include Norman B. Plummer, *Crow Indians* (New York: Garland, 1974); Joseph L. Cramer, "The Lean Site: An Historic Log Structure in Yellowstone County, Montana," *Plains Anthropologist* 6, no.14 (1961): 267–70; Rodney Frey, *The World of the Crow Indians: As Driftwood Lodges* (Norman: University of Oklahoma Press, 1987); Charles C. Bradley, Jr., *After the Buffalo Days*, vol. 1 (Lodge Grass, Mont.: Privately published, 1977); and Joe Medicine Crow, "The Effects of European Culture Contacts upon the Economic, Social, and Religious Life of the Crow Indians" (Master's thesis, University of Southern California, 1935).

3. Susan C. Vehik, "Late Prehistoric Plains Trade and Economic Specialization," *Plains Anthropologist* 35 (May 1990): 125–46; Donald J. Blakeslee, "The Plains Interband Trade System: An Ethnohistoric and Archaeological Investigation" (Ph.D. diss., University of Wisconsin, Milwaukee, 1975); Arthur J. Ray, "History and Archaeology of the Northern Fur Trade," *American Antiquity* 42 (January 1978): 26–34; idem, "Indians as Consumers in the Eighteenth Century," in *Old Trails and New Directions: Papers of the Third North American Fur Trade Conference*, ed. C. M. Judd and A. J. Ray (Toronto: University of Toronto Press, 1980), 255–71; idem, *Indians in the Fur Trade: Their Role as Trappers, Hunters, and Middlemen in the Lands Southwest of Hudson Bay, 1660–1870* (Toronto: University of Toronto Press, 1974); John C. Ewers, "Influence of the Fur Trade on Indians of the Northern Plains," in *People and Pelts: Selected Papers of the Second North American Fur Trade Conference*, ed. Malvina Bolus (Winnipeg: Peguis Publishers, 1972): 1–26; Charles E. Orser, Jr., "Trade Good Flow in Arikara Villages: Expanding Ray's 'Middleman Hypothesis,' " *Plains Anthropologist* 29 (February 1984): 1–12; Thomas F. Schilz, "Robes, Rum, and Rifles: Indian Middlemen in the Northern Plains Fur Trade," *Montana* 40 (Winter 1990): 2–13; W. Raymond Wood, "Plains Trade in Prehistoric and Protohistoric Intertribal Relations," in *Anthropology on the Great Plains*, ed. W. Raymond Wood and Margot Liberty (Lincoln: University of Nebraska Press, 1980), 98–109; David J. Wishart, *The Fur Trade of the Ameri-

can West, 1807–1840: A Geographical Synthesis (Lincoln: University of Nebraska Press, 1979); Keith Algier, "Robert Meldrum and the Crow Peltry Trade," Montana 36 (Summer 1986): 36–47. Although not directly related to the Yellowstone Valley region, the following two studies underscore the promise of a sensitive ethnohistorical approach to the economic relationships that defined the fur trade: Jennifer S. H. Brown, Strangers in Blood: Fur Trade Company Families in Indian Country (Vancouver: University of British Columbia Press, 1980), and Daniel Francis and Toby Morantz, Partners in Furs: A History of the Fur Trade in Eastern James Bay, 1600–1870 (Montreal: McGill-Queen's University Press, 1983).

4. Carroll Van West, "Coulson and the Clark's Fork Bottom: The Economic Structure of a Pre-Railroad Community, 1874–1881," Montana 35 (Autumn 1985): 42–55. For additional information on the early history of the valley, see William E. Lass, "Steamboats on the Yellowstone," ibid., 27–39; Clyde McLemore, "Fort Pease: The First Attempted Settlement in Yellowstone Valley," ibid. 2 (January 1952): 17–31; Colgate Hoyt, "'Roughing It Up the Yellowstone to Wonderland': An Account of a Trip through the Yellowstone Valley in 1878," ed. Carroll Van West, ibid. 36 (Spring 1986): 22–35; and Mark H. Brown, The Plainsmen of the Yellowstone: A History of the Yellowstone Basin (New York: G. P. Putnam, 1961).

5. West, "Coulson," 55; John C. Hudson, "Main Streets of the Yellowstone Valley: Town Building along the Northern Pacific in Montana," Montana 35 (Autumn 1985): 56–67; Carroll Van West, "Livingston: Railroad Town on the Yellowstone," ibid., 84–85; Walter A. Cameron, "Building the Northern Pacific in 1881," ibid. 33 (Summer 1983): 70–76; Waldo O. Kliewer, "The Foundations of Billings, Montana," Pacific Northwest Quarterly 31 (July 1940): 255–83; Lawrence Small, A Century of Politics on the Yellowstone (Billings: Rocky Mountain College, 1983), 20–21.

6. John M. Faragher, Sugar Creek: Life on the Illinois Prairie (New Haven: Yale University Press, 1986), 136. For similar-minded studies of the barter or "borrowing system," see Daniel H. Unser, Jr., "The Frontier Exchange Economy of the Lower Mississippi Valley in the Eighteenth Century," William and Mary Quarterly, 3d ser., 44 (April 1987): 165–92, and Christopher Clark, "The Household Economy, Market Exchange, and the Rise of Capitalism in the Connecticut Valley, 1800–1860," Journal of Social History 13 (Winter 1979): 169–90. For a collection of some of the best "new rural history" focusing on capitalistic evolution, and including an essay by Faragher on his Sugar Creek research, see Steven Hahn and Jonathan Prude, eds., The Countryside in the Age of Capitalistic Transformation (Chapel

Hill: University of North Carolina Press, 1985). On the development of in-land towns in the northern plains, see John C. Hudson, *Plains Country Towns* (Minneapolis: University of Minnesota Press, 1985), 26–38.

7. For the concept of civic capitalism, see John T. Cumbler, *A Social History of Economic Decline: Business, Politics, and Work in Trenton* (New Brunswick: Rutgers University Press, 1989), 3–5, 15. Lewis Atherton once observed, "Every country town had an inner circle whose own personal interests were so tightly interwoven with those of the community at large that one cannot determine where self-interest ended and public spirit began." See Atherton, *Main Street on the Middle Border* (Bloomington: Indiana University Press, 1954), 23.

8. For provocative interpretations of this transformation at the national level, see Martin J. Sklar, *The Corporate Reconstruction of American Capitalism, 1890–1916* (Cambridge: Cambridge University Press, 1988), especially chapter two, and Olivier Zunz, *Making America Corporate, 1870–1920* (Chicago: University of Chicago Press, 1990).

9. Duane A. Smith, *Rocky Mountain Mining Camps: The Urban Frontier* (Bloomington: Indiana University Press, 1967); Robert R. Dykstra, *The Cattle Towns* (New York: Knopf, 1968); Don H. Doyle, *The Social Order of a Frontier Community: Jacksonville, Illinois, 1825–1870* (Urbana: University of Illinois Press, 1978); Lawrence Larsen, *The Urban West at the End of the Frontier* (Lawrence: Regents Press of Kansas, 1978); John W. Reps, *Cities of the American West: A History of Frontier Urban Planning* (Princeton: Princeton University Press, 1979); Faragher, *Sugar Creek*; Kathleen Underwood, *Town Building on the Colorado Frontier* (Albuquerque: University of New Mexico Press, 1987); Timothy R. Mahoney, *River Towns in the Great West: The Structure of Provincial Urbanization in the American Midwest, 1820–1870* (Cambridge: Cambridge University Press, 1990).

10. Carl Abbott, "Frontiers and Sections: Cities and Regions in American Growth," in *American Urbanism: A Historiographical Review*, ed. Howard Gillette, Jr., and Zane L. Miller (Westport, Conn.: Greenwood Press, 1987): 278–79; Hudson, *Plains Country Towns*; Paula M. Nelson, *After the West Was Won: Homesteaders and Town-Builders in Western South Dakota, 1900–1917* (Iowa City: University of Iowa Press, 1986).

CHAPTER I

1. Brown, *Plainsmen*, 29; Meriwether Lewis, *History of the Expedition under the Command of Lewis and Clark*, Elliott Coues, ed., 3 vols. (New York:

York: Dover Books, 1965 [1893]), 3:1168–69. For Larocque's complete narrative, see W. Raymond Wood and Thomas D. Thiessen, eds., *Early Fur Trade on the Northern Plains: The Narratives of John Macdonell, David Thompson, Francois-Antoine Larocque, and Charles McKenzie* (Norman: University of Oklahoma Press, 1985).

2. I took the tribal name "Apsaa looke" from Frey's sensitive study *World of the Crow Indians*, 27–28.

3. G. Hubert Smith, *The Explorations of the La Vérendryes in the Northern Plains, 1738–43*, ed. W. Raymond Wood (Lincoln: University of Nebraska Press, 1980), 126, contains a map that details how historians have recreated the La Vérendrye route. Also see John W. Smurr, "A New La Vérendrye Theory," *Pacific Northwest Quarterly* 43 (January 1952): 51–64.

4. John C. Ewers, *Indian Life in the Upper Missouri* (Norman: University of Oklahoma Press, 1968), 20.

5. Ewers, "Influence of the Fur Trade," 2, summarizes some of the early conclusions. Donald J. Blakeslee's excellent dissertation, "The Plains Interband Trade System," is a thorough exploration of the topic.

6. Wood, "Plains Trade," 99–101; Frey, *World of the Crow Indians*, 12; William Wildschut, *Crow Indian Medicine Bundles* (New York: Museum of the American Indian, Heye Foundation, 1960), 109, 169.

7. R. Douglas Hurt called the Mandans and Hidatsas "the most agricultural people in this region." *Indian Agriculture: Prehistory to the Present* (Lawrence: University of Kansas Press, 1987), 58–61. Gilbert Wilson's *Buffalo Bird Woman's Garden* (St. Paul: Minnesota Historical Society Press, 1987 [1917]) is an excellent description of Hidatsa horticultural practices, told by an Indian woman born in about 1839. For an analysis of the relationship between the hunting and the horticultural tribes, see Preston Holder, *The Hoe and the Horse on the Plains: A Study of Cultural Development among North American Indians* (Lincoln: University of Nebraska Press, 1970).

8. Joe Medicine Crow, "The Crow Migration Story," *Archaeology in Montana* 20 (September-December 1979): 63–72; C. Adrian Heidenreich, "The Bearing of Ethnohistoric Data on the Crow-Hidatsa Separation," ibid., 87–111; Heidenreich, "Native Americans' Yellowstone," 7. Archaeological site reports include Mulloy, *Hagen Site*, and idem, "Indian Village near Pompey's Pillar Creek." A good summary of the debate is Frey, *World of the Crow Indians*, 10–12.

9. Lowie, *Crow Indians*, 274–96, contains an excellent description of the Crow tobacco society.

10. Hurt, *Indian Agriculture*, 62; Wood, "Plains Trade," 100.

11. Brown, *Plainsmen*, 15; Paul C. Phillips, *The Fur Trade*, 2 vols. (Norman: University of Oklahoma Press, 1961), 2: 234–35; John A. Alwin, "Pelts, Provisions, and Perceptions: The Hudson's Bay Company Mandan Indian Trade, 1795–1812," *Montana* 29 (Summer 1979): 17–22.

12. On the subject of the middleman in the fur trade, see Ray, "Northern Fur Trade"; Orser, "Trade Good Flow"; and Schilz, "Robes, Rum, and Rifles."

13. Larocque quoted in Brown, *Plainsmen*, 45; Wishart, *Fur Trade of the American West*, 29.

14. Arthur J. Ray and Donald Freeman, *"Give Us Good Measure": An Economic Analysis of Relations between the Indians and the Hudson's Bay Company* (Toronto: University of Toronto Press, 1978). Ewers discusses the Mandans' middleman role in the Crow trade in "Influence of the Fur Trade," 2–4. Also see Ray, "Indians as Consumers."

15. As a tribal historian later observed, the Crows "were very shrewd traders but were very poor users of money." Medicine Crow, "Effects of European Culture Contacts," 26.

16. Reuben G. Thwaites, ed., *Original Journals of the Lewis and Clark Expedition*, 8 vols. (New York: Arno Press, 1969 [1904–05]), 7:250; Brown, *Plainsmen*, 32–36; Jerome O. Steffen, "William Clark: A Reappraisal," *Montana* 25 (Spring 1975): 52–61; Ernest S. Osgood, "Clark on the Yellowstone, 1806," ibid. 18 (Summer 1968): 8–29.

17. Cited in Phillips, *Fur Trade* 2:257.

18. Ibid., 259–60; Thwaites, *Lewis and Clark Expedition*, 7:360; Burton Harris, *John Colter: His Years in the Rockies* (Basin, Wyo.: Big Horn Book Company, 1977 [1952]), 59–72; Merrill G. Burlingame, *The Montana Frontier* (Helena: State Publishing Company, 1942), 9.

19. Wishart, *Fur Trade of the American West*, 29; Richard E. Oglesby, *Manuel Lisa and the Opening of the Missouri Fur Trade* (Norman: University of Oklahoma Press, 1963), 192.

20. Oglesby, *Manuel Lisa*, 120–21.

21. Ibid., 54, 56; Phillips, *Fur Trade* 2:260.

22. Oglesby, *Manuel Lisa*, 55; Phillips, *Fur Trade* 2:260–61; Harris, *John Colter*, 82–114.

23. James P. Ronda, *Lewis and Clark among the Indians* (Lincoln: University of Nebraska Press, 1984), 238–45, is an excellent account of the Two Medicine fight and its consequences.

24. Phillips, *Fur Trade* 2:262–64, 390; John C. Ewers, *The Blackfeet: Raiders on the Northwestern Plains* (Norman: University of Oklahoma Press,

1958), 49–51; Wishart, *Fur Trade of the American West,* 46; Oglesby, *Manuel Lisa,* 117–18, 145–46.

25. Quotation in Phillips, *Fur Trade* 2:393; John E. Sunder, *Joshua Pilcher: Fur Trader and Indian Agent* (Norman: University of Oklahoma Press, 1968), 33–36.

26. Oglesby, *Manuel Lisa,* 172, 186–87; Brown, *Plainsmen,* 62–63: Phillips, *Fur Trade* 2:393–95; Ewers, *Blackfeet,* 53–54; Sunder, *Joshua Pilcher,* 40–41.

27. Richard M. Clokey, *William H. Ashley: Enterprise and Politics in the Trans-Mississippi West* (Norman: University of Oklahoma Press, 1980), 75; Wishart, *Fur Trade of the American West,* 49; Oglesby, *Manuel Lisa,* 188–89; Philips, *Fur Trade* 2:396. Also see the following biographies: Leroy R. Hafen, *Broken Hand: The Life of Thomas Fitzpatrick, Mountain Man, Guide, and Indian Agent* (Lincoln: University of Nebraska Press, 1973 [1931]); Dale L. Morgan, *Jedediah Smith and the Opening of the West* (Lincoln: University of Nebraska Press, 1953); John E. Sunder, *Bill Sublette: Mountain Man* (Norman: University of Oklahoma Press, 1959).

28. On the Arikara as middlemen, see Orser, "Trade Good Flow." An insightful account on the Arikara affair is Charles E. Orser, Jr., "Understanding Arikara Trading Behavior: A Cultural Case Study of the Ashley-Leavenworth Episode of 1823," in *Rendezvous: Selected Papers of the Fourth North American Fur Trade Conference, 1981,* ed. Thomas C. Buckley (St. Paul: Minnesota Historical Society Press, 1984), 101–8. A full exploration of the tribe's involvement in the plains trade is James J. Berry, "Arikara Middlemen: The Effects of Trade on an Upper Missouri Society" (Ph.D. diss., Indiana University, 1978).

29. Phillips, *Fur Trade* 2:396; Clokcy, *William H. Ashley,* 64, 134; Wishart, *Fur Trade of the American West,* 122–23; Sunder, *Bill Sublette,* 39–58; Morgan, *Jedediah Smith,* 64–95; Hafen, *Broken Hand,* 13–30.

30. Wishart, *Fur Trade of the American West,* 125; Leroy R. Hafen, ed., *Mountain Men and Fur Traders of the Far West* (Lincoln: University of Nebraska Press, 1982), is an informative introduction to the world of the mountain men and includes eighteen biographies.

31. The classic interpretation of the free trappers is William H. Goetzmann, "The Mountain Man as Jacksonian Man," *American Quarterly* 15 (Fall 1963): 402–15. A more complex reality is revealed in William O. Swagerty, "Marriage and Settlement Patterns of Rocky Mountain Trappers and Traders," *Western Historical Quarterly* 11 (April 1980): 159–80. "The fur trade," Swagerty observed, "was a reciprocal system which had to be bicultural and symbiotic in order to succeed in any given region of the West"

(179). Also see the differing perceptions of the geographer Wishart, *Fur Trade of the American West*, 206, and the historian Ray Allen Billington, *The Far Western Frontier, 1803–1860* (New York: Harper and Row, 1956), 41–55.

32. Phillips, *Fur Trade* 2:402–8, 417–20; Erwin N. Thompson, *Fort Union Trading Post: Fur Trade Empire on the Upper Missouri* (Medora, N.D.: Theodore Roosevelt Nature and History Association, 1986), 3–4, 10–12; Billington, *Far Western Frontier*, 56–57. The National Park Service has rebuilt Fort Union, basing its reconstruction on painstaking historic archaeological research.

33. Thompson, *Fort Union*, 15–16. Also see William J. Hunt, Jr., "The Fort Union Reconstruction Archaeology Project," *CRM Bulletin* 12, no.1, (1989): 2–4; Mary S. Culpin and Richard Borjes, "The Architecture of Fort Union: A Symbol of Dominance," in *Rendezvous: Selected Papers of the Fourth North American Fur Trade Conference*, ed. Thomas C. Buckley, 135–40, with the quote appearing on p.135.

34. Stanley Vestal, *Jim Bridger: Mountain Man* (Lincoln: University of Nebraska Press, 1970 [1946]), 68–69; Billington, *Far Western Frontier*, 57–58; Hafen, *Mountain Men*, 255–56.

35. Wishart, *Fur Trade of the American West*, 153–55; William H. Goetzmann, *Exploration and Empire: The Explorer and the Scientist in the Winning of the American West* (New York: Knopf, 1967), 165; Hafen, *Mountain Men*, 272–84, 313–26.

36. Sunder, *Bill Sublette*, 114–49; Billington, *Far Western Frontier*, 63–64.

37. Lewis O. Saum, *The Fur Trader and the Indian* (Seattle: University of Washington Press, 1965), 28, 39.

38. Cited in Heidenreich, "Native Americans' Yellowstone," 3, and Brown, *Plainsmen*, 17.

39. Everett Dick, *Vanguards of the Frontier* (Lincoln: University of Nebraska Press, 1965 [1941]), 5–6; Ewers, "Influence of the Fur Trade," 6–7; Saum, *Fur Trader and the Indian*, 213; Edwin T. Denig, *Five Indian Tribes of the Upper Missouri: Sioux, Arickaras, Assiniboines, Crees, Crows*, ed. John C. Ewers (Norman: University of Oklahoma Press, 1961), 204; James P. Beckwourth, *The Life and Adventures of James P. Beckwourth*, ed. T. D. Bonner (Minneapolis: Ross and Haines, 1965 [1856]), 365.

40. Wishart, *Fur Trade of the American West*, 60–61; Keith Algier, "Robert Meldrum," 42.

41. Wishart, *Fur Trade of the American West*, 58, 97; David Dary, *Entrepreneurs of the Old West* (New York: Knopf, 1986), 68–75.

42. Wishart, *Fur Trade of the American West*, 97; Lowie, *Crow Indians*, 77.

43. Dary, *Entrepreneurs*, 72–73.
44. Wishart, *Fur Trade of the American West*, 163–64, 187–88; Michael Malone and Richard Roeder, *Montana: A History of Two Centuries* (Seattle: University of Washington Press, 1976), 44–45; Hafen, *Montain Men*, 258–61; Vestal, *Jim Bridger*, 134–41; Heidenreich, "Native Americans' Yellowstone," 9.
45. Wishart, *Fur Trade of the American West*, 31.
46. Ewers, *Blackfeet*, 65–66; Ewers, "Influence of the Fur Trade," 20; Malone and Roeder, *Montana*, 47; Frey, *World of the Crow Indians*, 30; Frank B. Linderman, *Pretty-shield: Medicine Woman of the Crows* (Lincoln: University of Nebraska Press, 1972 [1932]), 45. Also see Alfred W. Crosby, *Ecological Imperialism: The Biological Expansion of Europe, 900–1900* (Cambridge: Cambridge University Press, 1986), for an excellent synthesis on this topic. His "Virgin Soil Epidemics as a Factor in the Aboriginal Depopulation in America," *William and Mary Quarterly*, 3d. ser., 33 (April 1976): 289–99, is a concise summary of his early findings.
47. John E. Sunder, *The Fur Trade on the Upper Missouri, 1840–1865* (Norman: University of Oklahoma Press, 1965), 55, 60, 94, 194.
48. Ibid., 126, 162, 164, 196; Thompson, *Fort Union*, 86–88.
49. Algier, "Robert Meldrum," analyzes Meldrum's evolving relationship with the Crows from the 1830s to the time of the Civil War.
50. Both quotations in Saum, *Fur Trader and the Indian*, 5; Algier, "Robert Meldrum," 43–44; Sunder, *Fur Trade*, 198; William F. Raynolds, *Exploration of the Yellowstone River* (Washington: Government Printing Office, 1868), 47–53.
51. "Fort Sarpy Journal, 1855–56," *Contributions to the Historical Society of Montana*, vol. 10 (Helena: Montana Historical Society, 1940), 115.
52. Goetzmann, *Exploration and Empire*, 311, 418; Brown, *Plainsmen*, 111–22; Phillips, *Fur Trade* 2:398; Sunder, *Fur Trade*, 174, 204.
53. Raynolds, *Exploration of the Yellowstone*, 47–48.
54. Ibid., 50–51.
55. Ibid., 53.
56. Wishart, *Fur Trade of the American West*, 215; John W. Stafford, "Crow Culture Change: A Geographical Analysis" (Ph.D. diss., Michigan State University, 1971), 88–90, contains an excellent discussion of the impact of the fur trade on the Crows.

CHAPTER 2

1. E. S. Topping, *Chronicles of the Yellowstone* (St. Paul: Pioneer Press, 1883), 28; Letter of March 15, 1865, by D. B. Weaver, cited in *An Illustrated History of Yellowstone Valley* (Spokane: Western Historical Publishing Com-

pany, 1907), 120–21. A map, "diagram showing site of Yellowstone City," in the MHS collections gives a layout of the placer mines, dwellings, and stores.

2. Topping, *Chronicles*, 29–30; *Illustrated History*, 123; John J. and Margaret Tomlinson, Logbooks, 1864, Iowa State Historical Society Collections, Iowa City.

3. For useful studies on the Bozeman Trail, see Merrill G. Burlingame, *John M. Bozeman: Montana Trailmaker* (Bozeman: Gallatin County Tribune, 1971); Dorothy M. Johnson, *The Bloody Bozeman* (New York: McGraw-Hill, 1971); Burton S. Hill, "Bozeman and the Bozeman Trail," *Annals of Wyoming* 36 (October 1964): 205–33; Robert A. Murray, *The Bozeman Trail: Highway of History* (Boulder: Pruett Publishing Company, 1988); and Susan Badger Doyle, "Journeys to the Land of Gold: Emigrants on the Bozeman Trail, 1863–1866," *Montana* 41 (Autumn 1991): 54–67. On the expansion of the Sioux in the Yellowstone country, see Richard White, "The Winning of the West: The Expansion of the Western Sioux in the Eighteenth and Nineteenth Century," *Journal of American History* 65 (September 1978): 319–43.

4. William K. Thomas Diary, Small Collections, MHS; Murray, *Bozeman Trail*, 45–47, 51–54, 56, 63–67, 75; Malone and Roeder, *Montana*, 95–97; Robert M. Utley, *The Indian Frontier of the American West, 1846–1890* (Albuquerque: University of New Mexico Press, 1984), 99–101, 104–5, 109–12, 118–20; Thomas W. Dunlay, *Wolves for the Blue Soldiers: Indian Scouts and Auxiliaries with the United States Army, 1860–90* (Lincoln: University of Nebraska Press, 1982), 39–40.

5. *Illustrated History*, 123–24; Murray, *Bozeman Trail*, 71; Brown, *Plainsmen*, 428–29; Thomas H. Leforge, *Memoirs of a White Crow Indian*, ed. Thomas B. Marquis (Lincoln: University of Nebraska Press, 1974 [1928]), 32, 71–72.

6. Leforge, *White Crow Indian*, 170; the close relationship between Leforge and Cherry is described on pp. 31–70.

7. Ibid., 63.

8. Ibid., 63–64.

9. Brown, *Plainsmen*, 429; *Centennial Scrapbook: Livingston, 1882–1982* (Livingston, Mont.: Livingston Enterprise, 1982), 12; *Illustrated History*, 126–27; Topping, *Chronicles*, 71, 99, 126; Park County *News*, March 3, 1955; Leforge, *White Crow Indian*, 42; Linderman, *Pretty-shield*, 136; Peter Nabokov, *Two Leggings: The Making of a Crow Warrior* (Lincoln: University of Nebraska Press, 1967), 76.

10. *Illustrated History,* 127; Michael A. Leeson, ed., *History of Montana, 1739–1885* (Chicago: Warner, Beers and Company, 1885), 532; Brown, *Plainsmen,* 336; Leforge, *White Crow Indian,* 45.

11. Ernest S. Osgood, *The Day of the Cattleman* (Minneapolis: University of Minnesota Press, 1929), 73; Louis T. Renz, *The History of the Northern Pacific Railroad* (Fairfield, Wash.: Ye Galleon Press, 1980), 46–50.

12. Addison M. Quivey, "The Yellowstone Expedition of 1874," *Contributions to the Historical Society of Montana,* vol. 1 (Helena: Montana Historical Society, 1876), 268–69; Bozeman *Avant Courier,* January 24, 1874.

13. Lass, "Steamboats on the Yellowstone," 27–30; Charles W. Bryan, Jr., "Dr. Lamme and His Gallant Little Yellowstone," *Montana* 15 (Summer 1965): 25–27, 38; Brown, *Plainsmen,* 203; Jerry Keenan, "Yellowstone Kelly: From New York to Paradise," *Montana* 40 (Summer 1990): 19.

14. The broadside has been reprinted in Merrill Burlingame, *Gallatin County's Heritage* (Bozeman: Gallatin County Historical Society, 1976), 40; Quivey, "Yellowstone Expedition," 283. Mark Brown argued that the expedition members "were pawns in the schemes of others," especially Territorial Governor Benjamin Potts, to instigate a war with the Native Americans. Brown, *Plainsmen,* 211–16.

15. Topping, *Chronicles,* 135–41; Brown, *Plainsmen,* 220–25; McLemore, "Fort Pease," 17–19; Lass, "Steamboats on Yellowstone," 27.

16. McLemore, "Fort Pease," 17, 22. On the organization of the landscape, see Mahoney, *River Towns in the Great West,* 4–5, 52–53.

17. Frank B. Linderman, *Plenty-coups: Chief of the Crows* (Lincoln: University of Nebraska Press, 1962 [1930]), 293–95.

18. *Centennial Scrapbook: Livingston,* 11–12; Brown, *Plainsmen,* 432–35; Topping, *Chronicles,* 126.

19. Bradley, *After the Buffalo Days,* 5; Leforge, *White Crow Indian,* 110–111.

20. Stafford, "Crow Culture," 97–98, 101; Leforge, *White Crow Indian,* 44, 57; Montana Historical Society, Crow Indian Collection, Accession numbers: x65.13.01, x82.18.10, x82.28.19, and x82.28.25.

21. Brown, *Plainsmen,* 435, contains Clapp's quote; Leforge, *White Crow Indian,* 203–4.

22. Burton M. Smith, "Politics and the Crow Indian Land Cessions, 1851–1904," *Montana* 36 (Autumn 1986): 25, 27–28; Heidenreich, "Native Americans' Yellowstone," 15.

23. Chief Blackfoot quoted in Smith, "Crow Indian Land Cessions," 28–30.

24. Brown, *Plainsmen,* 434; Smith, "Crow Indian Land Cessions," 30.

25. Smith, "Crow Indian Land Cessions," 30.

26. Chief Blackfoot quoted in Dunlay, *Wolves for the Blue Soldiers*, 113–14; Leforge, *White Crow Indian*, 206–8; Nabokov, *Two Leggings*, 187.

27. Robert M. Utley, *Frontier Regulars: The U. S. Army and the Indians, 1866–1891* (New York: Macmillan, 1973), 249–69.

28. Ibid. Also see Utley, *Indian Frontier*, 184, and idem, *Cavalier in Buckskin: George Armstrong Custer and the Western Military Frontier* (Norman: University of Oklahoma Press, 1988), 165–93; Loyd J. Overfield II, comp. *The Little Big Horn, 1876.* (1971; reprint, Lincoln: University of Nebraska Press, 1990); John S. Gray, *Custer's Last Campaign: Mitch Boyer and the Little Bighorn Reconstructed* (Lincoln: University of Nebraska Press, 1991); and Jerome A. Greene, *Yellowstone Command: Colonel Nelson A. Miles and the Great Sioux War, 1876–1877* (Lincoln: University of Nebraska Press, 1991).

29. For an authoritative overview of Forts Keogh and Custer, see Robert M. Utley, "War Houses in the Sioux Country: The Military Occupation of the Lower Yellowstone," *Montana* 35 (Autumn 1985): 18–25. The recommendation for a post at the mouth of the Tongue River dates to Lieutenant Colonel F. D. Grant to Lieutenant General P. H. Sheridan, June 23, 1875, Yellowstone River and Valley, 1875 Military Expedition, MHS Microfilm Collections.

30. Fort Keogh, MT (1876–1908), Records of United States Army Commands, Record Group 98, NA; "Fort Keogh, MT," National Register of Historic Places Nomination Form, State Historic Preservation Office, Helena, Mont.

31. George M. Miles Diary, Small Collections, MHS, 65–68; *Illustrated History*, 343; Topping, *Chronicles*, 197.

32. Miles Diary, MHS, 65–68; *Illustrated History*, 333; Opheim (Mont.) *Observer*, August 31, 1923.

33. Sherman's quote is cited in Utley, "War Houses," 19. Brisbin's quote is cited in *Office of the President, Northern Pacific Railroad Company, to Committee on the Judiciary, House of Representatives, July 6, 1882* (New York: Northern Pacific Railroad, 1882), 3. In that same pamphlet, General John Gibbon observed, "From 1870, when I first went to Montana, till 1876, that whole region was an almost unknown wilderness, where it was not safe for any but large and well-organized parties of white men to go" (4).

34. Brown, *Plainsmen*, 316–18; "General Orders No. 101, War Department, November 8, 1877," Record Group 98, NA.

35. Colonel O. M. Poe, Diary, July 25, 1877, cited in *Reports of Inspection Made in the Summer of 1877 by Generals P. H. Sheridan and W. T. Sherman of*

the Country North of the Union Pacific Railroad (Washington: Government Printing Office, 1878), 66.

36. W. T. Sherman to George W. McCrary, August 3, 1877, cited in ibid., 31; Bozeman *Avant Courier*, October 17, 1878; Stuart quote cited in Agnes L. Jones, *Crow Country* (Billings: Rocky Mountain College Print Shop, n.d.), 14; Mahoney, *River Towns of the Great West*, 32–36.

37. Robert Hine's observation that a community must have a "sense of place," be small enough for "face-to-face relations" and have "shared binding values" is certainly true for the Coulson/Clark Fork's Bottom area during these years. Robert V. Hine, *Community on the American Frontier* (Norman: University of Oklahoma Press, 1980), 32.

38. Helen Braum, "Life on the Yellowstone," unpublished typescript, BCMSU, 2; "Joseph M. V. Cochran," in O'Donnell, comp., "Montana Monographs," PBL; Yellowstone County, Montana, Homestead Tract Books of the General Land Office, 1878–82, National Records Center, Suitland, Md.; Bozeman *Avant Courier*, August 8, 1877; Billings *Gazette*, November 6, 1921, July 24, 1932, and April 18, 1991; *Illustrated History*, 269–71. The tendency to settle initially along the Yellowstone fit a well-established pattern on the Missouri and Mississippi rivers; see Mahoney, *River Towns of the Great West*, 47–48.

39. Bozeman *Avant Courier*, June 28, 1877. The government did not always play a positive role. In 1879, it forced Cochran and other early settlers to relinquish their homesteads in the Bottom. By mistake, they had been allowed to claim land already alloted as school land, and new claims had to be filed again. Joseph Cochran file, Coulson Biographies, WHC; Billings *Gazette*, April 18, 1991.

40. P. W. McAdow to L. Hershfield and Bro., July 1, 31, 1877, Merchants National Bank Collection, MHS; Leeson, *History of Montana*, 1142; Delores Morrow, "Our Sawdust Roots: A History of the Forest Products Industry in Montana," unpublished typescript, MHS, 9; Bozeman *Avant Courier*, July 26, 1877; K. Ross Toole, "Perry W. McAdow and Montana in 1861–1862," *Montana* 2 (January 1952): 41–53; Robert G. Dunbar, "The Economic Development of the Gallatin Valley," *Pacific Northwest Quarterly* 47 (October 1956): 118; Lewis H. Carpenter, July 2, 1877, and George W. Frost, August 9 and October 3, 1877 to P. W. McAdow, Crow Indian Agency Records, MHS.

41. Fred G. Bond, *Flatboating on the Yellowstone, 1877* (New York: New York Public Library, 1925), 4; Brown, *Plainsmen*, 182; John Opie, *The Law of the Land: Two Hundred Years of American Farmland Policy* (Lincoln: Univer-

sity of Nebraska Press, 1987), 105; John T. Ganoe, "Desert Land Act in Operation 1877–1891," *Agricultural History* 11 (April 1937): 142–57; Billings *Gazette*, July 24, 1932; Bozeman *Avant Courier*, September 19, 1878. As John Faragher noted in his study of Sugar Creek, Illinois, frontier entrepreneurs realized that "transportation development offered the best way to break into the market economy." Faragher, *Sugar Creek*, 178.

42. P. W. McAdow to Martin Maginnis, March 14, 1877, Martin Maginnis Papers, MHS.

43. In 1891 the federal government awarded Cochran $654.50 for the damages to his homestead, but Congress never formally appropriated the funds, and he never received any money. Billings *Gazette*, April 18, 1991.

44. Utley, *Frontier Regulars*, 310; Francis Haines, *The Nez Perces: Tribesmen of the Columbia Plateau* (Norman: University of Oklahoma Press, 1955), 299–304; Topping, *Chronicles*, 221–22; "Mrs. Alice Shock" and "Joseph M. V. Cochran," in O'Donnell, comp., "Montana Monographs," PBL; Utley, *Indian Frontier*, 189–91.

45. P. W. McAdow to L. Hershfield and Bro., November 13, 1877, Merchants National Bank Collection, MHS.

CHAPTER 3

1. Billings *Gazette*, September 30, 1928; Topping, *Chronicles*, 230; Waldo O. Kliewer, "The Foundations of Billings Montana," (Master's thesis, University of Washington, 1938), 3. On earlier competition between small settlements for transportation links, see Faragher, *Sugar Creek*, 177–78, and Mahoney, *River Towns of the Great West*, 110–28.

2. Bozeman *Avant Courier*, December 6, 1877, and January 3, 1878; Bryan, "Dr. Lamme," 42–43; Alonzo J. Young house, MHS Photo Archives, 945–51.

3. P. W. McAdow to Martin Maginnis, February 7, 1878, Maginnis Papers, MHS; Bozeman *Avant Courier*, February 14 and April 11, 1878; Billings *Gazette*, July 24, 1932; "Mrs. Alice Shock," in O'Donnell, comp., "Montana Monographs," PBL; Alice R. Shock file, Coulson Biographies, WHC.

4. Hudson, *Plains Country Towns*, 34.

5. Billings *Gazette*, April 2, 1907; Bozeman *Avant Courier*, April 11 and October 3, 1878, and March 6, 1890; Deer Lodge (Mont.) *New Northwest*, January 28, 1881.

6. "Forest Young" and "John Kinney," in O'Donnell, comp., "Montana Monographs," PBL; Bozeman *Avant Courier*, October 17, 1878.

7. Newman told his life story in the Billings *Gazette*, October 6, 1899; "Notes from the Newman Family Bible," Orson N. Newman Papers, BCMSU. Bil-

lings *Gazette*, December 13, 1921, contains Newman's obituary, which has some useful information but also has several errors. Patricia Nelson Limerick, *The Legacy of Conquest: The Unbroken Past of the American West* (New York: Norton, 1987), 152.

8. "Mary Newman Scott," Montana Monographs, PBL.

9. McAdow quoted in Richard Clarke file, PBL; Coulson Biographies, WHC; White Sulpher Springs (Mont.) *Rocky Mountain Husbandman*, December 7, 1939; Roy M. Crismas Scrapbook, MHS, 45; Bozeman *Avant Courier*, March 28, 1878; 1880 Census, Custer County, Montana Territory, NA; "Mrs. R. W. Clarke," Montana Pioneers Collection, MHS; Lamme quoted in R. W. Clarke, "The Bozeman Trail," Montana Monographs, PBL; Bryan, "Dr. Lamme," 38.

10. Leeson, *History of Montana*, 1364; *Illustrated History*, 271; John J. Alderson to P. W. McAdow, January 16, 1879, Maginnis Papers, MHS.

11. Bozeman *Avant Courier*, March 21 and October 17, 1878; Crismas Scrapbook, MHS; 1880 Census, Custer County, Montana Territory, NA; Coulson Biographies, WHC.

12. Coulson Files, PBL; 1877 Custer County Tax List, MHS. The author's calculations indicate the following: in the tax year 1877, there were 112 taxpayers paying a total of $3,452.53 in taxes, with a mean tax of $30.83. If the top 5 taxpayers are eliminated from the tax year 1877, the number of taxpayers was 107, paying a total of $1,668.64 with a mean tax of $15.59. The top 5 taxpayers were: O'Toole & Co., $900.00; H. R. Ninniger, $250.78; Matt Carroll & Co., $246.29; L. M. Black, $232.43 and Paul McCormick & Co., $154.39. These 5 compose 4.5 percent of the taxable population.

13. For a comparative discussion of "the mixture of private and communal that characterized the backcountry economy," see Faragher, *Sugar Creek*, 136.

14. 1878 Custer County Tax List, MHS. The author based his calculations on the following: There were 236 taxpayers, taxed for a total of $8,138.60. Once the top 10 taxpayers were eliminated, there were 226 taxpayers, assessed $3,702.29. The top 10 were Broadwater, Hubbell, & Co., $1,692.82; Morris Cohn, $219.47; William Grimes, $178.47; Jordan & Leighton, $131.53; Paul McCormick & Co., $379.39; P. W. McAdow, $125.42; H. R. Ninniger, $212.00; William O'Toole, $873.50; Donald Stephens, $519.08; and Tingley & Bros, $104.95. The McAdow brothers paid $375.30 in Gallatin County taxes. Bozeman *Avant Courier*, December 5, 1878.

15. 1879 Custer County Tax List. With the top 15 taxpayers eliminated, 308 people paid $3,928.92 in taxes, an average of $12.76. The top 15 taxpayers in 1879 were Thos. Burns, $99.82; Julius Basinski, $185.02; D. Burford,

$193.65; Ellis & Co., $336.09; J. B. Hubbell, $1,314.77; McGirl & Hoskins, $87.82; Jordan & Leighton, $155.92; G. W. Miles, $98.29; P. W. McAdow, $137.60; W. D. O'Toole Co., $1,148.45; H. H. Orschel, $159.00; Quigley Bros., $119.29; William Van Gasken, $74.17; Daniel Lebeben, $86.40; and Ninninger & Co., $669.29. In 1880, 421 people were assessed $12,915.25, an average of $30.68 per taxpayer. If the top 19 (who compose 4.5 percent of the taxable population, owning 50.3 percent of the taxable wealth) are eliminated, 402 people were assessed $6,420.05, an average of $15.97. The top 19 taxpayers were Broadwater, Hubbell & Co., $2,220.91; Julius Basinski, $154.60; D. Burford, $107.34; W. H. Burleigh, $166.12; Walter Cooper, $224.40; T. L. Dawes, $244.58; J. Ellis, $168.03; John Graham, $193.26; McGirl & Hoskins, $192.60; James McFarland, $170.51; P. W. McAdow, $145.36; G. W. Miles, $96.30; Ninninger & Co., $1,312.28; W. D. O'Toole & Co., $401.00; Issac Orschel, $268.34; Leighton & Jordan, $118.37; I. O. Sherell, $102.69; William Van Gasken, $120.79; and L. C. Silverman: $89.04.

16. Bozeman *Avant Courier*, January 2, 1879 and February 12, 1880; Leeson, *History of Montana*, 532, 973; Glendolin Damon Wagner and William A. Allen, *Blankets and Moccasins: Plenty Coups and His People, the Crows* (Lincoln: University of Nebraska Press, 1987 [1933]), 21.

17. Richard Clarke file, PBL.

18. Affidavit of Milton M. Russell, June 6, 1878, Letters Received by the Office of Indian Affairs, 1824–1880, Montana Superintendency, 1879, NA; H. C. Bulis to E. A. Hayt, December 22, 1878, Letters Received by Commissioner of Indian Affairs, Office of Indian Affairs, 1878–1881, NA; George W. Frost to Perry W. McAdow, August 9 and October 3, 1877, Crow Indian Agency Records, MHS; Horace Countryman, September 15, 1877, T. J. Dawes, September 18, 1877, L. M. Black, September 18, 1877, to George W. Frost, and bids from Black, Dawes, Countryman, Harvey Rea, and Lester E. Willson, File 275, Office of Indian Affairs Records, NA.

19. Bradley, *After the Buffalo Days*, 8; A. R. Keller to Capt. E. C. Gilbreath, December 31, 1879, Crow Indian Agency Records, MHS; David Kern to E. A. Hayt, October 29, 1878, File 253, Office of Indian Affairs Records, NA; A. R. Keller to E. A. Hayt, February 2, and to R. E. Trowbridge, August 2, 1880, Letters Received by Commissioner of Indian Affairs, NA; Leforge, *White Crow Indian*, 60.

20. A. R. Keller to R. E. Trowbridge, April 19 and October 24, 1880, to E. J. Brooks, March 8, 1880, and Keller's "Estimate for Stationery," November 21, 1879, Letters Received by Commissioner of Indian Affairs, NA; Bozeman *Avant Courier*, February 26, 1880; Stafford, "Crow Culture," 101–2.

On the general question of Indian reform in the 1870s and 1880s, see Frederick E. Hoxie, *A Final Promise: The Campaign to Assimilate the Indians, 1880–1920* (Lincoln: University of Nebraska Press, 1984), 16–21, 41–81; Francis P. Prucha, *The Great Father: The United States Government and the American Indians*, 2 vols. (Lincoln: University of Nebraska Press, 1984), 2:611–58; and Loring B. Priest, *Uncle Sam's Stepchildren: The Reformation of United States Indian Policy, 1865–1887* (New York: Octagon Books, 1969 [1942]). For the use of architecture as a tool of acculturation, see my essay "Acculturation by Design: Architectural Determinism and the Montana Indian Reservations, 1870–1930," *Great Plains Quarterly* 7 (Spring 1987): 91–102.

21. A. R. Keller to E. A. Hayt, February 2 and March 2, 1880, to Commissioner of Indian Affairs, February 14 and 23, 1880, and to R. G. Trowbridge, April 1, 14, and 27, 1880, Letters Received by Commissioner of Indian Affairs, NA.

22. A. R. Keller to R. E. Trowbridge, July 20, 1880, ibid.; Horace Countryman to Samuel Hauser, September 17, 1880, Samuel T. Hauser Papers, MHS.

23. "Mary Newman Scott," "Mrs. Alice Shock," and "Bill Mitchell," Montana Monographs, PBL; Medicine Crow, "European Culture Contacts," 27; Bozeman *Avant Courier*, November 7, 1878; Wagner and Allen, *Blankets and Moccasins*, 216–26.

24. "Bill Mitchell," Montana Monographs, PBL.

25. "Mary Newman Scott," Montana Monographs, PBL; A. R. Keller to E. A. Hayt, January 20 and March 26, 1880, Letters Received by Commissioner of Indian Affairs, NA; George Ellsworth Snell Diary, August 10–11, 1880, Small Collections, MHS.

26. Wagner and Allen, *Blankets and Moccasins*, 171–78.

27. A. R. Keller to E. A. Hayt, August 12, 1880, Letters Received by Commissioner of Indian Affairs, NA.

28. Thomson P. McElrath to George Stark, September 15, 1879, Northern Pacific Railway Company Papers, MNHS.

29. "Frank L. Summers," "George Danford," "Mrs. Maggie Story," and "V. J. Salisbury and John Reardon," Montana Monographs, PBL; "V. J. Salisbury," I. D. O'Donnell Papers, BCMSU; Salisbury Family file, PBL; Small, *Century of Politics*, 7; Braum, "Life on the Yellowstone," 6.

30. Small, *Century of Politics*, 7.

31. Elsie Johnston, *Laurel's Story: A Montana Heritage* (Billings: Artcraft Publishing, 1979), 12; "Joseph Cochran," Montana Monographs, PBL; Bozeman *Avant Courier*, December 12, 1878; John J. Alderson to P. W. McAdow, January 16, 1879, Maginnis Papers, MHS.

32. Bozeman *Avant Courier,* April 10, 17, June 26, and July 3, 1879; Wagner and Allen, *Blankets and Moccasins,* 206; Helena *Herald,* March 29, 1879; Braum, "Life on the Yellowstone," 7.

33. In his study of North Dakota towns of the early twentieth century, John Hudson used central place theory to analyze the development of individual settlements. He called a small trade center not connected to the railroad, a place like Coulson in 1879, an "inland" town. He observed, "Each business site was some entrepreneur's statement of hope that a town might grow there." See Hudson, *Plains Country Towns,* 37. Timothy Mahoney, in his analysis of upper Mississippi River towns of the midnineteenth century, rejected central place theory in favor of a regionally based model of urban development. From the 1850s forward, he concluded, the increasing "metropolitanization of American life" transformed many small settlements that had once been "the centers of small local worlds" into "'provincial' places." See Mahoney, *River Towns of the Great West,* 242; also see his "Urban History in a Regional Context: River Towns on the Upper Mississippi, 1840–1860," *Journal of American History* 72 (September 1985): 318–39. Both approaches provide valuable insight on the development of Coulson. In 1879, Coulson certainly had the institutions associated with Hudson's inland towns. The coming of the railroad eventually ended its inland town status as the center of a small local world. The railroad transformed the settlement into a new place, the city of Billings, with several of the characteristics of Mahoney's "provincial" town, a place where "the web of feedbacks and exchange, measured locally, appears open-ended on account of their being dependent on broad and distant regional interactions." See Mahoney, *River Towns of the Great West,* 242.

34. Bozeman *Avant Courier,* June 26, 1879; John J. Alderson to P. W. McAdow, January 16, 1879, Maginnis Papers, MHS; Billings *Gazette,* March 23, 1930.

35. Bozeman *Avant Courier,* July 24, 1879, January 1 and February 26, 1880; "V. J. Salisbury," O'Donnell Papers, BCMSU; "Frank L. Summers," Montana Monographs, PBL; John Summers Diary, 1880–90, BCMSU. It was not unusual for prosperous farmers to work as day laborers. In Sugar Creek, Illinois, men often "dedicate[d] their surplus labor to investment." See Faragher, *Sugar Creek,* 105.

36. Orson N. Newman Diary, 1879, typescript, MHS.

37. William A. Allen, *Adventures with Indians and Game* (Chicago: A. W. Bowen, 1903), 206–8; quotation in Braum, "Life on the Yellowstone," 10, 13–20; Johnston, *Laurel's Story,* 12.

38. Billings *Gazette,* March 23, 1930.

39. "L. A. Nutting and Family," Montana Monographs, PBL; Bozeman *Avant Courier*, March 19, 1881; John J. Alderson to P. W. McAdow, January 16, 1879, Maginnis Papers, MHS. Also see Mahoney, *River Towns of the Great West*, 209–10.

40. Newman Diary, 1879, MHS; Orson N. Newman Diary, 1880, typescript, PBL; "L. A. Nutting," Montana Monographs, PBL.

CHAPTER 4

1. Thomson P. McElrath, *The Yellowstone Valley* (St. Paul: Pioneer Press, 1880), 94–95.

2. Hoyt, "Roughing It Up the Yellowstone," 25–34.

3. McElrath, *Yellowstone Valley*, 47–48, 51, 78, 80, 83.

4. Wagner and Allen, *Blankets and Moccasins*, 22; A. R. Keller to E. A. Hayt, February 2, 1880, Letters Received by Commissioner of Indian Affairs, NA.

5. Bozeman *Avant Courier*, February 26, 1880; Smith, "Crow Indian Land Cessions," 30–31; A. R. Keller to E. A. Hayt, December 30, 1879, and to R. E. Trowbridge, April 19, 1880, Letters Received by Commissioner of Indian Affairs, NA; Linderman, *Plenty-coups*, 239–40.

6. P. W. McAdow to Martin Maginnis, May 5, 1880, Maginnis Papers, MHS; Smith, "Crow Indian Land Cessions," 30–31; "Crow Delegation Agreement to Sell a portion of their Res. in mountains," May 15, 1880, Letters Received by the Office of Indian Affairs, NA.

7. "Report of Council held with the Crows at Crow Agency, M. T. June 12th 1880," Letters Received by the Office of Indians Affairs, NA.

8. Ibid.

9. Northern Pacific Railroad, *Annual Report, 1881* (New York: Northern Pacific Railroad, 1881), 25; Smith, "Crow Indian Land Cessions," 31.

10. C. P. Blakeley to Hauser, October 23, 1880, Hauser Papers, MHS; Smith, "Crow Indian Land Cessions," 31.

11. The dates Newman mentioned were September 30 and November 5, 1880, Newman Diary, 1880, PBL; "An Indian Trading Adventure Told by Henry A. Frith," Montana Monographs, PBL; Coulson file, PBL; Summers Diary, October 12, 1880, BCMSU.

12. George D. Mueller, "Skookum Joe Anderson: A Prospector's Idol," unpublished typescript, MHS, 3–4.

13. P. W. McAdow to Martin Maginnis, May 5, 1880, Maginnis Papers, MHS.

14. Mueller, "Skookum Joe Anderson," 5; George D. Mueller, "Real and Fancied Claims: Joseph Richard 'Skookum Joe' Anderson, Miner in Central Montana, 1880–1897," *Montana* 35 (Spring 1985): 53–54; quotation in

Braum, "Life on the Yellowstone," 8; Bozeman *Avant Courier,* July 14, 1881; Muriel Wolfe, *Montana Pay Dirt: A Guide to the Mining Camps of the Treasure State* (Athens, Ohio: Sage Books, 1963), 349–51.

15. Braum, "Life on the Yellowstone," 10.

16. Bozeman *Avant Courier,* January 22, February 26, and March 25, 1880.

17. Summers Diary, 1880, BCMSU; 1880 Census, Custer County.

18. Bozeman *Avant Courier,* February 26, 1880.

19. Stuart's quote cited in Carroll Van West, *A Traveler's Companion to Montana History* (Helena: Montana Historical Society Press, 1986), 13–14; Burlingame, *Montana Frontier,* 71–72; Braum, "Life on the Yellowstone," 15–17; Linderman, *Pretty-shield,* 250.

20. "Frank L. Summers," Montana Monographs, PBL; "John Henry Dover," I. D. O'Donnell, comp., *Montana Monographs* (Billings: Yellowstone County Historical Society, 1984); Stafford, "Crow Culture," 103.

21. Braum, "Life on the Yellowstone," 15.

22. Ibid., 17–18; "George Danford," Montana Monographs, PBL.

23. "Frank Summers" and "Ben Hogan," Montana Monographs, PBL; Leeson, *History of Montana,* 522.

24. Bozeman *Avant Courier,* September 9, 1880; Colwell's quote cited in Coulson Biographies, WHC.

25. Quotations in this and the following five paragraphs are from Newman Diary, 1880, PBL.

26. Miles City *Yellowstone Journal,* October 2, 1979, and March 27, 1880; Jones, *Crow Country,* 27; "George Danford," Montana Monographs, PBL; Braum, "Life on the Yellowstone," 17–18.

27. Miles City *Yellowstone Journal,* April 23, 1881; Braum, "Life on the Yellowstone," 18–19.

28. Braum, "Life on the Yellowstone," 18–19; P. W. McAdow to T. C. Power, October 16, 1881, T. C. Power Papers, MHS.

29. Marie MacDonald, *Glendive: The History of a Montana Town* (Glendive, Mont.: Glendive Press, 1968), 14–15; Brown, *Plainsmen,* 357; Walter A. Cameron Reminiscences, Small Collections, MHS, published as Cameron, "Building the Northern Pacific in 1881," 70–76; Hudson, "Main Streets of the Yellowstone," 63–64. On the historic association between railroad workers and liquor, see Walter Licht, *Working for the Railroad: The Organization of Work in the Nineteenth Century* (Princeton: Princeton University Press, 1983), 236.

30. *Illustrated History,* 345; Brown, *Plainsmen,* 341; Miles City *Yellowstone Journal,* November 5, 1881.

31. Cameron Reminiscences, MHS.
32. Summers Diary, August 6, 1881, BCMSU; quotations in Braum, "Life on the Yellowstone," 20–21.
33. Braum, "Life on the Yellowstone," 21. The Western Heritage Center in Billings has a copy of the original Coulson town plan by Alderson. It has been reproduced in a comparison with the present-day layout of Billings in Myrtle E. Cooper, *Tent Town to City: A Chronological History of Billings, Montana, 1882–1935* (Billings: privately published, 1981).
34. Quotation in *American Field,* February 18, 1882; magazine article transcribed and filed in Coulson Biographies, WHC.

CHAPTER 5

1. What John Faragher noted for early-nineteenth-century Sugar Creek, Illinois—"with a remarkable degree of gregariousness, farm families reached out from their log cabins to their neighbors for work and play"—proved true for the Clark's Fork Bottom fifty years later. See Faragher, *Sugar Creek,* 131.
2. On the importance of visiting in rural northern plains culture, see Hudson, *Plains Country Towns,* 123.
3. Hoyt, "Roughing It Up the Yellowstone," 27.
4. "Mary Newman Scott," Montana Monographs, PBL. According to the author's calculations, of the 200 people listed as residents of the Clark's Fork Bottom in the 1880 census, 67.5 percent were male, and 32.5 percent were female. The historian Julie Roy Jeffrey has pointed out that the "sex ratio on the frontier meant that young women did not have to accept the first available suitor who presented himself but could bide their time and choose among several." See Jeffrey, *Frontier Women: The Trans-Mississippi West, 1840–1880* (New York: Hill and Wang, 1979), 66.
5. Glenda Riley, "Women's Responses to the Challenges of Plains Living," *Great Plains Quarterly* 9 (Summer 1989): 177–78. For a community perspective, see Faragher, *Sugar Creek,* 110–18; Billings *Gazette,* March 23, 1930.
6. Newman Diary, 1879, March 10, July 12, August 11 and 30, September 30, October 2, November 2, and December 3, 1879, MHS.
7. Quotation in Twin Bridges (Mont.) *Sentinel,* November 10, 1932; "Mary Newman Scott," Montana Monographs, PBL; Bozeman *Avant Courier,* June 26, 1879.
8. Twin Bridges (Mont.) *Sentinel,* November 10, 1932; "Mary Newman Scott," Montana Monographs, PBL; quotations in Bozeman *Avant Courier,* November 13 and December 11, 1879, and January 22 and February 12, 1880.

9. The poem is in the Orson N. Newman Family file, PBL.

10. Newman Diary, 1879, MHS; Bozeman *Avant Courier,* December 18, 1879, and January 1 and 15, 1880; Newman Diary, 1880, PBL.

11. Newman Diary, 1879, MHS; Newman Diary, 1880, PBL.

12. Riley, "Women's Responses," 179; Hudson, *Plains Country Towns,* 125.

13. Newman Diary, 1880, PBL; Braum, "Life on the Yellowstone," 9, 19.

14. Newman Diary, 1880, November 1 and December 31, 1880, PBL; 1880 Census, Custer County; Bozeman *Avant Courier,* January 22, 1880; Larsen, *Urban West,* 24.

15. Faragher, *Sugar Creek,* 101, 110.

16. Author's calculations taken from 1880 Census, Custer County.

17. Newman Diary, 1880, February 19, 1880; Alice Shock file, PBL; and "Mrs. Alice Shock," Montana Monographs, PBL.

18. Billings *Gazette,* March 23, 1930; Bozeman *Avant Courier,* August 4, 1881.

19. Summers Diary, August 1, 1880, and June 26, 1881, BCMSU; Faragher, *Sugar Creek,* 160, 170.

20. Summers Diary, October 19, 1880, and July 17, 1881, BCMSU; Billings *Gazette,* March 23, 1930; Deer Lodge (Mont.) *New Northwest,* January 28, 1881; Alice Shock file, PBL; Coulson *Post,* April 5, 1882.

21. Bozeman *Avant Courier,* February 12, 1880; Billings *Gazette,* March 23, 1930; Riley, "Women's Responses," 181.

22. Miles City *Yellowstone Journal,* May 29, 1880; Thompson's quote cited in Coulson Biographies, WHC; Wagner and Allen, *Blankets and Moccasins,* 21–29.

23. Wagner and Allen, *Blankets and Moccasins,* 179–203; Summers Diary, August 26, 1881, BCMSU.

24. Coulson file, PBL; Crismas Scrapbook, MHS, 36–37; Livingston *Post,* February 8, 1900; Billings *Gazette,* September 30, 1928; Senia C. Hart, ed., "Calamity Jane Spent Latter Part of Her Life in Billings," *Landmarks* 2 (1975): 26–29.

CHAPTER 6

1. For an informative comparison with the Coulson-Billings experience in 1882, see Kathleen Underwood's description of Grand Junction, Colorado, at the same time in her *Town Building,* 7–26. For an earlier account of the impact of railroads on small frontier towns, see Faragher, *Sugar Creek,* 178–80, and for a later account, see Hudson, *Plains Country Towns,* 37.

2. Bozeman *Avant Courier,* December 1 and 15, 1881.

3. Paul McCormick to T. C. Power, December 30, 1881, Power Papers, MHS.

4. Paul McCormick to T. C. Power, January 8, 1882, ibid.

5. Bozeman *Avant Courier*, January 12, 19, and 26, 1882.

6. Dary, *Entrepreneurs of the Old West*, 256–57; Daniel J. Boorstin, *The Americans: The National Experience* (New York: Vintage Books, 1965), 124–47; Larsen, *Urban West*, 5; Livingston *Post*, May 9, 1907; Great Falls *Tribune*, September 27, 1940.

7. Coulson *Post*, February 4, 1882.

8. Ibid., February 4 and 18, 1882.

9. Irene G. Breuchaud, *Memoirs of Montana, 1882* (New York: Privately published, 1958), 9–10, 17, 25.

10. Ibid.; Coulson *Post*, March 25, 1882.

11. Coulson *Post*, March 18, 1882.

12. "First Drug Store Battled Bravely against Elements," Coulson file, PBL; Billings *Gazette*, July 24, 1932; Coulson *Post*, April 1, 1882.

13. Hudson, *Plains Country Towns*, 42.

14. Roswell H. Mason to Frederick Billings, March 27, 1880, Northern Pacific Railway Company Papers (hereafter cited as NPR Papers), MNHS.

15. H. W. Rowley, "The Founding of Billings: Early Recollections and Experiences," Montana Monographs, PBL; Reps, *Cities of the American West*, 537; Robin Winks, *Frederick Billings: A Life* (New York: Oxford University Press, 1991), 54, 203–4, 264.

16. Rowley, "Founding of Billings," PBL; *Northern Pacific Railroad Report of the President to the Stockholders, September 20, 1883* (New York: Northern Pacific Railroad, 1883), 36; Kliewer, "Billings," 256–57; Winks, *Billings*, 257. The initial close relationship between the Northern Pacific and the land company at Billings differed from the experience in Grand Junction, Colorado. There the town company first established the city and then sold half interest in the town company to the Denver and Rio Grande Railroad; in exchange, the railroad built a division point there. See Underwood, *Town Building*, 7–26.

17. Coulson *Post*, April 1 and 8, 1882. On the "structure" model, see Hudson, *Plains Country Towns*, 71.

18. Hudson, "Main Streets of the Yellowstone," 64, and idem, *Plains Country Towns*, 88–89. On the impact of railroad designs on western towns, see Zunz, *Making America Corporate*, 152.

19. Coulson *Post*, April 1 and 8, 1882; *Illustrated History*, 291; Kliewer, "Billings," 258–60.

20. Coulson *Post*, April 8 and 22, 1882; "Town Lot Sales, Billings, M. T.," 1882–83, WHC.

21. T. F. Oakes to J. M. Hannaford, March 31, 1882, NPR Papers, MNHS; E. V. Smalley, "The New Northwest," *Century Magazine* 24 (September 1882): 769–79.

22. Billings and Coulson *Post*, April 15, 1882.

23. Ibid., April 22, 1882.

24. Small, *Century of Politics*, 22; Hudson, *Plains Country Towns*, 106.

25. Coulson *Post*, February 4, 11, 18, March 18, 25, and April 1, 1882.

26. "First Drug Store," Coulson file, PBL; Helena *Herald*, April 6, 1882; Johnson's quote is cited in Billings *Gazette*, July 24, 1932, and September 18, 1960.

27. Billings *Gazette*, March 23, 1940 (Shock quote), and September 18, 1960; Billings *Post*, September 30, 1882.

28. Coulson *Post*, February 11 and March 18, 1882; Billings and Coulson *Post*, May 20, 1882; Coulson Biographies, WHC.

29. Coulson *Post*, February 18 and March 18 and 25, 1882; Otto Maerdin to sister, June 25, 1882, in L. B. Mirrielees, ed., "Pioneer Ranching in Central Montana," *Sources of Northwest History*, no.10 (Missoula: University of Montana, n.d.), 5.

30. Billings *Gazette*, October 6, 1899, and May 7, 1933; Billings and Coulson *Post*, April 29 and May 6, 1882; P. W. McAdow to T. C. Power, May 6, 1882, Power Papers, MHS.

31. Billings and Coulson *Post*, April 29, 1882; Hudson, "Main Streets of the Yellowstone," 63; "Stebbins, Post and Mund Circular," Box 319, folder 11, Power Papers, MHS; Kliewer, "Billings," 261; Cooper, *Tent Town to City*, 3; James B. Hedges, "The Colonization Work of the Northern Pacific Railroad," *Mississippi Valley Historical Review* 13 (December 1926): 335–36.

32. Benjamin Shuart, "Reminiscences of a Home Missionary," in *First Congregational United Church of Christ: Our First One Hundred Years* (Billings: First Congregational Church, 1982), 27–29.

33. "Highlights and Incidences in My Life by H. B. Wiley," H. B. Wiley Papers, Small Collections, MHS.

34. Smalley, "New Northwest," 770–72.

35. Breuchaud, *Memoirs*, 39–40.

36. Coulson Biographies, WHC; Cooper, *Tent Town to City*, 3; Smalley, "New Northwest," 770; Small, *Century of Politics*, 20.

37. Billings and Coulson *Post*, May 6, 13, and 20, 1882; Summers Diary, May 22, 1882, and October 12, 1883, BCMSU; Billings *Herald*, November 16, 1882.

38. Billings and Coulson *Post*, May 20, 1882.

39. Small, *Century of Politics*, 20; Coulson Town file, WHC; Kliewer, "Billings," 270–71.

40. Billings *Post*, March 12, 1885; Fergus County (Mont.) *Argus*, November 4, 1921; Raymond Gozzi, "A Short History of Coulson," unpublished typescript, 1983, WHC.

CHAPTER 7

1. Billings *Herald*, June 1, 1882; Billings *Post*, June 3, 1882. The land ownership percentages given in these newspaper accounts are confirmed by the single remaining "Town Lots Sales" book for 1882 at the Western Heritage Center. Of its first two hundred contracts, only one in five went to local residents.

2. Billings *Post*, June 10 (Clark quote) and 17, 1882; Cooper, *Tent Town to City*, 4.

3. Shuart, "Reminiscences," 29–30; Walter Burke to T. C. Power, August 4, 1882, Power Papers, MHS (this letter is on the official stationery of the library association and lists the officers); Small, *Century of Politics*, 22. On the western urban tradition of replicating eastern cultural institutions, see Larsen, *Urban West*, 33–34.

4. Billings *Herald*, June 29, 1882; Kliewer, "Billings," 263. To compare the problems of Billings with those of other communities, see Larsen, *Urban West*, 69–70, and Stanley K. Schultz, *Constructing Urban Culture: American Cities and City Planning, 1800–1920* (Philadelphia: Temple University Press, 1989), 162–67.

5. V. Bannister (?) to Wilbur F. Sanders, June 11, 1882, Wilbur Fisk Sanders Papers, MHS.

6. Billings *Post*, July 15, 1882; Breuchaud, *Memoirs*, 67–68.

7. Billings *Post*, July 1, 1882. Mund's circular is cited in "As It Was in Billings 45 Years Ago Today," Billings *Gazette*, July 5, 1927.

8. "Highlights and Incidences," Wiley Papers, MHS; Walter Burke to T. C. Power, July 18, 20, and 24 and August 4, 1882, Power Papers, MHS.

9. Henry J. Winser to George B. Hulme, August 10, 1882, and to Thomas F. Oakes, August 22, 1882, NPR Papers, MNIIS.

10. Small, *Century of Politics*, 10; Cooper, *Tent Town to City*, 6-7; "Joseph M. V. Cochran," Montana Monographs, PBL.

11. Billings *Post*, July 8 and August 5, 1882; Marriage Records, 1882, Custer County, Montana Territory, transcribed list at PBL; Cooper, *Tent Town to City*, 6–7.

12. Billings *Herald*, August 24, 1882; Billings *Post*, August 12, 19, and 26, 1882;

Cooper, *Tent Town to City,* 6–7; Kliewer, "Billings," 264; "Highlights and Incidences," Wiley Papers, MHS.

13. Office of Land Assistant, Northern Pacific Railway, *Revised Corporate History of Northern Pacific Railway Company* (St. Paul: Northern Pacific Railway, 1921), 23; Billings *Post,* September 16 and October 7, 1882; Cooper, *Tent Town to City,* 7–8. The Northern Pacific rate circular of October 10, 1882, is in Box 155, folder 3, Power Papers, MHS.

14. Lucius Whitney, September 25, and C. W. Horr, October 6, 1882, to T. C. Power, Power Papers, MHS.

15. Diary extract quoted in Jane Curtis, et al., *Frederick Billings: Vermonter, Pioneer, Lawyer, Businessman, Conservationist* (Woodstock, Vt.: Woodstock Foundation, 1986), 114; Billings *Post,* October 28, 1882.

16. Billings *Post,* October 7 and 28, 1882; Billings *Herald,* October 22, 1882; C. W. Horr to T. C. Power, October 30, 1882, Power Papers, MHS; Cooper, *Tent Town to City,* 8; Kliewer, "Billings," 264.

17. Billings *Post,* November 4, 1882; Thomas F. Oakes to James S. Brisbin, November 6, 1882, NPR Papers, MNHS; Small, *Century of Politics,* 17–18.

18. Billings *Post,* November 5 and 25, 1882, and February 3, 1883 (editorial); Cooper, *Tent Town to City,* 8.

19. Curtis, *Frederick Billings,* 114; Winks, *Billings,* 258.

20. Benjamin F. Shuart to Frederick Billings, November 29 and December 4 and 23, 1882, Northern Pacific Railroad: Correspondence Concerning Land Dealings, carton A 23, Billings Mansion and Archives, Woodstock, Vt.

21. Small, *Century of Politics,* 12–15.

22. Billings *Post,* April 26, 1883; Cooper, *Tent Town to City,* 9–10.

23. Cooper, *Tent Town to City,* 9, 13; Shuart to Billings, March 28, 1883, Billings Mansion and Archives; Kliewer, "Billings," 267.

24. Polly's quote cited in "Pilgrims First Impression of Town Terrified," *Landmarks* 2 (August 1975): 14; Cooper, *Tent Town to City,* 12.

25. Breuchaud, *Memoirs,* 76; Deer Lodge (Mont.) *New Northwest,* February 7, 1896.

26. Shuart to Billings, March 23, 1883, Billings Mansion and Archives.

27. Shuart to Billings, March 1, 14, 15, and 17, 1883, ibid.

28. Shuart to Billings, March 17, 23, and 28 and April 4 and 24, 1883, ibid.; Real Estate Tax Records, 1888, Yellowstone County, Montana Territory, WHC.

29. Shuart to Billings, May 2, 1883; Greene and Peck, July 31, and Stebbins, Post, and Mund to T. C. Power, May 18, 1883, Power Papers, MHS.

30. Kliewer, "Billings," 276.

31. Billings *Post*, March 10, 17, and 31, 1883; Cumbler, *Social History of Economic Decline*, 5 and 15.
32. "Billings, Montana," Circular dated April 1883 included in George B. Hulme to T. C. Power and Bro., July 21, 1883, Power Papers, MHS.
33. Benjamin F. Shuart to Frederick Billings, December 23, 1882, March 26 and April 24, 1883, Billings Archives; Cumbler, *Social History of Economic Decline*, 5. For the bureaucratic nature of the railroad corporations of the 1880s, see the description of the Chicago, Burlington, and Quincy in Zunz, *Making America Corporate*, 37–66, and of the industry in general in Alfred D. Chandler, Jr., *The Visible Hand: The Managerial Revolution in American Business* (Cambridge: Belknap Press, 1977).
34. Memorandums from Charles B. Lamborn and G. K. Barnes to Thomas F. Oakes, April 7, 1883, Billings Mansion and Archives; Billings *Post*, April 14, 1883; Billings *Herald*, April 2, 1883.
35. Shuart to Billings, December 26, 1882, and April 14, 1883, Billings Mansion and Archives.
36. Shuart to Billings, April 16, 1883, ibid.
37. Shuart to Billings, May 3 and 8, 1883, ibid.
38. Shuart to Billings, May 27, 1883, ibid.
39. *Post* editorial quoted in Kliewer, "Billings," 274; Yerkes's quote is from Small, *Century of Politics*, 26; Cooper, *Tent Town to City*, 11–12.
40. Larsen, *Urban West*, 62–66, 71; Schultz, *Constructing Urban Culture*, 116.
41. Shuart to Billings, May 12, 1883, Billings Mansion and Archives.
42. Billings *Post*, May 3 and June 24, 1883.
43. Billings *Herald*, April 10, 1883; Cooper, *Tent Town to City*, 11. Entrepreneurial infighting was, of course, nothing new in western cities. See Dykstra's comments on Wichita, Kansas, in his *Cattle Towns*, 361–63.
44. Small, *Century of Politics*, 25–26; Cooper, *Tent Town to City*, 11; Charles B. Lamborn to Leonard R. Kidder, June 24, 1883, and to Thomas F. Oakes, June 5, 1882, NPR Papers, MNHS; Shuart to Billings, May 1 and 10 (Mund quote), 1883, Billings Mansion and Archives.
45. Billings *Post*, July 26, 1883; Kliewer, "Billings," 268–69; Cooper, *Tent Town to City*, 13.
46. Shuart to Billings, May 1 and 12 and August 6, 1883, Billings Mansion and Archives; Billings *Post*, May 1, 1883.
47. Billings *Post*, March 31, April 7, July 12, and September 14, 1883; Shuart to Billings, April 17 and June 25, 1883, Billings Mansion and Archives.
48. Kliewer, "Billings," 273.
49. Shuart to Billings, May 2, 1883, and Frederick Billings to Samuel E. Kil-

ner (?), August 22, 1883, Billings Mansion and Archives; Cooper, *Tent Town to City*, 13; Winks, *Billings*, 258.

50. Edward W. Nolan, "'Not Without Labor and Expense': The Villard-Northern Pacific Last Spike Excursion, 1883," *Montana* 33 (Summer 1983): 4–5; Billings *Post*, September 6, 1883; Curtis et al., *Frederick Billings*, 115; Winks, *Billings*, 254–55.

51. Nolan, "Not Without Labor," 5; Billings *Post*, September 6 and 13, 1883; Summers Diary, September 6, 1883, BCMSU; Billings's speech cited in Curtis et al., *Frederick Billings*, 115–16; Winks, *Billings*, 255–56.

52. Billings *Post*, September 6 and 13, 1883; Small, *Century of Politics*, 28; Winks, *Billings*, 256.

53. Billings *Herald*, September 15, 1883; Kliewer, "Billings," 267; Cooper, *Tent Town to City*, 14; Small, *Century of Politics*, 25.

54. Billings *Post*, July 12, 1883; Billings *Herald*, September 27 and November 27, 1883; Benjamin F. Shuart to Samuel E. Kilner, October 4, 1883, Billings Mansion and Archives; N. C. Smith to T. C. Power, October 9, 1883, Power Papers, MHS.

55. Shuart to Billings, May 12, 14, and 15 and June 6, 1883, Billings Mansion and Archives.

56. Shuart to Billings, July 31, 1883, ibid.; T. F. Oakes to Herman Haupt, October 30, 1883, NPR Papers, MNHS.

57. Kliewer, "Billings," 270; Herman H. Mund to Land Committee, Northern Pacific Railroad, December 17, 1883, NPR Papers, MNHS.

58. The 1883 city directory has been reprinted as volumes 3 and 4 of *Landmarks* (1976), a historical magazine published in Billings during the bicentennial period. The quote is from *Landmarks* 3 (1976): 3.

59. Doyle, *Social Order of a Frontier Community*, 12–13, 181; Small, *Century of Politics*, 11–12, 15–16.

60. "Billings City Directory of 1883," *Landmarks* 3 (1976): 9.

CHAPTER 8

1. Cooper, *Tent Town to City*, 16; photograph of the North School, Photograph Collections, WHC.

2. Underwood, *Town Building*, 25–27.

3. Shuart to Billings, January 25 and February 1, 1884, Billings Mansion and Archives.

4. Shuart to Billings, February 20, 1884, ibid.

5. Benjamin F. Shuart to Samuel Kilner, March 18, 1884, ibid.

6. Billings *Post*, April 3, 1884; Benjamin F. Shuart to S. E. Kilner, April 7 and

November 25, 1884, Billings Mansion and Archives. In this last letter, Shuart gave Billings's landholdings as 4545.1 acres.

7. Charles B. Lamborn to L. R. Kidder, December 8, 1884, and January 8, 1885, NPR Papers, MNHS; Benjamin F. Shuart to S. E. Kilner, April 22 and May 7, 1884, Billings Mansion and Archives.

8. Shuart to Billings, May 7, 1884, Billings Mansion and Archives.

9. Shuart to Billings, May 31 and June 20 and 24, 1884, ibid.

10. Curtis et al., *Frederick Billings*, 124–25.

11. Ibid., 126; Benjamin F. Shuart to Samuel Kilner, August 1 and 26, 1884, Billings Mansion and Archives.

12. Benjamin F. Shuart to Samuel Kilner, August 26 and September 2 and 18, 1884, Joseph Zimmerman to Parmly Billings, September 11, and Edward Bailey to Frederick Billings, September 19, 1884, Billings Mansion and Archives.

13. Instructions to Arbitors, November 12, 1884, Shuart to Billings, November 28 and December 3, 1884, and January 17, 1885, Billings Mansion and Archives. These last two letters contain Shuart's version of the Johnson affair; Billings to Shuart (telegraph), November 25, 1884, ibid.

14. Shuart to Billings, December 3, 1884, and Affidavits from Edward Johnson, January 9, 1885, and Benjamin F. Shuart, January 28, 1885, ibid.

15. Affidavits from Parmly Billings, February 1885, and Edward Bailey, February 1885, ibid.; Cooper, *Tent Town to City*, 15; Winks, *Billings*, 209–10.

16. Billings *Post*, March 12 and 19, 1885; O'Donnell, comp., "Parmly Billings," *Montana Monographs*.

17. Helen F. Sanders, *A History of Montana* (Chicago: Lewis Publishing Company, 1913), 1193; "I. D. O'Donnell," Montana Pioneers Collection, MHS.

18. Sanders, *History of Montana*, 1193–94; also see the brief biographical sketch in Small, *Century of Politics*, 45–46.

19. The letter from Parmly to Mary Billings is cited in Curtis et al., *Frederick Billings*, 127; Small, *Century of Politics*, 29.

20. Billings *Post*, March 12, 1885; Cooper, *Tent Town to City*, 18–19.

21. Billings *Gazette*, May 6 and December 20, 1886; Curtis et al., *Frederick Billings*, 127. By this point, the local control exercised by the faraway New York capitalists resembled the situation in the mining towns of western Pennsylvania, documented in Anthony F. C. Wallace, *St. Clair: A Nineteenth-Century Coal Town's Experience with a Disaster-Prone Industry* (New York: Knopf, 1987).

22. C. W. Horr to T. C. Power, October 20, 1886, Power Papers, MHS.

23. Billings *Post*, July 3 and 24, 1884; Lucius Whitney to T. C. Power, March 9, 1887, Powers Papers, MHS.

24. Cooper, *Tent Town to City*, 21; Billings *Stock Gazette*, April 21, 1887.

25. Billings *Gazette*, December 16, 23, and 30, 1886.

26. John W. Hakola, "Samuel T. Hauser and the Economic Development of Montana: A Case Study in Nineteenth-Century Frontier Capitalism" (Ph.D. diss., Indiana University, 1961), 124, 153–59; Thomas F. Oakes to Samuel T. Hauser, June 2, 1885, Hauser Papers, MHS.

27. Billings *Gazette*, January 15 and March 10, 1887.

28. Ibid., April 21 and 28, 1887.

29. Thomas F. Oakes, January 22 (telegram), Frederick Billings, January 25, and E. G. Bailey, March 22, 1888, to Samuel T. Hauser, Hauser Papers, MHS.

30. Curtis et al., *Frederick Billings*, 128; Billings *Gazette*, July 19, 1888; "I. D. O'Donnell," Montana Pioneers Collection, MHS; Winks, *Billings*, 259.

31. "Agreement between Northern Pacific Railroad and Helena and Livingston Smelter and Reduction Company," May 28, 1888, Box 54, Hauser Papers, MHS; S. E. Kilner to Samuel T. Hauser, July 18, 1889, ibid.; Hakola, "Hauser and the Economic Development," 179–80.

32. Hakola, "Hauser and the Economic Development," 179–80.

33. Thomas F. Oakes to Samuel T. Hauser, February 18 and 19, 1889 (telegrams), and Henry Villard to John W. Buskett, July 15, 1889, and to Samuel T. Hauser, July 13, 1891, Hauser Papers, MHS.

34. Linderman, *Plenty-coups*, 227.

35. Colin G. Calloway, "Sword Bearer and the 'Crow Outbreak,' 1887," *Montana* 36 (Autumn 1986): 40–42.

36. Billings *Gazette*, October 18, 1887; Calloway, "Sword Bearer," 44–51.

37. LeRoy Barnett, "The Ghastly Harvest: Montana's Buffalo Bone Trade," *Montana* 26 (Summer 1975): 4–5. The bones were an important source of hard currency for homesteaders throughout the northern plains. See Hudson, *Plains Country Towns*, 33.

38. P. W. McAdow to Power and Co., May 3, 1884, and Lucius Whitney to T. C. Power, October 21, 1885, Power Papers, MHS; Billings *Post*, March 12, 1885.

39. Wolfe, *Montana Pay Dirt*, 351; J. F. Keating, August 11 and September 2 and 4, 1885 and P. W. McAdow, August 27, 1890, to T. C. Power, Power Papers, MHS.

40. Miles City *Yellowstone Journal*, February 6, 1886; Billings *Gazette*, March 5, 1889; P. W. McAdow to Granville Stuart, January 9, 1889, Hauser Papers, MHS.

41. Summers Diary, 1882 to 1889, BCMSU.

42. Small, *Century of Politics*, 47.

43. The Billings *Gazette* editorial is cited in ibid., 36.

44. The town shared its fire problems with many other northern plains communities; see Hudson, *Plains Country Towns*, 108. Billings *Post*, July 17, 1884; Kliewer, "Billings," 272–74; Cooper, *Tent Town to City*, 20–21; Lucius Whitney, July 18, 1885, and Lesley Bates, January 20, 1886, to T. C. Power, Power Papers, MHS; photograph of Grand Hotel, Photograph Collections, WHC.

45. Paul McCormick, January 8, February 7, 11, 14, and 25 and Lucius Whitney, May 12, 1887 to T. C. Power, Power Papers, MHS.

CHAPTER 9

1. E. G. Campbell, *The Reorganization of the American Railroad System, 1893–1900* (New York: AMS Press, 1968 [1938]), 13.

2. Billings *Gazette*, October 2, 1890; Curtis et al., *Frederick Billings*, 128–29; Winks, *Billings*, 311.

3. Office of Land Assistant, *Corporate History of Northern Pacific*, 28.

4. The writings of Fernand Braudel have influenced my understanding of the evolving economic structure found in the Clark's Fork Bottom in the nineteenth century. Braudel has established three levels of economic structure—material life, the market economy, and capitalism—to account for the economic development of preindustrial Europe from 1400 to 1800. To Braudel, capitalism was the highest level of development, in which "certain groups of privileged actors were engaged in circuits and calculations that ordinary people knew nothing of." See Braudel, *The Structures of Everyday Life: The Limits of the Possible* (New York: Harper, 1979), 23–24. The impact of the Northern Pacific Railroad's reorganization on the future development of Billings and Yellowstone County is an interesting example of Braudel's "privileged actors" at work at the highest stages of capitalist activity. For a provocative synthesis of this period, especially insightful on the impact of industrialism on the northern plains, see William G. Robbins, " 'At the end of the cracked whip': The Northern West, 1880–1920," *Montana*, 38 (Autumn 1988): 2–11, and for a national context, see Sklar, *Corporate Reconstruction of American Capitalism*.

5. Billings *Gazette*, March 12, 1891.

6. Paul McCormick to T. C. Power, February 11, 1890, Power Papers, MHS.

7. Paul McCormick to T. C. Power, July 9, 1890, ibid.

8. Plenty Coups's quote is cited in Smith, "Crow Indian Land Cessions," 34–35.

9. Paul McCormick to T. C. Power, December 8, 1890 (telegram), Power Papers, MHS; Ted Townsend, "Pioneer Home at Magic City," *Montana* 4 (Spring 1954): 50–51.

10. P. C. Weare to T. C. Power, December 26, 1890, Power Papers, MHS.

11. Smith, "Crow Indian Land Cessions," 34; James W. Noble to T. C. Power, October 17, 1892, ibid.

12. J. M. Hannaford to T. C. Power, November 17, 1890, ibid.

13. Anneke-Jan Boden, *Billings: The First 100 Years* (Billings: First Bank, 1982), 30; Cooper, *Tent Town to City*, 25; *Illustrated History*, 301.

14. Billings *Gazette*, March 5, 1891; Licht, *Working for the Railroad*, 79–80.

15. Billings *Gazette*, July 23, 1891, and March 24, 1892.

16. O. F. Goddard to T. C. Power, December 19, 1891, Power Papers, MHS; Cooper, *Tent Town to City*, 25; "I. D. O'Donnell," Montana Pioneers Collection, MHS; Sanders, *History of Montana*, 1194; Billings *Gazette*, May 18, 1893.

17. Sanders, *History of Montana*, 1194. PBL has a copy of the original stock certificate of the Yellowstone Fair Association, signed by I. D. O'Donnell as president.

18. *Illustrated History*, 301; *The Official Northern Pacific Railroad Guide* (St. Paul: W. C. Riley, 1893), 218.

19. W. W. Baldwin, *Corporate History of the Chicago, Burlington, and Quincy Railroad Company and Affiliated Companies* ([Chicago]: Chicago, Burlington, Quincy, 1917), 373, and railroad map of Wyoming and Montana lines; Richard C. Overton, *Burlington Route: A History of the Burlington Lines* (New York: Knopf, 1965), 229.

20. Baldwin, *Corporate History*, 373; Paul McCormick to T. C. Power, February 17, 1892, Power Papers, MHS.

21. Paul McCormick to T. C. Power, December 13, 1892, and January 22 and February 5, 1893, Power Papers, MHS.

22. R. Lockey, March 8, and O. F. Goddard, March 9 and 21, 1893, to T. C. Power, ibid.; Small, *Century of Politics*, 23; Overton, *Burlington Route*, 229.

23. Paul McCormick to T. C. Power, March 2, 7, and 28, 1893, Power Papers, MHS.

24. Billings *Gazette*, May 4 and 11, 1893.

25. P. B. Weare to T. C. Power, June 10, 1893, Power Papers, MHS; Campbell, *Reorganization*, 24–25.

26. Renz, *History of the Northern Pacific*, 175; Hoyt, "Roughing It Up the Yellowstone," 24.

27. T. Barth, "Report on the Investigation of the Northern Pacific Railroad, Made During a Trip over the Road (October 24th to November 9th 1893)," James J. Hill Papers, James J. Hill Reference Library, St. Paul, Minn.; *Report of Receiver Henry C. Rouse, December 11, 1893* (New York: Northern Pacific Railroad, 1893), 15, 19.

28. Renz, *History of the Northern Pacific,* 176–80. What happened to the Northern Pacific during these years was part of a larger movement in corporate America to reorganize itself after the disaster of 1893. See Naomi R. Lamoreaux, *The Great Merger Movement in American Business, 1895–1904* (New York: Cambridge University Press, 1985).

29. *40th Annual Report of the Board of Directors of the Chicago, Burlington, and Quincy Railroad Company* (Cambridge: Wilson and Son, 1894), 17; Billings *Gazette,* April 21, 1894.

30. Billings *Gazette,* April 28, 1894; telegram cited in Thomas A. Clinch, *Urban Populism and Free Silver in Montana* (Missoula: University of Montana Press, 1970), 106–10. For a regional review of the Coxey movement, see W. Thomas White, "A History of Railroad Workers in the Pacific Northwest, 1883–1934" (Ph.D. diss., University of Washington, 1981), 82–123.

31. W. Thomas White, "Boycott: The Pullman Strike in Montana," *Montana* 29 (October 1979): 4–5.

32. Jennings quoted in ibid., 6–7; Billings *Gazette,* July 7, 1894; Billings *Daily Times,* July 7, 1894.

33. Zunz, *Making America Corporate,* 64.

34. White, "Pullman Strike," 8–11.

35. Billings *Gazette,* October 6, 1894; *41st Annual Report of the Board of Directors of the Chicago, Burlington, and Quincy Railroad Company* (Cambridge: Wilson and Son, 1895), 14; Overton, *Burlington Route,* 229–30. For an earlier account of how competing railroad lines boomed a Midwest town, see Doyle, *Social Order of a Frontier Community,* 84–85.

36. *Northwest Magazine,* September 1894, typescript in PBL.

37. Opie, *Law of the Land,* 106, 120; Billings *Gazette,* April 7, 1894, and March 10 and 21, 1899; Small, *Century of Politics,* 49; Sanders, *History of Montana,* 1194.

38. The quote is from Small, *Century of Politics,* 37.

39. Campbell, *Reorganization,* 195; Stuart Daggett, *Railroad Reorganization* (New York: A. M. Kelley, 1967 [1908]), 293–94.

40. Excellent biographies have been prepared on both Hill and Stephen: Albro Martin, *James J. Hill and the Opening of the Northwest* (New York: Oxford University Press, 1976), and Heather Gilbert, *The Life of Lord Mount Stephen,* vol. 2, *The End of the Road, 1891–1921* (Aberdeen, Scotland: Aberdeen University Press, 1977).

41. George Stephen to James J. Hill, October 18, and Hill to Stephen, October 20 and 25, 1894, and to Jacob Schiff, January 4, 1895, Hill Papers; Gilbert, *Mount Stephen,* 73–74. Just over a week after Stephen's initial communi-

cation to Hill, the New York banker Jacob Schiff wrote a financial ally of the Deutsche Bank: "Your friends of the Deutsche Bank could do nothing better than to induce Mr. James J. Hill to interest himself in the affairs of the Northern Pacific Company. No one else so thoroughly understands everything concerning the traffic of the territory through which the N. P. runs, and he has proven in the management of the affairs of the Great Northern what can be done by thorough attention and management on strict business principles, even in the face of the most adverse circumstances." Quoted in Gilbert, *Mount Stephen,* 75.

42. Edward D. Adams to Dr. Georg Siemens, March 15, 1895, Northern Pacific Reorganization file, Hill Papers; James J. Hill to George Stephen, March 19 and April 6, and Stephen to Hill, April 8, 9 (two communications), and 10, and Gaspard Farrar to Hill, April 10, 1895, ibid.; Campbell, *Reorganization,* 195–97; and see copy of letter from Adams to Siemens in George Stephen to James J. Hill, April 19, 1895, Hill Papers.

43. George Stephen to James J. Hill, April 19, 25, and 26, Arthur Gwinner to Stephen, May 2, Hill to St. Paul Office, May 10, and Edward D. Adams to Hill, with attached memorandum, May 9–10, 1895, Hill Papers; Gilbert, *Mount Stephen,* 81–83.

44. Marcus Daly, May 20, Charles A. Pillsbury, May 21, and John G. Moore, May 29, 1895, to James J. Hill, Hill Papers.

45. E. T. Nichols, May 22 and June 5, and George Stephen, May 31 and June 8, 1895, to Hill, Hill Papers. W. P. Clough, the Great Northern's vice-president, reported that the company's staff believed that the unification of the two railroads was legal in Minnesota law; see Clough to Hill, June 12, 1895, ibid. On the legal questions, also see Martin, *James J. Hill,* 446–50. On Morgan's increasing involvement, see Hill to Stephen, June 24, 1895, Hill Papers. Vincent P. Carosso has given one reason Morgan so feared a lawsuit—it might call into question his integrity and that of private bankers worldwide. Morgan was "a conservative merchant banker, bold and resourceful but opposed to any practices that might bring disrepute to his firms or to private banking and finance generally." See Carosso, *The Morgans: Private International Bankers* (Cambridge: Harvard University Press, 1987), 287.

46. Jacob Halstead to Henry J. Horn, August 20, Horn to Halstead, September 4, James J. Hill to E. T. Nichols, August 16, and to Jacob Schiff, November 11, and Schiff to Hill, November 18, 1895, Hill Papers; Martin, *James J. Hill,* 447. Henry W. Cannon, president of the Chase National Bank of New York City, also urged Hill to drop the agreement and asked him to have a per-

sonal interview with Morgan. "If you personally confer with him at outset, [I] feel confident he will work for best interests [of] all concerned." See H. W. Cannon to Hill, November 29, 1895, Hill Papers.

47. James J. Hill to George Stephen, December 17, 1895, and February 10 and 15, 1896, and J. P. Morgan, January 21 and February 25, H. W. Cannon, January 25, and E. T. Nichols, February 7, 1896, to Hill, Hill Papers. Lewis Corey, *The House of Morgan: A Social Biography of the Masters of Money* (New York: G. H. Watt, 1930), 157, popularized the phrase "Morganized"; Carosso, *The Morgans*, 364–68, 384.

48. Martin, *James J. Hill*, 455; Gilbert, *Mount Stephen*, 94–96; "Memorandum of a Conference held in London on the 2nd of April, 1896," Hill Papers.

49. For a sample of the controversies, see Edward D. Adams, June 25 and Charles H. Coster and Adams, July 31, 1896, to James J. Hill, Hill to Adams, June 25 and August 2, and to Adams and Coster, August 8, and J. W. Kendrick to E. W. Winter, August 28, 1896, NPR Papers, MNHS.

50. Renz, *History of the Northern Pacific*, 205–6; *Illustrated History*, 156–58; *We Will Welcome You to Livingston. . . .* (Livingston, Mont.: Privately published, 1909).

51. Billings *Gazette*, October 6, 1899 (special edition, with pages 1–2, 9, 13–14, 19); Small, *Century of Politics*, 94.

52. Small, *Century of Politics*, 56; Billings *Gazette*, July 7, 1894 (Illustrated Edition), March 10 and 21 and October 6, 1899.

53. *Illustrated History*, 301–2; Cooper, *Tent Town to City*, 34; Billings *Gazette*, October 6, 1899.

54. Billings *Gazette*, October 6, 1899.

55. Small, *Century of Politics*, 48–49; *Illustrated History*, 278; Billings *Gazette*, October 23, 1900.

56. Reps, *Cities of the American West*, 540.

57. Billings *Gazette*, October 16, 23, 26, and 30, 1900, and March 19, 1901; *Trails and Tales: South of the Yellowstone* (Billings: Midland Printing, 1983), 689–92; Small, *Century of Politics*, 48–49.

58. Billings *Gazette*, October 9 and 12, 1900; *Illustrated History*, 302; Winks, *Billings*, 304.

59. Kathryn Wright, *Historic Homes of Billings* (Billings and Helena: Falcon Press Publishing Company, 1981), 3; "Moss Mansion," National Register of Historic Places Nomination Form, State Historic Preservation Office, Helena, Mont.

60. Johnston, *Laurel's Story*, 91–93; Ralph W. Hidy et al., *The Great Northern Railway: A History* (Boston: Harvard Business School Press, 1988), 100–

105, 114; W. Thomas White, "Commonwealth or Colony? Montana and the Railroads in the First Decade of Statehood," *Montana* 38 (Autumn 1988): 22–23; Hudson, "Main Streets," 65–67.
61. *Illustrated History*, 302.
62. Ibid.

Bibliography

◻

PRIMARY SOURCES
Manuscripts and Documents
Billings Mansion and Archives, Woodstock, Vermont
    Frederick Billings–Benjamin Shuart Correspondence.
James J. Hill Reference Library, St. Paul, Minnesota
    James J. Hill Papers
Iowa State Historical Society Collections, Iowa City
    John J. and Margaret Tomlinson, Logbooks, 1864
Minnesota Historical Society, St. Paul
    Northern Pacific Railway Company Papers
Montana Historical Society, Helena
    Walter A. Cameron Reminiscences, Small Collections
    Roy M. Crismas Scrapbook
    Crow Indian Agency Records
    Crow Indian Collection
    Samuel T. Hauser Papers
    Martin Maginnis Papers
    Merchants National Bank Collection
    George M. Miles Diary, Small Collections

Montana Pioneers Collection

Morrow, Delores, "Our Sawdust Roots: A History of the Forest Products Industry in Montana," typescript, vertical files

Mueller, George D., "Skookum Joe Anderson: A Prospector's Idol," typescript, vertical files

Orson N. Newman Diary, 1879, typescript

T. C. Power Papers

Wilbur Fisk Sanders Papers

George Ellsworth Snell Diary, Small Collections

Tax Lists, 1877–80, Custer County, Montana Territory

William K. Thomas Diary, Small Collections

H. B. Wiley Papers

Yellowstone River and Valley, 1875 Military Expedition, Microfilm Collections

Montana State Historic Preservation Office, Helena

"Fort Keogh, MT," National Register of Historic Places Nomination Form

"Moss Mansion," National Register of Historic Places Nomination Form

Montana State University Library, Bozeman: Merrill G. Burlingame Special Collections

Braum, Helen, "Life on the Yellowstone," typescript

Orson N. Newman Papers

I. D. O'Donnell Papers

John Summers Diary, 1880–90

National Archives, Washington, D.C.

Correspondence of the Quartermaster, Fort Custer, Montana Territory, 1878–82

1880 Census, Custer County, Montana Territory

Fort Keogh, Mont. (1876–1908), Records of United States Army Commands, Record Group 98

"General Orders No. 101, War Department, November 8, 1877," Records of United States Army Commands, Record Group 98

Homestead Tract Books of the General Land Office, 1878–82, Yellowstone County, Montana. National Records Center, Suitland, Maryland

Letters Received by Commissioner of Indian Affairs, Office of Indian Affairs, 1878–81

Letters Received by the Office of Indian Affairs, 1824–80, Montana Superintendency, 1879

Office of Indian Affairs Records, Files 253 and 275
Parmly Billings Library, Billings, Montana
   Richard Clarke file, vertical files
   Coulson file, vertical files
   Marriage Records, 1882, Custer County, Montana Territory, transcribed
   Montana Pioneer Biographies, vertical files
   O'Donnell, I. D., comp., "Montana Monographs," typescript
   Orson N. Newman Diary, 1880, typescript
   Orson N. Newman Family file, vertical files
   Salisbury Family file, vertical files
   Alice Shock file, vertical files
Western Heritage Center, Billings, Montana
   Coulson Biographies
   Coulson Town file
   Gozzi, Raymond, "A Short History of Coulson," typescript, 1983
   Photographic Collections
   Real Estate Tax Records, 1888–90, Yellowstone County, Montana
   "Town Lot Sales, Billings, M. T.," 1882–83

Newspapers

Billings *Daily Times*, 1894
Billings *Gazette*, 1886–1991
Billings *Herald*, 1882–83
Billings *Post*, 1882–85
Billings *Stock Gazette*, 1887
Billings and Coulson *Post*, 1882
Bozeman *Avant Courier*, 1874, 1877–82
Coulson *Post*, 1882
Deer Lodge (Mont.) *New Northwest*, January 28, 1881
Fergus County (Mont.) *Argus*, November 4, 1921
Great Falls *Tribune*, September 27, 1940
Helena *Herald*, March 29, 1879, and April 6, 1882
Livingston *Post*, February 8, 1900, and May 9, 1907
Miles City *Yellowstone Journal*, 1879–86
Opheim (Mont.) *Observer*, August 31, 1923
Park County (Mont.) *News*, March 3, 1955

Twin Bridges (Mont.) *Sentinel*, November 10, 1932

White Sulpher Springs (Mont.) *Rocky Mountain Husbandman*, December 7, 1939

SECONDARY SOURCES

Articles

Abbott, Carl. "Frontiers and Sections: Cities and Regions in American Growth." In *American Urbanism: A Historiographical Review*, ed. Howard Gillette, Jr., and Zane L. Miller, 271–90. Westport, Conn.: Greenwood Press, 1987.

Algier, Keith. "Robert Meldrum and the Crow Peltry Trade." *Montana* 36 (Summer 1986): 36–47.

Alwin, John A. "Pelts, Provisions, and Perceptions: The Hudson's Bay Company Mandan Indian Trade, 1795–1812." *Montana* 29 (Summer 1979): 17–22.

Barnett, LeRoy. "The Ghastly Harvest: Montana's Buffalo Bone Trade." *Montana* 26 (Summer 1976): 14–25.

Bryan, Charles W., Jr. "Dr. Lamme and His Gallant Little Yellowstone." *Montana* 15 (Summer 1965): 24–43.

Calloway, Colin G. "Sword Bearer and the 'Crow Outbreak,' 1887." *Montana* 36 (Autumn 1986): 38–51.

Cameron, Walter A. "Building the Northern Pacific in 1881." *Montana* 33 (Summer 1983): 70–76.

Clark, Christopher. "The Household Economy, Market Exchange, and the Rise of Capitalism in the Connecticut Valley, 1800–1860." *Journal of Social History* 13 (Winter 1979): 169–90.

Conner, Stuart. "Prehistoric Man in the Yellowstone Valley." *Montana* 14 (Spring 1964): 14–21.

Cramer, Joseph L. "The Lean Site: An Historic Log Structure in Yellowstone County, Montana." *Plains Anthropologist* 6, no. 14 (1961): 267–70.

Crosby, Alfred W. "Virgin Soil Epidemics as a Factor in the Aboriginal Depopulation in America." *William and Mary Quarterly*, 3d ser., 33 (April 1976): 289–99.

Culpin, Mary S., and Richard Borjes. "The Architecture of Fort Union: A Symbol of Dominance." In *Rendezvous: Selected Papers of the Fourth North American Fur Trade Conference, 1981*, ed. Thomas C. Buckley, 135–40. St. Paul: Minnesota Historical Society Press, 1984.

Doyle, Susan Badger. "Journeys to the Land of Gold: Emigrants on the Bozeman Trail, 1863–1866." *Montana* 41 (Autumn 1991): 54–67.

Dunbar, Robert G. "The Economic Development of the Gallatin Valley." *Pacific Northwest Quarterly* 47 (October 1956): 117–23.

Ewers, John C. "Influence of the Fur Trade on Indians of the Northern Plains." In *People and Pelts: Selected Papers of the Second North American Fur Trade Conference*, ed. Malvina Bolus, 1–26. Winnipeg: Peguis Publishers, 1972.

Forbes, Jack D. "Frontiers in American History and the Role of the Frontier Historian." *Ethnohistory* 15 (Spring 1968): 203–35.

"Fort Sarpy Journal, 1855–56." *Contributions to the Historical Society of Montana*, vol. 10 (Helena: Montana Historical Society, 1940).

Ganoe, John T. "Desert Land Act in Operation, 1877–1891." *Agricultural History* 11 (April 1937): 142–57.

Goetzmann, William H. "The Mountain Man as Jacksonian Man." *American Quarterly* 15 (Fall 1963): 402–15.

Hart, Senia C., ed. "Calamity Jane Spent Latter Part of Her Life in Billings." *Landmarks* 2 (1975): 26–29.

Hedges, James B. "The Colonization Work of the Northern Pacific Railroad." *Mississippi Valley Historical Review* 13 (December 1926): 311–42.

Heidenreich, C. Adrian. "The Bearing of Ethnohistoric Data on the Crow-Hidasta Separation." *Archaeology in Montana* 20 (September-December 1979): 87–111.

———. "The Native Americans' Yellowstone." *Montana* 35 (Autumn 1985): 2–17.

Hill, Burton S. "Bozeman and the Bozeman Trail." *Annals of Wyoming* 36 (October 1964): 205–33.

Hoyt, Colgate. "'Roughing It Up the Yellowstone to Wonderland': An Account of a Trip through the Yellowstone Valley in 1878." Edited by Carroll Van West. *Montana* 36 (Spring 1986): 22–35.

Hudson, John C. "Main Streets of the Yellowstone Valley: Town Building along the Northern Pacific in Montana." *Montana* 35 (Autumn 1985): 56–67.

Hunt, William J., Jr. "The Fort Union Reconstruction Archaeology Project." *CRM Bulletin* 12, no. 1 (1989): 2–4.

Keenan, Jerry. "Yellowstone Kelly: From New York to Paradise." *Montana* 40 (Summer 1990): 14–27.

Kliewer, Waldo O. "The Foundations of Billings, Montana." *Pacific Northwest Quarterly* 31 (July 1940): 255–83.

Lass, William E. "Steamboats on the Yellowstone." *Montana* 35 (Autumn 1985): 27–39.

McLemore, Clyde. "Fort Pease: The First Attempted Settlement in Yellowstone Valley." *Montana* 2 (January 1952): 17–31.

Mahoney, Timothy R. "Urban History in a Regional Context: River Towns on the Upper Mississippi, 1840–1860." *Journal of American History* 72 (September 1985): 318–39.

Medicine Crow, Joe. "The Crow Migration Story." *Archaeology in Montana* 20 (September-December 1979): 63–72.

Mirrielees, L. B., ed. "Pioneer Ranching in Central Montana." *Sources of Northwest History,* no. 10 (Missoula: University of Montana, n.d.).

Mueller, George D. "Real and Fancied Claims: Joseph Richard 'Skookum Joe' Anderson, Miner in Central Montana, 1880–1897." *Montana* 35 (Spring 1985): 50–59.

Mulloy, William. "An Indian Village near Pompey's Pillar Creek, Montana." *Plains Anthropologist* 14, no. 4 (1969): 95–102.

Nolan, Edward W. "'Not Without Labor and Expense': The Villard–Northern Pacific Last Spike Excursion, 1883." *Montana* 33 (Summer 1983): 2–11.

Orser, Charles E., Jr. "Trade Good Flow in Arikara Villages: Expanding Ray's 'Middleman Hypothesis.' " *Plains Anthropologist* 29 (February 1984): 1–12.

———. "Understanding Arikara Trading Behavior: A Cultural Case Study of the Ashley-Leavenworth Episode of 1823." In *Rendezvous: Selected Papers of the Fourth North American Fur Trade Conference, 1981,* ed. Thomas C. Buckley, 101–8. St. Paul: Minnesota Historical Society Press, 1984.

Osgood, Ernest S. "Clark on the Yellowstone, 1806." *Montana* 18 (Summer 1968): 8–29.

"Pilgrims First Impressions of Town Terrified." *Landmarks* 2 (August 1975): 14–15.

Quivey, Addison M. "The Yellowstone Expedition of 1874." *Contributions to the Historical Society of Montana,* vol. 1 (Helena: Montana Historical Society, 1876).

Ray, Arthur J. "History and Archaeology of the Northern Fur Trade." *American Antiquity* 42 (January 1978): 26–34.

―――. "Indians as Consumers in the Eighteenth Century." In *Old Trails and New Directions: Papers of the Third North American Fur Trade Conference,* ed. C. M. Judd and A. J. Ray, 255–71. Toronto: University of Toronto Press, 1980.

Riley, Glenda. "Women's Responses to the Challenges of Plains Living." *Great Plains Quarterly* 9 (Summer 1989): 174–84.

Robbins, William G. " 'At the end of the cracked whip': The Northern West, 1880–1920." *Montana* 38 (Autumn 1988): 2–11.

Schilz, Thomas F. "Robes, Rum, and Rifles: Indian Middlemen in the Northern Plains Fur Trade." *Montana* 40 (Winter 1990): 2–13.

Shuart, Benjamin. "Reminiscences of a Home Missionary." In *First Congregational United Church of Christ: Our First One Hundred Years.* Billings: First Congregational Church, 1982.

Smalley, E. V. "The New Northwest." *Century Magazine* 24 (September 1882): 769–79.

Smith, Burton M. "Politics and the Crow Indian Land Cession, 1851–1904." *Montana* 36 (Autumn 1986): 24–37.

Smurr, John W. "A New La Verendrye Theory." *Pacific Northwest Quarterly* 43 (January 1952): 51–64.

Steffen, Jerome O. "William Clark: A Reappraisal." *Montana* 25 (Spring 1975): 52–61.

Swagerty, William O. "Marriage and Settlement Patterns of the Rocky Mountain Trappers and Traders." *Western Historical Quarterly* 11 (April 1980): 159–80.

Toole, K. Ross. "Perry W. McAdow and Montana in 1861–1862." *Montana* 2 (January 1952): 41–53.

Townsend, Ted. "Pioneer Home at Magic City." *Montana* 4 (Spring 1954): 50–51.

Unser, Daniel H., Jr. "The Frontier Exchange Economy of the Lower Mississippi Valley in the Eighteenth Century." *William and Mary Quarterly,* 3d ser., 44 (April 1987): 165–92.

Utley, Robert M. "War Houses in the Sioux Country: The Military Occupation of the Lower Yellowstone." *Montana* 35 (Autumn 1985): 18–25.

Vehik, Susan C. "Late Prehistoric Plains Trade and Economic Specialization." *Plains Anthropologist* 35 (May 1990): 125–46.

Ward, James A. "Image and Reality: The Railway Corporate-State Metaphor." *Business History Review* 55 (Winter 1981): 491–516.

Waselkov, G. A., and R. E. Paul. "Frontiers and Archaeology." *North American Archaeologist* 2, no. 4 (1980–81): 309–31.

West, Carroll Van. "Acculturation by Design: Architectural Determinism and the Montana Indian Reservations, 1870–1930." *Great Plains Quarterly* 7 (Spring 1987): 91–107.

———. "Coulson and the Clark's Fork Bottom: The Economic Structure of a Pre-Railroad Community, 1874–1881." *Montana* 35 (Autumn 1985): 42–55.

———. "Livingston: Railroad Town on the Yellowstone." *Montana* 35 (Autumn 1985): 84–85.

White, Richard. "The Winning of the West: The Expansion of the Western Sioux in the Eighteenth and Nineteenth Century." *Journal of American History* 65 (September 1978): 319–43.

White, W. Thomas. "Boycott: The Pullman Strike in Montana." *Montana* 29 (October 1979): 2–13.

———. "Commonwealth or Colony? Montana and the Railroads in the First Decade of Statehood." *Montana* 38 (Autumn 1988): 12–23.

Wood, W. Raymond. "Plains Trade in Prehistoric and Protohistoric Intertribal Relations." In *Anthropology on the Great Plains*, ed. W. Raymond Wood and Margot Liberty, 98–109. Lincoln: University of Nebraska Press, 1980.

Books

Allen, William A. *Adventures with Indians and Game*. Chicago: A. W. Bowen, 1903.

Atherton, Lewis. *Main Street on the Middle Border*. Bloomington: Indiana University Press, 1954.

Baldwin, W. W. *Corporate History of Chicago, Burlington, and Quincy Railroad Company and Affiliated Companies*. [Chicago]: Chicago, Burlington, Quincy, 1917.

Beckwourth, James P. *The Life and Adventures of James P. Beckwourth*. Edited by T. D. Bonner. Minneapolis: Ross and Haines, 1965 [1856].

Billington, Ray Allen. *The Far Western Frontier, 1830–1860*. New York: Harper and Row, 1956.

Boden, Anneke-Jan. *Billings: The First 100 Years*. Billings: First Bank, 1982.

Bond, Fred G. *Flatboating on the Yellowstone, 1877*. New York: New York Public Library, 1925.

Boorstin, Daniel J. *The Americans: The National Experience.* New York: Vintage Books, 1965.

Bradley, Charles C., Jr. *After the Buffalo Days.* Vol. 1. Lodge Grass, Mont.: Privately published, 1977.

Braudel, Fernand. *The Structures of Everyday Life: The Limits of the Possible.* New York: Harper, 1979.

Breuchaud, Irene G. *Memoirs of Montana, 1882.* New York: Privately published, 1958.

Brown, Jennifer S. H. *Strangers in Blood: Fur Trade Company Families in Indian Country.* Vancouver: University of British Columbia Press, 1980.

Brown, Mark H. *The Plainsmen of the Yellowstone: A History of the Yellowstone Basin.* New York: G. P. Putnam, 1961.

Burlingame, Merrill G. *Gallatin County's Heritage.* Bozeman: Gallatin County Historical Society, 1976.

——. *John M. Bozeman: Montana Trailmaker.* Bozeman: Gallatin County Tribune, 1971.

——. *The Montana Frontier.* Helena: State Publishing Company, 1942.

Campbell, E. G. *The Reorganization of the American Railroad System, 1893–1900.* New York: AMS Press, 1968 [1938].

Carosso, Vincent P. *The Morgans: Private International Bankers.* Cambridge: Harvard University Press, 1987.

Centennial Scrapbook: Livingston, 1882–1982. Livingston, Mont.: Livingston Enterprise, 1982.

Chandler, Alfred D., Jr. *The Visible Hand: The Managerial Revolution in American Business.* Cambridge: Belknap Press, 1977.

Clinch, Thomas A. *Urban Populism and Free Silver in Montana.* Missoula: University of Montana Press, 1970.

Clokey, Richard M. *William H. Ashley: Enterprise and Politics in the Trans-Mississippi West.* Norman: University of Oklahoma Press, 1980.

Cooper, Myrtle E. *From Tent Town to City: A Chronological History of Billings, Montana, 1882–1935.* Billings: Privately published, 1981.

Corey, Lewis. *The House of Morgan: A Social Biography of the Masters of Money.* New York: G. H. Watt, 1930.

Crosby, Alfred W. *Ecological Imperialism: The Biological Expansion of Europe, 900–1900.* Cambridge: Cambridge University Press, 1986.

Cumbler, John T. *A Social History of Economic Decline: Business, Poli-*

tics, and Work in Trenton. New Brunswick: Rutgers University Press, 1989.

Curtis, Jane, et al. *Frederick Billings: Vermonter, Pioneer, Lawyer, Businessman, Conservationist.* Woodstock, Vt.: Woodstock Foundation, 1986.

Daggett, Stuart. *Railroad Reorganization.* New York: A. M. Kelley, 1967 [1908].

Dary, David. *Entrepreneurs of the Old West.* New York: Knopf, 1986.

Denig, Edwin T. *Five Indian Tribes of the Upper Missouri: Sioux, Arickaras, Assiniboines, Crees, Crows.* Edited by John C. Ewers. Norman: University of Oklahoma Press, 1961.

Dick, Everett. *Vanguards of the Frontier.* Lincoln: University of Nebraska Press, 1965 [1941].

Doyle, Don H. *The Social Order of a Frontier Community: Jacksonville, Illinois, 1825–1870.* Urbana: University of Illinois Press, 1978.

Dunlay, Thomas W. *Wolves for the Blue Soldiers: Indian Scouts and Auxiliaries with the United States Army, 1860–90.* Lincoln: University of Nebraska Press, 1982.

Dykstra, Robert R. *The Cattle Towns.* New York: Knopf, 1968.

Ebner, Michael H. *Creating Chicago's North Shore: A Suburban History.* Chicago: University of Chicago Press, 1988.

Ewers, John C. *The Blackfeet: Raiders on the Northwestern Plains.* Norman: University of Oklahoma Press, 1958.

———. *Indian Life in the Upper Missouri.* Norman: University of Oklahoma Press, 1968.

Faragher, John M. *Sugar Creek: Life on the Illinois Prairie.* New Haven: Yale University Press, 1986.

40th Annual Report of the Board of Directors of the Chicago, Burlington, and Quincy Railroad Company. Cambridge: Wilson and Son, 1894.

41st Annual Report of the Board of Directors of the Chicago, Burlington, and Quincy Railroad Company. Cambridge: Wilson and Son, 1895.

Francis, Daniel, and Toby Morantz. *Partners in Furs: A History of the Fur Trade in Eastern James Bay, 1600–1870.* Montreal: McGill-Queen's University Press, 1983.

Frey, Rodney. *The World of the Crow Indians: As Driftwood Lodges.* Norman: University of Oklahoma Press, 1987.

Frison, George C. *Prehistoric Hunters of the High Plains.* New York: Academic Press, 1978.

Gilbert, Heather. *The Life of Lord Mount Stephen.* Vol. 2, *The End of the Road, 1891–1921.* Aberdeen, Scotland: Aberdeen University Press, 1977.

Goetzmann, William H. *Exploration and Empire: The Explorer and the Scientist in the Winning of the American West.* New York: Knopf, 1967.

Gray, John S. *Custer's Last Campaign: Mitch Boyer and the Little Bighorn Reconstructed.* Lincoln: University of Nebraska Press, 1991.

Greene, Jerome A. *Yellowstone Command: Colonel Nelson A. Miles and the Great Sioux War, 1876–1877.* Lincoln: University of Nebraska Press, 1991.

Grodinsky, Julius. *Transcontinental Railway Strategy, 1869–1893: A Study of Businessmen.* Philadelphia: University of Pennsylvania Press, 1962.

Hafen, Leroy R. *Broken Hand: The Life of Thomas Fitzpatrick, Mountain Man, Guide, and Indian Agent.* Lincoln: University of Nebraska Press, 1973 [1931].

———, ed. *Mountain Men and Fur Traders of the Far West.* Lincoln: University of Nebraska Press, 1982.

Hahn, Steven, and Jonathan Prude, eds. *The Countryside in the Age of Capitalistic Transformation.* Chapel Hill: University of North Carolina Press, 1985.

Haines, Francis. *The Nez Perces: Tribesmen of the Columbia Plateau.* Norman: University of Oklahoma Press, 1955.

Harris, Burton. *John Colter: His Years in the Rockies.* Basin, Wyo.: Big Horn Book Company, 1977 [1952].

Hedges, James B. *Henry Villard and the Railways of the Northwest.* New York: Russell and Russell, 1967 [1930].

Hidy, Ralph W., et al. *The Great Northern Railway: A History.* Cambridge: Harvard Business School Press, 1988.

Hine, Robert V. *Community on the American Frontier.* Norman: University of Oklahoma Press, 1980.

Holder, Preston. *The Hoe and the Horse on the Plains: A Study of Cultural Development among North American Indians.* Lincoln: University of Nebraska Press, 1970.

Hoxie, Frederick E. *A Final Promise: The Campaign to Assimilate the Indians, 1880–1920.* Lincoln: University of Nebraska Press, 1984.

Hudson, John C. *Plains Country Towns.* Minneapolis: University of Minnesota Press, 1985.

Hurt, R. Douglas. *Indian Agriculture: Prehistory to the Present*. Lawrence: University of Kansas Press, 1987.

An Illustrated History of the Yellowstone Valley. Spokane: Western Historical Publishing Company, 1907.

Jeffrey, Julie Roy. *Frontier Women: The Trans-Mississippi West, 1840–1880*. New York: Hill and Wang, 1979.

Johnson, Dorothy M. *The Bloody Bozeman*. New York: McGraw-Hill, 1971.

Johnston, Elsie. *Laurel's Story: A Montana Heritage*. Billings: Artcraft Publishing, 1979.

Jones, Agnes L. *Crow Country*. Billings: Rocky Mountain College Print Shop, n.d.

Lamar, Howard R. *The Trader on the American Frontier: Myth's Victim*. College Station: Texas A&M University Press, 1977.

Lamar, Howard, and Leonard Thompson, eds. *The Frontier in History: North America and South Africa Compared*. New Haven: Yale University Press, 1981.

Lamoreaux, Naomi R. *The Great Merger Movement in American Business, 1895–1904*. New York: Cambridge University Press, 1985.

Larsen, Lawrence. *The Urban West at the End of the Frontier*. Lawrence: Regents Press of Kansas, 1978.

Leeson, Michael A., ed. *History of Montana, 1739–1885*. Chicago: Warner, Beers and Company, 1885.

Leforge, Thomas H. *Memoirs of a White Crow Indian*. Edited by Thomas B. Marquis. Lincoln: University of Nebraska Press, 1974 [1928].

Lewis, Meriwether. *History of the Expedition under the Command of Lewis and Clark*. Edited by Elliott Coues. 3 Vols. New York: Dover Books, 1965 [1893].

Licht, Walter. *Working for the Railroad: The Organization of Work in the Nineteenth Century*. Princeton: Princeton University Press, 1983.

Limerick, Patricia Nelson. *The Legacy of Conquest: The Unbroken Past of the American West*. New York: Norton, 1987.

Linderman, Frank B. *Plenty-coups: Chief of the Crows*. Lincoln: University of Nebraska Press, 1962 [1930].

———. *Pretty-shield: Medicine Woman of the Crows*. Lincoln: University of Nebraska Press, 1972 [1932].

Lowie, Robert. *The Crow Indians*. New York: Farrar and Rinehart, 1935.

———. *Indians of the Plains.* Garden City, N.Y.: Natural History Press, 1963 [1954].

MacDonald, Marie. *Glendive: The History of a Montana Town.* Glendive, Mont.: Glendive Press, 1968.

McElrath, Thomson P. *The Yellowstone Valley.* St. Paul: Pioneer Press, 1880.

Mahoney, Timothy R. *River Towns in the Great West: The Structure of Provincial Urbanization in the American Midwest, 1820–1870.* New York: Cambridge University Press, 1990.

Malone, Michael, and Richard Roeder. *Montana: A History of Two Centuries.* Seattle: University of Washington Press, 1976.

Martin, Albro. *James J. Hill and the Opening of the Northwest.* New York: Oxford University Press, 1976.

Morgan, Dale L. *Jedediah Smith and the Opening of the West.* Lincoln: University of Nebraska Press, 1953.

Mulloy, William. *The Hagen Site: A Prehistoric Village on the Lower Yellowstone.* Missoula: University of Montana, 1942.

Murray, Robert A. *The Bozeman Trail: Highway of History.* Boulder: Pruett Publishing Company, 1988.

Nabokov, Peter. *Two Leggings: The Making of a Crow Warrior.* Lincoln: University of Nebraska Press, 1967.

Nelson, Paula M. *After the West Was Won: Homesteaders and Town-Builders in Western South Dakota, 1900–1917.* Iowa City: University of Iowa Press, 1986.

Northern Pacific Railroad. *Annual Report, 1881.* New York: Northern Pacific Railroad, 1881.

Northern Pacific Railroad Report of the President to the Stockholders, September 20, 1883. New York: Northern Pacific Railroad, 1883.

O'Donnell, I. D., comp. *Montana Monographs.* Billings: Yellowstone County Historical Society, 1984.

Office of Land Assistant, Northern Pacific Railway. *Revised Corporate History of Northern Pacific Railway Company.* St. Paul: Northern Pacific Railway, 1921.

Office of the President, Northern Pacific Railroad Company, to Committee on the Judiciary, House of Representatives, July 6, 1882. New York: Northern Pacific Railroad, 1882.

The Official Northern Pacific Railroad Guide. St. Paul: W. C. Riley, 1893.

Oglesby, Richard E. *Manuel Lisa and the Opening of the Missouri Fur Trade*. Norman: University of Oklahoma Press, 1963.

Opie, John. *The Law of the Land: Two Hundred Years of American Farmland Policy*. Lincoln: University of Nebraska Press, 1987.

Osgood, Ernest S. *The Day of the Cattleman*. Minneapolis: University of Minnesota Press, 1929.

Overfield, Loyd J. II, comp. *The Little Big Horn, 1876*. 1971 Reprint. Lincoln: University of Nebraska Press, 1990.

Overton, Richard C. *Burlington Route: A History of the Burlington Lines*. New York: Knopf, 1965.

Phillips, Paul C. *The Fur Trade*. 2 vols. Norman: University of Oklahoma Press, 1961.

Plummer, Norman B. *Crow Indians*. New York: Garland, 1974.

Priest, Loring B. *Uncle Sam's Stepchildren: The Reformation of United States Indian Policy, 1865–1887*. New York: Octagon Books, 1969 [1942].

Prucha, Francis P. *The Great Father: The United States Government and the American Indians*. 2 vols. Lincoln: University of Nebraska Press, 1984.

Ray, Arthur J. *Indians in the Fur Trade: Their Role as Trappers, Hunters, and Middlemen in the Lands Southwest of Hudson Bay, 1660–1870*. Toronto: University of Toronto Press, 1974.

Ray, Arthur J., and Donald Freeman. *"Give Us Good Measure": An Economic Analysis of Relations between the Indians and the Hudson's Bay Company*. Toronto: University of Toronto Press, 1978.

Raynolds, William F. *Exploration of the Yellowstone River*. Washington: Government Printing Office, 1868.

Renz, Louis T. *The History of the Northern Pacific Railroad*. Fairfield, Wash.: Ye Galleon Press, 1980.

Report of Receiver Henry C. Rouse, December 11, 1893. New York: Northern Pacific Railroad, 1893.

Reports of Inspection Made in the Summer of 1877 by Generals P. H. Sheridan and W. T. Sherman of the Country North of the Union Pacific Railroad. Washington: Government Printing Office, 1878.

Reps, John W. *Cities of the American West: A History of Frontier Urban Planning*. Princeton: Princeton University Press, 1979.

Ronda, James P. *Lewis and Clark among the Indians*. Lincoln: University of Nebraska Press, 1984.

Sanders, Helen F. *A History of Montana.* Chicago: Lewis Publishing Company, 1913.

Saum, Lewis O. *The Fur Trader and the Indian.* Seattle: University of Washington Press, 1965.

Schultz, Stanley K. *Constructing Urban Culture: American Cities and City Planning, 1800–1920.* Philadelphia: Temple University Press, 1989.

Sklar, Martin J. *The Corporate Reconstruction of American Capitalism, 1890–1916.* Cambridge: Cambridge University Press, 1988.

Small, Lawrence. *A Century of Politics on the Yellowstone.* Billings: Rocky Mountain College, 1983.

Smith, Duane A. *Rocky Mountain Mining Camps: The Urban Frontier.* Bloomington: Indiana University Press, 1967.

Smith, G. Hubert. *The Explorations of the La Verendryes in the Northern Plains, 1738–43.* Edited by W. Raymond Wood. Lincoln: University of Nebraska Press, 1980.

Sunder, John E. *Bill Sublette: Mountain Man.* Norman: University of Oklahoma Press, 1959.

———. *The Fur Trade on the Upper Missouri, 1840–1865.* Norman: University of Oklahoma Press, 1965.

———. *Joshua Pilcher: Fur Trader and Indian Agent.* Norman: University of Oklahoma Press, 1968.

Thompson, Erwin N. *Fort Union Tradng Post: Fur Trade Empire on the Upper Missouri.* Medora, N.D.: Theodore Roosevelt Nature and History Association, 1986.

Thwaites, Reuben G., ed. *Original Journals of the Lewis and Clark Expedition.* 8 vols. New York: Arno Press, 1969 [1904–5].

Topping, E. S. *Chronicles of the Yellowstone.* St. Paul: Pioneer Press, 1883.

Trails and Tales: South of the Yellowstone. Billings: Midland Printing, 1983.

Underwood, Kathleen. *Town Building on the Colorado Frontier.* Albuquerque: University of New Mexico Press, 1987.

Utley, Robert M. *Cavalier in Buckskin: George Armstrong Custer and the Western Military Frontier.* Norman: University of Oklahoma Press, 1988.

———. *Frontier Regulars: The U.S. Army and the Indians, 1866–1891.* New York: Macmillan, 1973.

———. *The Indian Frontier of the American West, 1846–1890*. Albuquerque: University of New Mexico Press, 1984.

Vestal, Stanley. *Jim Bridger: Mountain Man*. Lincoln: University of Nebraska Press, 1970 [1946].

Wagner, Glendolin Damon, and William A. Allen. *Blankets and Moccasins: Plenty Coups and His People, the Crows*. Lincoln: University of Nebraska Press, 1987 [1933].

Wallace, Anthony F. C. *St. Clair: A Nineteenth-Century Coal Town's Experience with a Disaster-Prone Industry*. New York: Knopf, 1987.

West, Carroll Van. *A Traveler's Companion to Montana History*. Helena: Montana Historical Society Press, 1986.

We Will Welcome You to Livingston. . . . Livingston, Mont.: Privately published, 1909.

Wildschut, William. *Crow Indian Medicine Bundles*. New York: Museum of the American Indian, Heye Foundation, 1960.

Wilson, Gilbert. *Buffalo Bird Woman's Garden*. St. Paul: Minnesota Historical Society Press, 1987 [1917].

Winks, Robin. *Frederick Billings: A Life*. New York: Oxford University Press, 1991.

Wishart, David J. *The Fur Trade of the American West, 1807–1840: A Geographical Synthesis*. Lincoln: University of Nebraska Press, 1979.

Wolfe, Muriel. *Montana Pay Dirt: A Guide to the Mining Camps of the Treasure State*. Athens, Ohio: Sage Books, 1963.

Wood, W. Raymond, and Thomas D. Thiessen, eds. *Early Fur Trade on the Northern Plains: The Narratives of John Macdonell, David Thompson, Francois-Antoine Larocque, and Charles Mckenzie*. Norman: University of Oklahoma Press, 1985.

Wright, Kathryn. *Historic Homes of Billings*. Helena and Billings: Falcon Press Publishing Company, 1981.

Zunz, Olivier. *Making America Corporate, 1870–1920*. Chicago: University of Chicago Press, 1990.

Dissertations and Theses

Berry, James J. "Arikara Middlemen: The Effects of Trade on an Upper Missouri Society." Ph.D. diss., Indiana University, 1978.

Blakeslee, Donald J. "The Plains Interband Trade System: An Ethnohistoric and Archaeological Investigation." Ph.D. diss., University of Wisconsin, Milwaukee, 1975.

Hakola, John W. "Samuel T. Hauser and the Economic Development of Montana: A Case Study in Nineteenth-Century Frontier Capitalism." Ph.D. diss., Indiana University, 1961.

Kliewer, Waldo O. "The Foundations of Billings Montana." Master's thesis, University of Washington, 1938.

Loendorf, Lawrence. "Prehistoric Settlement Patterns in the Pryor Mountains." Ph.D. diss., University of Missouri, 1973.

Medicine Crow, Joe. "The Effects of European Culture Contacts upon the Economic, Social, and Religious Life of the Crow Indians." Master's thesis, University of Southern California, 1935.

Stafford, John W. "Crow Culture Change: A Geographical Analysis." Ph.D. diss., Michigan State University, 1971.

Vincent, William B. "The Late Prehistoric and Historic Periods in Northern Yellowstone County: A Comparison of Archaeological and Historical Evidence." Master's thesis, Washington State University, 1976.

White, W. Thomas. "A History of Railroad Workers in the Pacific Northwest, 1883–1934." Ph.D. diss., University of Washington, 1981.

Index